Parades and Power

Street Theatre in Nineteenth-Century Philadelphia

Parades and Power

Street Theatre in Nineteenth-Century Philadelphia

Susan G. Davis

Temple University Press

PHILADELPHIA

The frontispiece is a detail from the 1832 lithograph,
"The Gold & Silver Artificers of Phil[a.]," by M. E. D. Brown.
Courtesy of the Library Company of Philadelphia

Temple University Press, Philadelphia 19122
© 1986 by Susan G. Davis. All rights reserved
Published 1986

Printed in the United States of America

Library of Congress Cataloging-in-Publication Data

Davis, Susan G., 1953–
Parades and power.

Bibliography: p.
Includes index.
1. Processions—Pennsylvania—Philadelphia.
2. Philadelphia—Festivals, etc. 3. Street theater—
Pennsylvania—Philadelphia. 4. Philadelphia (Pa.)—
Politics and government. 5. Philadelphia (Pa.)
—Social conditions. I. Title.
GT4011.P46D38   1985   394'.5'0974811   85-14675
ISBN 0-87722-394-7

For Dan

Contents

Acknowledgments

It is a pleasure to acknowledge the help of many skilled archivists and librarians without whose efforts my research would have been impossible. At the Historical Society of Pennsylvania, Pennsylvania history librarians Maxine Brennan and Waldo Tulk answered my questions and guided me to primary and secondary sources with efficiency and patience. No less important, Ms. Brennan and Mr. Tulk spent months locating the heavy bound volumes of nineteenth-century newspapers and carrying them to the reading room where I could examine them. Linda Stanley, of the manuscript division of the Historical Society of Pennsylvania, helped me research visual materials. Phil Lapsansky and Kenneth Finkel of the Library Company of Philadelphia shared their knowledge of Philadelphia's graphic record. I am grateful to the Historical Society and the Library Company, to the Free Library of Philadelphia, the Philadelphia Museum of Art, the New-York Historical Society, and the Library of Congress for permission to reproduce prints, drawings, and paintings in their collections.

Jane Bryan and the reference staff at the University of Pennsylvania Library, especially Julie Miller and Joan Anderson, helped me sort through folklore and historical sources. At the University of California, San Diego, Anita Schiller, Susan Galloway, and Helen Wykle rendered bibliographic aid; Larry Cruse helped me explore Philadelphia's cartography.

My teachers at the University of Pennsylvania extended unconditional support and friendship to me. It is a pleasure to thank my advisers, Professors Henry Glassie, Michael B. Katz, and John F. Szwed (now at Yale University), and members of the Department of Folklore and Folklife, Professors Dell Hymes, Kenneth Goldstein, Dan Ben-Amos, Don Yoder, Barbara Kirshenblatt-Gimblett (now at New York University), and Theresa Pyott.

Work on this book was substantially aided by a postdoctoral fellowship at the Philadelphia Center for Early American Studies and a research grant from the Faculty Senate Committee on Research, University of California, San Diego. At the Philadelphia Center, Michael Zuckerman, Richard Beeman, and Richard Dunn provided moral support and intellectual challenge. Participants in the Center's seminars on early American history and culture helped me clarify my ideas, and Susan Klepp, Billy Smith, Michael Meranze, Ric Northrup, Allen Steinberg, and Jack Michel shared research leads and unpublished work with me.

Many folklorists and historians helped generously with this project. Folklorists include Edward Ives, Roger Abrahams, Simon Lichman, John McGuigan, Sam Schrager, John Dorst, Robert St. George, and the late Richard Dorson. Among historians, I owe thanks to Lynn Lees, Lee Benson, Peter Buckley, David Montgomery, Michael Frisch, Steven Rosswurm, Roy Rosenzweig, Alfred Young, Peter Linebaugh, Drew Faust, Gary Nash, Cynthia Shelton, Lawrence Levine, and David Glassberg, many of whom shared unpublished work with me.

All my colleagues in the Department of Communication at the University of California at San Diego have given me unreserved support; I owe particular thanks to Helene Keyssar, Michael Cole, Herbert Schiller, Chandra Mukerji, and Michael Schudson for their enthusiasm. Farther afield at the University of California, San Diego, Tom Dublin, Fred Lonidier, Robert Ritchie, Robyn Hunt, and Jehanne Teilhet make the Sun Belt hospitable to a Philadelphian.

At Temple University Press, I have been guided by two highly skilled editors, Janet Francendese and Mary D. Capouya.

Many friends have helped me take parades seriously. Diana Natko, Mimi Zarsky, Stuart Ewen, Ridie Ghezzi, Janet Wasko, Vincent Mosco, Cathy McKercher, and Nick and Virginia Westbrook offered wit, good humor, and encouragement. Marcus Rediker has been deeply implicated in this project for years. Nancy Hewitt lent me solid support and her own example.

I owe my grandmothers, Esther Green and the late Margaret Evans Davis, a debt of thanks for teaching me to care about the past. Maggie Hayden helped me find a quiet and beautiful place to work. Herb, Anita, and Zach Schiller and Aaron Rosenbaum shared their enthusiasm and criticisms. Mary Ann and Dave Davis have been in on this caper since the beginning, and have used their wide variety of talents to help me complete it. Although Kay Davis was not nearby as I wrote, I have benefitted from her hope and kindness. To all my family, my dearest thanks.

My biggest debt is to Dan Schiller, for being consistent, critical, and generous. Perhaps Dan's greatest contribution has been to remind me constantly that our social world, in Huddie Ledbetter's words, "Ain't no iron, ain't no solid rock."

Parades and Power

Street Theatre in Nineteenth-Century Philadelphia

CHAPTER ONE

A History of Parades and Ceremonies

On February 22, 1832, the centennial of George Washington's birthday, thousands of Philadelphians took part in an elaborate commemoration that commenced with resounding cannon fire. Streamers decorated ships in the harbor, and banners hung prominently from city buildings. Nearly every Philadelphian took a day off from work to see the central event, a grand civic procession that drew visitors and reporters from nearby towns. The streets were thronged with people, and householders rented their second storeys to spectators eager for a good view.[1]

The colorful spectacle presented a ceremonious image of the city's social makeup. Planned by local committees, authorized by the City Councils, and produced during weeks of flurried activity, the procession that honored Washington revealed the forces shaping Philadelphians' lives. As Chief Marshal Clement Biddle led the procession up Third Street to the State House, four distinct divisions fell into line. First came a cadre of citizens powerful in governmental and private capacities, joined by colleagues, friends, and subordinates in a delineation of the city's leadership. Clearing the way for the chief marshal and Mayor Benjamin Richards, "eighteen stout pioneer axemen," marched "in white frocks with blue ribbons [and] strong leather caps."[2] City police and watchmen, wearing badges and sashes and accompanied by marching bands, heralded good order and the dignified barouche carrying the Committee of Arrangements. These prominent citizens and councilmen were joined by distinguished senior men of the city: the Reverend Clergy, including the venerable minister William White, William Rawle, the reader of Washington's Farewell Address, and members of the elite Society of the Cincinnati. Underlining the day's historical references, surviving Revolutionary War veterans also held a place of honor. Behind contemporary and rediscovered heroes, a vast array of federal, state, and municipal officials brought up the rear of the first division.

The parade's second division—the military—marched under a banner bearing the city's seal, "Philadelphia" and "Plenty" personified as women, flanking a shield displaying the scales of justice, a plough, and a merchant ship. The size and elegance of this division, with the city's standard in its keeping, announced the importance of voluntary militia troops in local social and political life. Led by the popular Colonel C. G. Childs and a corps of volunteers from the War of 1812, the militias strode in an enormous cavalcade. Cavalry troops on fine horses led off, displaying badges, banners, and sabres and rifles. Each company, distinguished by elaborate ceremonial uniform, marched to its own band of musicians.

The third division, masters and employees of more than forty trades, celebrated the city's industrial prowess. Labor and its products were made vivid and festive as tradesmen displayed their skills on horse-drawn carriages. Copperplate printers struck portraits of Washington on squares "of white satin with a pink edge" and tossed them into the crowd.[3] Tanners and morocco dressers portrayed themselves "hard at it . . . fleshing and working hides, shaving leather, coloring and polishing morocco."[4] Coopers built hogsheads on a rolling stage, hatters made hats, and shipwrights built three scaled-down vessels. In these displays, products ranked as important as processes: Men from "Mr. McCauley's manufactory" presided over a rich display of new carpets. Workers masquerading as Turks and Indian chiefs held up the finest wares for the crowd's inspection.

More than thirty companies of volunteer firemen, each fully equipped with new ceremonial paraphernalia, brought up the rear. The outstanding display included painted leather buckets, hats and cloaks, spanners and hoses, and each company's engine, gilded and painted with figures of

Washington or Lafayette, as well as Hope, Perseverance, Good Intent, and Diligence. The press considered this colorful cavalcade of civic virtue and selfless action especially appropriate for Washington's commemoration. The companies, "[a]rrayed as they were with all their means of doing good," represented patriotic heroism.[5] Encouraged by their enthusiastic reception, the firemen voted to make their parade an annual event.

On the following day the press declared the Washington Centennial a public event of unprecedented respectability and elegance. Soldiers and civilians, laborers and employers, public bodies and private associations had joined in a flamboyant but dignified salute to a historic leader. Selfless patriotism and memories of the Revolution were combined with the imagery of economic growth and prosperity. Not only had all the performers done themselves proud with their costly displays, but a salubrious sobriety had prevailed among the spectators![6]

How would a cultural historian look at the Washington Centennial parade? What was the street drama's relationship to the social context in which it was performed, and to the larger patterns in the history of American public ceremonial culture? Parades and public ceremonies have been neglected by scholars, few of whom have systematically investigated the relationship between social life and public enactments; thus, little is known about how the public ceremonies we think of as traditional have come to be so.

Parades were an important, varied, and popular mode of communication in nineteenth-century cities. Although spectacles like the Washington Centennial were reserved for special events of national importance, parades in general were familiar urban events. Philadelphians often organized parades to advertise economic ventures or express political protest, partisan support, or community solidarity. Parades were modes of propaganda, recreation, local celebration, and national commemoration. The Centennial Procession of 1832 combined elements and techniques of all these modes and was both familiar and spectacular at the same time.

Although print media became unprecedentedly important in the early nineteenth century, the period's social history reveals that American city dwellers often used collective gatherings and vernacular dramatic techniques—reading aloud, oratory, festivals, work stoppages, mass meetings, and parades—to propose ideas about social relations. While great spectacles are mentioned in community histories or accounts of political movements, less elaborate parade traditions, such as July Fourth military marches, street ceremonies for local anniversaries, or the mobile proselytizing parades of reform movements, have remained outside scholarly scrutiny. Historians have analyzed great events and social movements, but they have often ignored the nonliterate, nonelectronic communication through which movements and events are accomplished, interpreted, and remembered.

Inattention to parades and ceremonies can be attributed to how we view collective activities. First impressions of public ceremonies are often shaped by the common-sense belief that such events are straightforward reflections of notions shared by all the performers. At first glance, the Washington Centennial seems self-evidently meaningful, a simple representation of consensus and unity, shared pride and patriotism. Upon closer examination, however, the procession's meanings for performers and audience seem less unified. This procession was a selective version of local social relations that hardly represented all communities, all points of view, and all versions of patriotism. Although private associations, from firemen to the Cincinnati, made up the parade, many of Philadelphia's community associations were denied participation.

Philadelphia's blacks, who held strong hopes for equal rights in the North, honored the great day in their churches with fasting, sermons, and prayer, but found no role in the public drama. Despite their protests, women were also excluded from participating in street processions, even on grand republican holidays. In commemorating a defender of freedom and democracy, was it right that hereditary groups of wealthy men, like the Society of the Cincinnati, should take pride of place? Although skilled workers participated in displays sponsored by well-to-do employers and master craftsmen, the vast unskilled majority were expected only to make up the spectacle's audience. Further, images of the relations between masters and men were distorted and wishful. While men enacted hearty, happy toil under their masters' benign eyes, in the city's real work-places, long-simmering tensions between capital and labor boiled over. These tensions fed the spirit of insurrection in Philadelphia's textile districts, gave strength to the nascent labor movement, and found full expression in a citywide general strike four years later.[7]

Thus even so broadly inclusive a celebration as the Washington Centennial was shaped by power relations in the city. Images of social relations were filtered through a complex process of inclusion, exclusion, influence, and planning, until the parade expressed power and special interest more than unity and consensus. If all public events in the city were shaped by such filtering processes, the answers to questions of what parades meant, how performers intended their dramas, and how audiences understood street displays are much more complex than a first look indicates.

This case study of parades and ceremonies in early-nine-teenth-century Philadelphia reveals how and why public events are problematic and significant for social history. The conceptual tools of folklore, social history, and communication will enable us to examine parades and ceremonies as political actions, rhetorical means by which performers attempted to accomplish practical and symbolic goals.[8] This approach helps interpret the usual, repetitive events of urban public culture, as well as the startling and unusual ones—the July Fourth parades as well as the strike demonstrations—as kinds of communication that are part of the social forces that shape our lives. Looking at parades in their social-historical context—in this period a context of change and conflict—reveals that parades do more than reflect society. Such public enactments, in their multiplici-tous and varied forms, are not only patterned by social forces—they have been part of the very building and challenging of social relations.

PARADES AS POLITICAL ACTIVITIES

As dramatic representations, parades and public ceremonies are political acts: They have pragmatic objectives, and concrete, often material, results. People use street theatre, like other rituals, as tools for building, maintaining, and confronting power relations. The amplification of power through performance is often viewed as unimportant because it takes place largely through the construction and presentation of images. But even trite, frequently repeated images can be critical to political policies and mobilization. Parades are public dramas of social relations, and in them performers define who can be a social actor and what subjects and ideas are available for communication and consideration. These defining images in turn shape the actions and alternatives people can imagine and propose. Street performances, then, are both shaped by the field of power relations in which they take place, and are attempts to act on and influence those relations. In the nineteenth-century city, parades were used to define what society was or might be. In Philadelphia, for example, in the 1840s, nativist political organizers mounted enormous Fourth of July spectacles to create anti-immigrant sentiment and call for the contraction of Irish-American civil rights. Public processions linking the symbols of patriotism with the nativist platform resulted in anti-Irish rioting and justified anti-Irish prejudice. This and subsequent examples support the argument that public ceremonialism as a practice needs to be held open to historical analysis as much as the ideologies of nativism and patriotism.

As political acts, parades and ceremonies take place in a context of contest and confrontation. Even a cursory reading of primary sources on nineteenth-century cities discloses that street dramas drew not only extraordinary interest, but also violent antagonism and horrified concern from many citizens. In practice, the streets of Philadelphia, like all other contexts for communication, had limits. Precisely because parades were such a powerful mode of communication, the range of meanings they could be used to communicate was constrained by society and politics. Constraint on meaning was effected through custom, opinion, example, the law, and, sometimes, force.

Recognizing parades as political activities enables us to grasp the significance of street theatre and to formulate key questions: What role did public representation of social relations play in American history? How did social history —especially relations among groups and classes—shape traditions of ritualization? New insight into the history of American social structure and class relations makes it ever more difficult to view American culture as the product of consensus and accommodation through participation.⁹ If conflict among economic groups and social classes has existed throughout American history, what does this mean for a history of how Americans made public images of social life?¹⁰ Conversely, if parades were a form of communication, they were meaningful, even within conflicting and controversial contexts. Terming parades a mode of communication means that an audience existed, and that observers and performers had ways of knowing what was intended by performances. If parades were kinds of communication, how did they communicate? What kinds of communication were they?

Concepts for the Study

The concepts framing this study flow from the ongoing dialogue shared by folklore, history, and sociolinguistics. E. P. Thompson, Henry Glassie, Dell Hymes, and Raymond Williams, among others, have presented ways to think historically about culture and anthropologically about history, extending our understanding of the relationship between culture and communication.¹¹ My theses about public performances rest on several concepts, the first of which is context. Defining context requires considering parades and ceremonies within social history and the history of communication; it is also necessary to discuss the nature of the immediate social-historical context for a case study of public culture. Other central concepts include popular culture and vernacular communication, the problem of tradition and how it is selectively shaped and built, style and its relation to vernacular communication, and the notion of public culture. Analysis of the history and patterns of parades and ceremonies in nineteenth-century Philadelphia will develop and refine these notions and clarify their links to the problematic relationship between enactment and power.

Context: History and the Traditions of Street Theatre

If public ceremonies are politically grounded, useful modes of communication, they must have evolved as societies developed new forms of authority, power, and media; thus, parades and ceremonies figure in the social history of communication. Such a history of communication genres, still largely unwritten, would include the relations between societies and their communicative practices, as well as the changing internal relations between kinds or genres of communication.[12]

A preliminary survey reveals a long history and a multitude of shifting uses for parades and processions, a diversity that is itself evidence of untraced historical processes.[13] Throughout history, street dramas have been used by those in power and by those out of official power. The history of drama yields examples of this use, since drama and power have long been closely linked. In the ancient world, and medieval and early modern Europe, the wielders of authority—the church and the state—developed expertise in the techniques of display; the relationship between theatre and monarchy, processions and power, was intimate.[14] Processions were elaborately planned exercises of church and state power in early modern Italy; in England state sponsorship and personal patronage combined to foster the development of the stage.[15]

Parades also figure in the history of European vernacular or popular culture as the symbolic, expressive modes of communication developed among and transmitted by peasants and common people. In the realm of the older European vernacular culture—from the earliest peasant revolts through the English Chartist movement to the demonstrations and "indignations" of nineteenth-century London— parades and processions have a long genealogy. This popular culture, Peter Burke argues, declined in Europe after 1800. Weakened by its rejection by elite patrons, routed by social upheavals and Protestant prejudice against superstition and irrationality, the genres of popular culture began to be displaced by new communications media. What happened to the popular culture and processional traditions of early modern Europe when faced with change in the New World? The study of public enactments in early-nineteenth-century Philadelphia provides some clues.[16]

In the United States, the years between the Revolution's end and the Civil War form a definitive period in the social history of public communication. Philadelphia, a leading commercial and industrial city, became a key site in the transformation and invention of street theatrical traditions. With its Revolutionary historical associations, unique spatial arrangements, international mix of immigrants, and the pace of its industrialization, Philadelphia was a center for cultural production, popular as well as elite, vernacular as well as commercial.

Building Traditions of Public Culture

The years between 1790 and 1860 were crucial for public culture and public performances because the nation was new; the direction of government, economy, and society still seemed open and uncertain. During these decades, Philadelphians played a prominent part in a process Eric Hobsbawm has called the invention of tradition.[17] Hobsbawm argues that modern nation states, in the transformation from monarchy to republic, solidify their power by constructing modes of communication and edification, including rituals and ceremonies, to help citizens understand the relationships between government and the people as well as people and history. As the United States underwent this process, citizens of the new republic invented traditions, such as Washington's Birthday, to fit their view of the nation's role in world history. But in the United States this process was somewhat different from that in other places, for example, early-nineteenth-century France. After 1798 the French Republic established institutions and offices to produce monuments, festivals, and spectacles to interpret the Revolution to citizens; this official production of ceremonial life has been continuous.[18] In the United States generally, and notably in Philadelphia, the creation of traditions of display was laissez-faire, to be taken up by those who could use spectacles and performances to suit their own purposes.

New possibilities for public culture and enactment burgeoned at the Revolution's end, but a central problem loomed. Were rituals and ceremonies appropriate to life in a republic? How would they be structured and used? In general, Philadelphians accepted the precedent of dramatizing social relations in public, but clashes of ideology as well as new social relations transformed older enactments and started divergent traditions. Even though royalist rituals seemed dead (indeed, they had been symbolically "executed" during the Revolution),[19] some Philadelphians, recognizing ceremonies' power, thought they smacked of popery and monarchy and had no place in the future republic.[20] In practice, a mélange of techniques was chosen from the past. Philadelphians rejected some older corporate and civic ceremonials, accepted others, and invented new ones. For example, Washington's Birthday was a bona fide local holiday before 1800, but even in the late eighteenth century it was no simple expression of patriotic consensus. The day became a holiday in part because some citizens who favored monarchy resurrected Georgian honors to highlight the president's kingly qualities. As the first candidate for hereditary rule, Washington himself wavered, favoring first a severe anticeremonialism, as with his New York inauguration in 1789, and later showing enthusiasm for courtly conduct at his birthday receptions and balls in Philadelphia. As criticisms of the February hubbub surfaced, ceremonial practices could be part of a debate about society. Would the new nation draw on English popular royalism, with all its excesses, and add adulation to its public life?[21]

The Washington's Birthday question resolved itself when he died. After 1800 the anniversary became less an honor to an individual and more a commemoration of a hero and the ideal of a disinterested farmer–soldier Cincinnatus. Still, Washington's memory crystalized in conflicting images: Some would see him as one of many republican heroes and others revere him as a godlike father. The twenty-second of February was commemorated with solemn processions by the Society of the Cincinnati, sermons and orations, workingmen's dinners, and apprentices' revels. The question persisted: What would republican rituals look like? Contradictions between the available repertoire of ceremonial traditions, the acceptance of public display, and republican suspicion of the motives behind spectacles nettled social critics and radicals.[22]

The decades before the Civil War saw a burst of national and local historical consciousness, expressed in the educated patriciate's publications and societies. There was much popular historicizing in vernacular forms, such as anniversaries and holidays, commemorations, and mythologizing. While Alexis de Tocqueville postulated that

America had no authentic traditions, urban Americans were elaborating strong patterns of festivity and ceremony, and vernacular commemorations frequently included parades and public ceremonies to connect past, present, and future.[23] These events were usually produced by men outside the patriciate who held no national prominence—contemporary men of letters denigrated popular historicizing as rude, inaccurate, and unsophisticated. The "ordinary" origins of ceremony were likely a source of learned disdain.

Since there is no history of any city's ceremonial life, much less the nation's, little is known about how commemorations developed. Laissez-faire ceremonial production meant that urban traditions were marked by regional and local differences. Philadelphians, proud of their ties to world history, made Independence Day a big event. In the early decades of the century, Evacuation Day (the twenty-fifth of November) became New York City's great historical holiday.[24] New England communities celebrated what is now called Patriots' Day on the anniversary of the Battle of Lexington (the nineteenth of April is still a legal holiday in Maine and Massachusetts). Bostonians have annually commemorated the Boston Massacre of March 5, 1770.[25]

Analysis of pre–Civil War Philadelphia reveals how urban Americans used the known, shared cultural pasts and reinvented parts of those pasts for use in the present. Which parts did they use, and for what purposes? Philadelphia's parade repertoire was based on older strains of street theatre. Sources were urban and mostly English, including Tudor, Stuart, and Hanoverian royal and civic pageantry. For example, George Washington's grand national tour in 1799 and his entrance into Philadelphia, although replete with republican trappings, still resembled an Elizabethan royal progress.[26] Philadelphians were familiar with corporate ceremonials in the eighteenth century, including dinners and celebrations of the king's birthday, receptions and banquets for investitures and visiting officials.[27] Seventeenth- and eighteenth-century guild rituals, although little known before the Revolution, were revived for later ceremonials.[28] Popular culture also contributed precedents for nineteenth-century street theatre. Rural and urban immigrants brought folk dramas to Pennsylvania, and while these unofficial and impious enactments suffered under

Quaker suppression of performances, folk dramatic techniques of European and African origin persisted in maskings and mummings, festive revelry, and burlesques.[29] Philadelphians also recast eighteenth-century English and American techniques of radical and royalist plebeian protest.[30]

The Immediate Historical Context, 1788–1860

Parades must be considered as products of an immediate social-historical context, as well as part of a larger history. The meaning of parades in early-nineteenth-century cities was as specific to context as speech or painting. No way of communicating can be understood from formal or stylistic characteristics alone, and dramatic production must be seen as particular to and developed to suit the context in which it is performed. Simply, ceremonies and rituals are human-made things. They must be studied in the time and space in which they are created.

How can we comprehend the context of vernacular media like street dramas? How big or small do we make context?[31] Philadelphia's antebellum parades were made in a world different from one that had used royal progresses, and different from one that can invent a Rose Bowl Parade. But what are the important differences? Layers or levels of context can be distinguished and analyzed. At the same time, context is more than a backdrop to be colored in. If street dramas are ways of acting on the world, they are related to social-historical situations, and they can affect the world that makes them.

Consider, as context, North America's economy. Ceremonies like the Washington Centennial proclaimed and helped strengthen the just and natural status of industrial capitalism in a period of momentum and crisis. But parades were also used to attack capitalism's effects and seeming inevitability. Another stratum of context is the type of urban industrialization taking place before 1860. Philadelphia's uneven but decisive development into a major manufacturing center created patterns of labor and daily life that promoted a distinctive calendar of festivity and public events. Industrialization provoked intense local controversies over group relations, even as it drew many ethnic groups with different performative traditions to the city. Parades were both tactics in and the subject of new and ongoing contro-versies: Who should have the right to display themselves collectively in the streets?

The Context of the Public Sphere

Parades and ceremonies can be called "public communi-cation" in common-sense acknowledgment of where they occur—in the streets. Performed outdoors in streets or squares or fields, such dramas seem to unfold before the eyes of all, open to the widest possible range of meaning and interpretation. But the visibility of parades should not be conflated with an absolute and unproblematic openness of communication. That parades have large and often widely inclusive audiences does not mean that they are open to everyone's influence and participation, or that all participation is equal. Nor should we assume that audi-ences for public events interpret what they observe in either uniform or randomly divergent ways. Rather, the nature of the domain called "the public sphere" helps structure what can be known and communicated publicly.

The domain in which public performances take place must be viewed as structured and contested terrain, rather than as a neutral field or empty frame for social action, and the public nature of street parades should be ana-lyzed rather than assumed. The institutions, practices, be-haviors, spaces and places we call the public sphere include the very idea that there can and should exist social inter-action open and accessible to the widest popular partici-pation and influence.[32]

Because of its links to the history of liberal democracy, the concept of the public sphere is infused with an ideology of neutrality. The notion of neutrality is useful for side-stepping the persistent question of whether or not system-atic, structural inequalities of power exist in democracies, as well as for masking or explaining away the struggles for power that take place among groups and classes.[33] The neutrality of the public sphere underscores the definition of democracy (and freedom) as the range of all possible indi-vidual choices for action. Further, this stance obviates the need to study the interrelationship of conflict, constraint, and meaning in communication.

As Émile Durkheim emphasized, no social space (or

behavior) can be neutral, precisely because it has been specified as social.[34] The street may be a confusing example because it gives its users the illusion of freedom. This illusion has been fostered for young working-class men because they have historically used the street to temporarily construct alternative social rules.[35] But social constraints on uses of the street have varied for different people, and even young white males have found their prerogatives challenged. The public realm of nineteenth-century Philadelphia is best seen as contested terrain, shifting and continually being redefined. Conflicting social relationships shaped the range of public possibilities, institutions, places, and events. This conflict infused parades with meaning, parades, which, in turn, were part of the contests shaping the public sphere.

Generic Context: The Ceremonial Repertoire

Philadelphians performed street ceremonies in what folklorists call a "generic context."[36] A parade was one of a range of urban communicative events: orations, lectures, sermons, elections, riots, demonstrations, balloon ascensions, commercial promotions, charitable balls, executions and punishments, market days, building dedications, concerts, and political meetings. Parades took some of their meaning from their relation to and contrast with other kinds of performance. Was a Christmas masking, perhaps, one of a slew of plebeian entertainments that drew import from their contrast with a cotillion ball? More specifically, any individual procession was part of a range of street theatrical devices current at any time and developed and maintained over time. Performances took place, in theory and reality, in relation to all other performances, contemporaneous and historical. This generic context must be reconstructed in order to describe the interrelationships of styles and kinds of public events, their typical uses, and the common frames of reference used to interpret performances. Generic context relates to style and the manipulation of conventions, for it is partly in reference to generic context that styles can be identified and understood.

Generic context can be illuminated by reconstructing the city's repertoire of events, its annual festivities, and other occasions when parades were possible, warranted, or indispensable. Generic comparison also includes study of how marches unfolded and who took part in them. Seeing these details within a communicative whole clarifies the choices made in the invention of traditions. When generic relations are considered as context, absence, omission, neglect, and suppression can emerge as critical forces as influential as invention and inclusion.

PARADES AS POPULAR CULTURE
AND VERNACULAR COMMUNICATION

Defining parades as "a popular mode of communication in the nineteenth-century city" provokes an examination of what is meant by "popular" or "vernacular culture."[37] Parades were well attended and frequent; their new popularity was linked to the invention of tradition, and public displays were acquiring new meanings in antebellum Philadelphia. By the Civil War, Philadelphians had an elaborate repertoire of parades, a recurring calendar of festivities and special events marked with street ceremonies. Thousands witnessed and participated in the city's procession advocating the adoption of the Constitution (1788), receptions for the Marquis de Lafayette (1824), demonstrations during the Bank War (1834), and fire-department extravaganzas, among others. Between 1788 and 1860, a variety of less spectacular parades punctuated everyday life.

Parades were popular, vernacular culture in the sense that they were informal, interactive communication. Philadelphians developed characteristic parade events, forms, and styles through nongovernmental and noncommercial processes, although commercial forces sometimes influenced public displays before 1860. Such unofficial cultural production defines our objects of study, folklore, and folk culture. Noncommercial communication processes, folklorists argue, differ qualitatively from industrial, commercial, and official modes of communication and media, and they have particular histories. Vernacular cultural production occurred when Philadelphians defined and refined methods for making appropriate and creditable parades. They had inherited many ideas from older cultural milieux. Parade styles, dramatic techniques, devices and symbols were established through experimentation, borrowed from the stage, or simply invented. Parades evolved from older traditions and were adapted for contemporary exigencies and

performers' experiences. These processes, which made parades popular and traditional, distinguish them, as kinds
of communication, from newspapers and radio broadcasts.
So, too, do the reasons for their performance. Unlike other
media, parades were not items for consumption, regardless
of the performers' ideologies and intentions.

Parades qualify as popular culture in another sense. A
wide variety of people could use the streets as a medium for
potent collective expression. They understood that group
motion could convey a message or image to the city at large.
This accessible mode of broadcasting required only shoe
leather, and did not rely on literacy for effectiveness. But I
do not claim that street theatre was a radically democratic
or even fully participatory art form, although it certainly
had democratic potential. While Philadelphians from freed
slaves to Freemasons used marches to convey messages
and claim power, the uses of the street had limitations—
often implicit, sometimes explicit, and sometimes articulated through force. Limits hedged in the popular uses of
public space for communication. This study emphasizes the
shifting freedoms and constraints on street dramas, the
social contours of popularity.

TRADITION AND SELECTIVITY

Parades were products of vernacular culture; they took place
frequently and were often associated with ceremonies commemorating history. Therefore, parades were traditional
practices, even in light of the frequency with which citizens
of the early republic invented traditions. The notion of invented traditions contrasts with everyday uses of the word:
Tradition is usually thought of as something directly (and
sometimes unthinkingly) handed down from the past, and
valued precisely because of that process of transmission.
Similarly, the tautology implied in many definitions of tradition states that people do traditional things because they
are traditional. Dell Hymes has offered a more precise view
of tradition, proposing that humans have a propensity to
"traditionalize." Hymes argues that in unofficial cultural
processes people validate practices, ideas, and activities by
naming them traditions from a heritable, shared past.[38]
Clearly, such processes are also at work in the official
invention of traditions. Furthermore, Raymond Williams

views traditions and processes of traditionalizing, whether official, vernacular, or fugitive, as selective; selectivity is a key process in the production of culture and communication.[39] Not all cultural patterns are traditionalized, and not all traditions persist.

The relationship between official invention of traditions and vernacular "traditionalizing" has not been well studied. Both processes must employ selectivity differently and have different qualities, characteristics, and aims. Governments and institutions sometimes allow parts of unofficial culture to be shared and transmitted, even while they discourage other strains and build official traditions. Vernacular culture sometimes draws on official culture for models and parodies; at other times, vernacular culture is oppositional, a "culture of contestation."[40] For now, it is sufficient to stress that all culture and communication depend on omission as much as inclusion. Like modern sculpture, meaning in expression is shaped by voids as well as solids. No matter how much modernism pronounces an irreducible individuality of meaning, everything said or done, built or stitched, or enacted is formed not only by individual choices but also by social definitions of what is, is not, cannot, or may not be done. The forces of selectivity include denial and forgetting, as well as suppression and distortion. Parades, like all cultural forms, are also products of selectivity in transmission.

Another contributing factor in selective transmission—the rise of commercial culture—gathered strength in the nineteenth century. The older vernacular culture described by Peter Burke and E. P. Thompson died slowly in the nineteenth century. Its demise did not result from some ineluctable process called "modernization," but from social and economic changes that ripped older rural and urban ways of life apart, and sustained and principled assaults by reformers and the state.[41] In this transformation of everyday life and symbolic modes, commercial culture played an ill-understood role.[42] The commercialization of festivals and music halls, fairs and markets; the development of a national market for entertainment; the invention of commodified recreation; and the rise of commercial journalism all helped destroy older modes of communication.

While parades and ceremonies were largely noncommercial communication before the 1860s, wholly commercial traditions were being developed. The Gilded Age factory picnic, employees' celebrations for the boss's birthday, and paternalist sponsorship of workers' holidays at company-owned recreational parks all sprang from antebellum experiments.[43] Standardized national traditions tied to commerce, consumption, and advertising, as well as to government, are recognizable after the Civil War—for example, Thanksgiving Day. These commercial–official traditions were the antecedents of present-day patterns of public ceremony produced by private enterprise, which blend with state and national traditions, and vice versa.[44]

Selectivity was at work in the invention of traditional occasions, the development of parade repertoire, and ways of being on parade: If ceremonies gave people ways of acting on their world, some ways were chosen, others rejected. In street theatre, invention, rejection, and validation were complexly bound.

Tradition Builders

Examination of tradition builders and bearers is indispensable to the analysis of traditionalizing processes.[45] Who made street ceremonies, in what varieties, and for what purposes? Unlike other art forms, street dramas do not seem to have individuated creators. If the Weccacoe Hose Company or the Butchers' Guild had parade masters, their identities are still secret. Uncovering processes of dramatic production is a matter of finding the social identities of people and organizations listed as performers and sponsors. Answers to these questions lie in mundane daily newspaper reports and advertisements, although diaries and account books are sometimes useful. These reports were used to build a broad, general account of a Philadelphia ceremonial repertoire, but descriptions of parades, though common, are usually terse. Newspaper accounts show that street performances were evaluated along a narrow range of values. Parades were rarely the subjects of paeans to genius.

Philadelphia's festive calendar and its ceremonial repertoire were shaped by many people's efforts. The local business class, many of whom held public office, voluntary associations, reform movements, clubs, struggling trades associations and occupational groups, the poor and anonymous bearers of folk traditions—all performed in the streets. The most significant division of street performers and repertoires followed class lines. When Philadelphia's economic and political leaders performed in the streets, they tended to do so separately and exclusively; alternatively, propertied citizens led, and played exemplary roles in more inclusive social dramas. Different groups contributed distinct repertoires to the city's public culture; at times, however, groups shared styles, and repertoires overlapped social boundaries.

Parade Styles and Conventions

In these informal processes, Philadelphians built a repertoire of parade conventions, a range of techniques for concerted symbolic action in public. This repertoire of conventions included competing ways of parading; though never codified, these ways were available for elaboration, revision, and assessment. I call these ways of parading "styles," and place their development at the center of this history.

Folklorists and historians argue that style and convention communicate meaningfully—in all social contexts—in genres as diverse as bread riots, sermons, and domestic architecture.[46] Conventions are the building blocks of style, details of which can be manipulated to make meaning; style is the recognition of conventional difference. Style was social information in nineteenth-century Philadelphia. Street performers and audiences perceived styles as existing within a range of possibilities, always as socially and politically meaningful choices. In some cases, choices of style in music, marching, banners, or dress were objects of scrutiny and debate, and were linked to the argument over public culture and behavior that grew out of shifting class relations. In the 1820s, working-class critics of social inequality often mentioned the legitimating use of public events to display employers' wealth and distinction. (These writers resisted the now-common pitfall of viewing style as an isolated, esthetic category.) One such critic, "Peter Single," proposed that while appearance was not everything, it proved useful in creating a belief in the naturalness of inequality. The powerful and affluent, he wrote, "originally poor in money and influence, succeeded by speculating in human misery," and "now ride in their carriage, give balls and act the rich nabob."[47]

The "respectable" ceremonies of the propertied and the "rowdy" rituals of working-class citizens comprised two styles infused with meanings that transcended the theatrical realm. *Respectability* set standards for public and private behavior that extended downward in the social hierarchy, to be imposed on, grasped, or rejected by different segments of workers and the poor. *Rowdiness* refers to old and new modes of behavior that opposed stylistically, if not always politically, business-class versions of appropriate behavior and social order. Although interests and styles often distinguished the parades of the powerful from those of the populace, the different ways of performing in public influenced each other mutually but unequally.

OUTLINE OF THE STUDY

This book begins with a broad definition of context. Chapter Two describes the city's streets and public spaces as stages for performances and outlines the forces defining the annual cycle of festivals and holidays. In the early nineteenth century, older uses of open spaces and festive times were being reshaped by the city's changing economy and by political and ideological shifts. The painful transition to industrial capitalism restructured individual and collective patterns of social life, work, and leisure. These changes are described in relation to each other and street theatre. Possibilities for street theatre were determined over time by law and custom, by the old and new allocations of space, and by patterns of the seasons and industrial time.

Chapters Three, Four, and Five delineate Philadelphia's parade performers and analyze their performances. Although many different types of Philadelphians took part in street theatre, newspapers rarely identified rank-and-file marchers. Nevertheless, sources reveal that social class, organizational activities, and street dramas are related. Three important parade-making traditions developed in the city after 1790; each had its own social location, history, and transformations.

The most prominent performers, whose marches thoroughly influenced the city's public culture, were the militia volunteers. Chapter Three examines the militia's ceremonious activities in relation to local social and class connotations of private military association. Militia training drills were elaborated into a popular art form, and as the volunteers created their own cycle of holidays, they began to invent or traditionalize local public events.

Chapter Four examines the fugitive, alternative, and disapproved parades of poor and working-class Philadelphians. Drawing on older folk traditions of masking and disguise, combined with political protest and direct action, and performed by young men, these dramas brought laughter and the imagery of popular justice into the streets. The history of alternative traditions sheds light on Philadelphia's Mummers, who have been perceived as bearers of an eternal, universal, and ahistorical folk custom.

Chapter Five outlines modes of representing labor as a social force. In its solemn and respectable tradition, the imagery of labor had a hard-earned legitimacy. Occupational theatricality and the enactment of work processes could embellish economic events, such as the opening of a canal, or inject labor's icons into a patriotic ceremony. Craftsmen and laborers used parades to further occupational and working-class interests in strikes and protests, and workingmen frequently took part in enormous marches by associations and reform movements that drew members from across class bounds. Comparison of these uses of the street illuminates the range of possibilities for representing class relations at a time when class difference (and the experience of class difference) was changing, heightened, and undeniable.

Chapter Six examines and compares the city's parade conventions and analyzes the parade repertoire as a mode of social communication. Analysis and comparison of styles show how social forces defined the making of a good parade. The two basic performance styles—respectable and rowdy —were not rigid; they combined with and took meaning from other social styles that Philadelphians called "republican" and "aristocratical," "black," "Irish," and "native American." The attribution of rowdy or respectable, legitimate or illegitimate, depended on the perceived identities and purposes of performers, as well as an immediate spatial or temporal context. Interpretation—the way paraders' messages were understood and acted upon—hinged as much on social context and audience knowledge as on style. Parades, though ephemeral, were more than entertainment: As communication they were ways of influencing perceptions and ideas, and, as such, important social actions. Examining parades and ceremonies, their performers, and their uses expands our knowledge of how public events communicate. In turn, familiar public rituals and their uses come to seem less natural and normal, more problematic and troubling. Today, as much as in the past, parades and ceremonies are media that shape how history and the future are understood.

CHAPTER TWO

The Setting in
Space and Time

Philadelphia's parade traditions were formed during a radical restructuring of urban economic and social life. What could, could not, and did take place in the city streets resulted from the interactions of a changing physical world, an explosive social environment, and shifting definitions of appropriate public behavior. More particularly, the city's festive calendar formally and informally codified the reasons people found to make street theatre. At the same time, changes in and conflicts over the calendar, festivals, and the popular uses of public space reveal how powerfully the city's transformation molded its parade traditions. This complicated context framed the gatherings, parades, and ceremonies of the populace and infused public performances with particular and general social meanings.

ECONOMIC CHANGE AND SOCIAL STRUCTURE

Between 1790 and 1860, Philadelphia shed its character as a center for the exchange of goods and money and became a powerful manufacturing metropolis. The rise of manufactures broke down and restructured older ways of life, affecting all levels of social life and culture. Spurred by the construction of canals and railways, the opening of new markets for urban manufactures drove the transition to industrial capitalism. The city began to produce light consumer goods for its own population, the region, and the rural hinterland.[1] Between 1800 and 1850, migrants in search of new kinds of work followed transport networks to Philadelphia, increasing the population at an unprecedented rate. The urban area quintupled its population—from 81,000 to 408,000—in five decades. Especially after 1820, the city absorbed many newcomers from the British Isles and still more from the Pennsylvania countryside.[2] As the city's industrial system changed unevenly but decisively, migrants sought work in a growing number of factories, manufactories, and workshops. Textile factories, introduced first as an experiment in "bettering" local paupers, soon became the centers of Manayunk, Spring Garden, and Kensington, tightly clustered working-class neighborhoods.[3] Other innovations in making glass, iron, furniture, shoes, and clothes brought large numbers of workers under one roof and one master, beginning the destruction of domestic industries and the restructuring of work patterns.

The transition to industrial capitalism widened older social and economic inequalities. Despite recurrent and devastating depressions, Philadelphia's rate of economic growth rose steadily between 1800 and 1850, and per capita wealth increased strikingly; but beneath the rosy measures of expansion lay desperation. The city housed more poor and working people than ever before, and growing numbers of workers depended solely on wage labor for their livelihood.

Wealth burgeoned, but its distribution grew more lopsided as a shrinking number of people controlled a swelling share of invested capital, property, and goods for export, in addition to personal income.[4] Although a stratum of merchants and professionals was emerging to ally with the wealthy and propertied, few rose from small beginnings to great wealth. The myth of the self-made man notwithstanding, most of Philadelphia's wealthy and powerful citizens had inherited their riches and social status from their fathers. Members of Philadelphia's patriciate kept their hands in the world of commerce and finance as they speculated in manufactures, transport, and private corporations.[5]

Although eighteenth-century Philadelphia had a large stratum of propertyless poor people, in the early nineteenth century differences between rich and poor sharpened. The worker's living standard did not rise with the merchant's swelling wealth, and industrial labor and overcrowding fostered impoverishment and health problems. A new kind of social relationship was being created, defining the amount and kinds of control people had over their lives. As more workers were less likely to own their own tools and dwellings, and as skills were devalued and reorganized in new modes of production, fewer people found the independent means of subsistence so valued by eighteenth-century workers. To live, most had to work for someone else, and for many, powerlessness to change their material situations defined their lives. Neither could the wealthy fully control the changes wrought by industrial capitalism: During economic crises, urban leaders were unable to alleviate widespread destitution and unrest.[6]

POLITICAL DEVELOPMENT AND SOCIAL CONFLICT

Differences in wealth and power were countered by a hopeful sign, the extension of political rights. Whereas in the eighteenth century political activity had been the domain of men of wealthy families and well-to-do artisans, nineteenth-century political participation took novel, extended forms. In Pennsylvania, white males enjoyed manhood suffrage, and by the 1830s they participated enthusiastically in political parties. Political participation, although broadened, may have masked widening class differences. In the first decades of the century, political leaders were still drawn from the city's wealthy and respectable families; by the 1830s merchants, businessmen, master artisans, and lawyers and other professionals dominated elective offices and political parties as they would for the rest of the antebellum period.[7]

In this period of fluidity and uncertainty, new forces and ideas entered the political arena. Men organized not only to influence the machinery of government, but also to challenge and control the pace and direction of social and economic change. Workers' associations, labor organizations, and a short-lived but important workingmen's movement injected urban, working-class concerns into politics, analyzing and attacking the forces reshaping workers' lives. Mechanics and artisans argued that the growing inequalities of wealth and power could not be ignored; they ad-

dressed the morality of accumulation, monopoly, and speculation, and they questioned the place of private economic
power in a democracy.[8]

Philadelphians participated enthusiastically in another
kind of nongovernmental political activity, the voluntary
association built upon neighborhood life and concerns.
Ethnic benefit societies, temperance and reform groups,
churches, and clubs bound men and women in networks
of sociability and special interest. However, Tocqueville's
hope that voluntary associations would mediate tensions
and rival the power of the "mercantile aristocracy" was
unfulfilled. Associations and clubs were more than means
for advancing ideas and platforms: The most elite of them
provided the means by which Philadelphia gentlemen
maintained control over important issues and institutions.
At lower levels, neighborhood reform societies and clubs
were structures through which merchants, businessmen,
and professionals became respected authorities and local
leaders. So, the purposes and activities of voluntary organizations that bound men across class lines tended to be
defined by men allied with business.[9]

Economic and social changes provoked bitter, almost
constant social conflict, and Philadelphia's associations expressed and engaged in more conflicts than they mediated.
Hibernians and Orangemen, abolitionists and slavery's
advocates, Whigs and Democrats, nativists and Catholics,
teetotalers and tipplers, workers and factory masters all
used associations to propagandize their positions and
attack each other. The city's streets were the prime location
for public expression of conflict, in both symbolic and physical modes. If most clubs and societies attacked their opponents only in the symbolic realm, many Philadelphians
communicated social antagonism with bricks, lathe, cobble-
stones, and bullets in the city's riots. Philadelphia was
wracked by mob violence in the 1840s and 1850s; its notorious street upheavals frightened the gentle, antagonized
the propertied, and contradicted Thackeray's praise for its
"grave, calm, kind" atmosphere.[10]

SPATIAL CHANGE AND THE USES OF THE STREET

Before the Civil War, the city underwent dramatic physical and social–geographic changes. In a sense, the city's

parade traditions were themselves ways people found to make the altered street and the expanding city understandable and knowable. Like other settlements, Philadelphia was initially conceived as a combined garrison and commercial venture, and its form reveals these mixed purposes. The shapes of medieval European cities and their early modern rebuildings recognized the performances central to church and state power. North American commercial cities, in contrast, were designed to move traffic and develop land, not house spectacles.[11]

Spaces formally designed for public activities were part of Philadelphia's seventeenth-century heritage, although they were not used as planned. William Penn's draftsman laid out a grid of streets, with two avenues intersecting at a midpoint forming Center Square, and four smaller squares defining the town's quadrants. Penn reserved Center Square for governmental buildings and activities; the other four were declared public domain, reserved for future recreation and gatherings of all the people.[12] As it worked out, Center Square was far removed from the hub of everyday life, the Delaware docks, and a half-timbered courthouse met government's needs in the city's markets at Second and High (now Market) streets. In the 1730s the city corporation moved the business of government out of the disorderly docks into orderly Georgian offices on a square surrounded by Fifth, Sixth, Walnut, and Chestnut streets. The yard around these buildings opened a sixth formal public space inside Philadelphia's boundaries, and the new State House became the site of corporate ceremony.[13]

In the eighteenth century, the squares served as commons with recreational and symbolic uses. Center Square boasted a tavern, a race course, and a militia parade ground. The city corporation used the large open field to stage public hangings, its infrequent but most popular spectacles, and twice-yearly fairs. The southeastern square found use as a potter's field, a burial ground for black and white paupers, and as a spot for slaves' festive dances.[14] The northeastern, northwestern, and southwestern squares served informally as drill, play, and burial grounds and offal dumps, uses which city leaders later rejected and reformed.

Throughout the eighteenth century and well into the next, privately owned, multifunctional open space lay at the city's edge. The city was surrounded by the outlying villages and a rural landscape of marshes and farmland, which Philadelphians used for fishing, swimming, hunting, and skating. Within walking distance of a city dwelling, open ground sheltered customary illegal sports such as bearbaiting, cockfighting, horseracing, and pugilism, and forage in the countryside buffered the poor in hard times. Semirural areas existed within the city in open yards and lots used as cow pastures, gardens and orchards, playgrounds, and work areas.[15]

Economic growth altered Philadelphia's colonial appearance and older spatial patterns. Open space was increasingly exploited for commercial use, and private property rights took precedence over older, informal uses. Open lots were filled with new buildings and the city moved outward, replacing farms and fields. The downtown surrounded the old city on the Delaware River, but private builders and speculators erected fine buildings on the westward streets, concentrating, investing, and displaying wealth in handsome domestic structures.[16] A great deal of money could be made by housing workers and the poor; thus blacks and Irish immigrants were crowded into suburbs and into the city's newly opened alleys and courts. Whole working-class districts sprang up around factories on the fringe of the urban grid. As the compact and walkable city, once an incomplete plan, became a large, densely populated terrain, neighborhoods acquired separate identities based on industry or ethnicity. Territorialities or specific conflicts were expressed in the streets, in fights, brawls, and riots.[17]

In the nineteenth century, the streets were the most accessible open space in the city; their layout and size testified to the city's preoccupation with the manufacture and movement of goods. Conduits for commodities and information, Philadelphia's streets extended in a grid of right angles north and south (between Vine and Cedar streets) and east and west (from the Delaware River to Center Square, and later to the Schuylkill). Some visitors found this rectangular plan monotonous. Frances Trollope, for example, declared her short downtown walk boring, and Rebecca Harding Davis felt oppressed and confined by her downtown neighborhood. But regular streets aided traffic flow, and the easy movement of goods to shipping points was important as Philadelphia became a major manufacturing center.[18]

The regularity and spacing of the streets made them easy, walkable transit ways. Houses faced the street, and doors fronted on the traffic, with only a few steps between interior and exterior. To step out one's door was to step into an intensely social milieu. Information, goods, experience, neighborliness (and perhaps anonymity) could be had for the walking.[19] To enter the street was to join and help create social communication.

Social life in neighborhoods and downtown streets took shape around a variety of commercial establishments, from grand to modest, and these multiplied along the transit ways and in side streets. Corner taverns flourished, and new institutions—oyster cellars, pleasure gardens, dance halls—hedged the street with sociability. Bow windows advertised goods of all kinds, and commercial theatres, forbidden in the eighteenth century, flowered first at the city's southern boundary and later in the district around the State House. By 1830 the theatre district featured the work of the most popular playwright of the period, Shakespeare, on the same stage with pantomimes and fairy shows, with blackface minstrelsy, circuses, panoramas, and automata.[20]

Street Life and Class Perception

The density of buildings and people and cultural, human, and commercial variety swelled and pressed on the street, amplifying its possibilities as a milieu for communication. Yet this variety and openness were problematic. Affluent and respectable Philadelphians were discomfitted by the disgusting scenes of vernacular culture unfolding in theatre and pub, street and square. The commercial theatre now played to a strongly working-class audience; refined theatre-goers, horrified by conduct in the galleries, sought refined theatrical spheres for themselves. At the same time, they decried the moral effects of stage spectacles on the excitable plebs.[21]

Moral reformers noted that working and poor people conducted much of their social, domestic, and working lives outdoors. As Christine Stansell has argued, the uses of nondomestic space for activities seen as properly familial and private became evidence of working-class ignorance and degeneracy.[22] People whose occupations depended on the street came under attack. Ragpickers, food vendors, hawkers, beggars, scavengers, and petty criminals used the street's rich resources but were increasingly harassed by the city watch and laws.[23]

Degeneracy was perceived everywhere in the public sphere, but especially in working-class social life and petty economic activities. Reformers made piecemeal efforts to banish unseemly customs and trades. For example, City Councils attempted to suppress street vendors' cries, bells, and horns as early as the 1830s. Others, often radical artisans, defended the rights of perambulating sellers, asserting that tradesmen's noise was a kind of public information.[24] There was also local defense of neighborhood street use: Vendors fought for the right to keep carts and stalls, and residents resisted the introduction of railroad and streetcar tracks that ruptured familiar residential patterns and fractured street life. People from the same districts banded together and sometimes fought to keep their streets free of watchmen, fine collectors, and strikebreakers, even as they defended their territories against foreigners, blacks, and outsiders.[25]

With more leisure and domestic space at its command, the business class responded to the street's culture by creating distance. Men moved their occupations out of the house, and family life and domestic labors withdrew from public view, to be defended by new standards of domestic manners, privacy, and gentility.[26] Try as they might, genteel citizens could not fully escape. Residential space was increasingly stratified by class and ethnicity, but the city was densely populated and poor neighborhoods persisted in alleys, courts, and the back streets of fashionable blocks. While separation was incomplete, an irritating physical proximity influenced perceptions and prompted more differentiation of behaviors and manners. Back alleys and working-class blocks were seen as "regions" populated by "demons" who menaced peace and morality.[27]

REORGANIZATION AND REINTERPRETATION OF SPACE

Lacking the ability to "renew" whole neighborhoods, affluent Philadelphians concentrated on accessible and symbolic spaces, notably the squares and, later, through the establishment of the police, the central streets. The potter's field, for example, was a miasma of collapsed graves and polluted water by the 1820s. In 1832 the Washington Centennial gave City Council members and militia volunteers the impetus to complete a proposed redesign of the square. William Strickland was commissioned to design a monument and commemorative square that would serve as a patriotic shrine and a fashionable resort for the neighborhood. Although the monument was never erected, the cornerstone was laid with military fanfare, and the square refurbished. Franklin, Logan, and Rittenhouse squares, in poor condition by the 1830s, were similarly reinvented in the nineteenth century. Logan and Rittenhouse had been used for decades as offal dumps, and Franklin had been illegally annexed for a churchyard. Poor neighbors around Rittenhouse Square complained of its condition as a threat to their health and safety, but it was the desire of affluent new residents for parks that finally spurred improvements.[28]

Throughout the nineteenth century, Philadelphians treated State House Square as the city's symbolic heart and most sacred site. The place was laden with local memories of the Revolution. On the day the Declaration of Independence was read, the crowd dragged the king's arms out of the hall and publicly burned them, making the square thoroughly revolutionary and North American.[29] During the war, the meetings of Congress, the speeches, and frequent military drills there had firmly attached the city's "affections" to the State House. Before the Civil War, the Democratic Party favored State House Square as a ceremonial spot and the city corporation used it as a reception hall for dignitaries and honored patriots. Philadelphians voted there and gathered there in civil emergencies; during strikes workingmen and unionists used Independence Hall's steps as a stage from which to read declarations of independence from their masters.[30] The Square served as the starting and ending point for many of the city's parades.

Paradoxically, while the social life of the city became more complicated and varied, some of the uses of open space were more contested, as the propertied worried about how public spaces should be used and what public events communicated. The squares were a case in point. State

House Square had recreational as well as ceremonial uses. As the five squares became parks, however, problems arose over recreation in these public places. In the 1830s, John Watson recalled a history of complaints about the uses of State House Square dating back to "the year of the war's conclusion [1783]," when the yard became "a place of general resort," "the haunt of many idle and profligate people." [31] In nineteenth-century City Council meetings, Philadelphia's leaders continually debated monitoring the behavior of the idle and profligate as well as protecting public spaces from indecorous users.

Collective uses of open space prompted more anxiety and were less susceptible to constraint than individual cases of inappropriate behavior. Center Square always drew working-class crowds on holidays, especially the Fourth of July. Officials repeatedly tried to restrain festivities, and finally banned booths and tents there in 1823. Expressing concern over crowds at spectacles, the state legislature removed hangings from public view. After the last open-air public execution in 1837, hangings were conducted inside Cherry Hill Prison. [32]

SPACE FOR WORKING-CLASS POLITICAL ACTIVITIES

From the working-class point of view, access to space for political activities was constrained in the antebellum period. Any trade union gathering could be labeled conspiratorial in the early nineteenth century; although workingmen relied on taverns and hotel dining rooms for regular meetings, their leaders had trouble finding halls for larger ceremonies and speeches. As Robert Dale Owen pointed out, workers needed their own spaces if they were to construct a fully autonomous political movement:

> You will be told there are public buildings enough in your city already. There are buildings enough, but whose are they? . . . [Churches] offer teaching without challenge or reply . . . and are not churches closed six days a week? . . . Neither the churches nor the State House are under the control of the people, the strange unrepublican fact is that while each of your hundred ministers of religion has a public building at his command, the people have not one at theirs. [33]

As the general strike of 1835 taught workers, the clergy often sided with employers. In that year, tens of thousands of men massed regularly in State House Square to hear speeches, but demonstrators ordinarily had to ask city officials for permission to use the yard and building.[34] Workingmen and the unemployed customarily held large meetings on street corners and in lots, where the back of a wagon served as a podium. On one hand, open-air gatherings could reach the city at large; on the other, weather could thwart such efforts, and it was difficult to conduct business with regularity.

As Owen emphasized, obtaining a building for collective use required money, resourcefulness, and a cause that those in power considered legitimate. Ironically, this limitation contrasted with an increase in the construction of "public" buildings—lycea, lecture halls, theatres, and museums—by businessmen, merchants, and private associations.[35] Black congregations, for example, struggled for decades to erect churches in which to center their communities.[36] Once constructed, black churches were given no guarantee that the city would protect them from racist mobs. Opponents of slavery—black and white, male and female—were always in danger when they held meetings, as the burning of the abolitionists' Pennsylvania Hall in 1838 demonstrated.[37]

THE POPULAR USES OF THE STREET

The streets enabled workers, poor people, and racial minorities to broadcast messages to large numbers of people, which partly explains the vibrant popularity of parades of all kinds and the variety of autonomously produced mobile performances. The street was shared more equally than any other space. A decision to strike, a meeting's outcome, or a festive gathering could move quickly from an assembly into a marching line that conveyed a message to coworkers, neighbors, and the city at large.

The grid of streets built for commerce suited the circulation of important messages, and parades fit the informal milieu of the street. Parades and processions occupied a crucial terrain of behavior between personal interactions at corners or dooryards and more formal ritual behavior, such as commemorations, oratory, or reenactments. Especially in the dense downtown area where work and domestic life were adjacent, parades took place within sight of home and neighbors, and within view of wide varieties of people. Characteristically, the early nineteenth-century line of march repeatedly doubled back on itself as it wound around familiar residential blocks.

Some of the deep, entwined roots of hostility to popular gatherings can be traced to colonial times. European historians have shown that Puritan antagonism to early modern vernacular culture led to recurrent attempts at suppression and reform.[38] In North America, the battle between the older superstitious plebeian culture and Protestant rationality, between Carnival and Lent, was often drawn around the issues of dramatic enactment and popular festivity. Because Pennsylvania's Quakers, like other Puritans, opposed marking any day as more sacred than another, they viewed the "irrational" behavior and revelries of traditional holidays and rituals as obnoxious and morally corrupting. Seventeenth- and eighteenth-century Quaker authorities had tried to eliminate festive Christmas customs, such as disguise, drumbeating, firing guns, noisemaking, drinking, and feasting.[39] Distrust of enactments and entertainments lay behind a long tradition of restricting theatre within Philadelphia.

Dramas and gatherings were neither easily contained nor easily abolished. The "[g]reat gatherings of people," the twice-yearly fairs in Center Square, were sources of complaint as early as the 1690s, and were called disruptions of the peace and corrupting influences on apprentices, servants, and youth. At such festive times, slaves, too, had permission to hold dances. But the fairs' economic functions made them difficult to abolish until the 1770s; like fairs, Afro-American revels were outlawed on the eve of the Revolution and never revived.[40]

Uneasiness over the regular gatherings of poor people stemmed as much from the social organization of labor in the city, and the social makeup of crowds, as from religious or cultural hostility to "irrational" behavior. The city depended heavily on unfree labor in the eighteenth century, that is, the labor of slaves, indentured servants, and apprentices. From the 1740s, petitioners urged City Councils to suppress "tumultuous meetings and disorderly doings of Negroes, Mullatoes, Indians, Servants and Slaves" who met in the marketplace after dark to talk and play music. Such demands for legal controls on the uses of the marketplace were repeated throughout the eighteenth century.[41] Antagonism to gatherings, fairs, and dances expressed owners' and masters' understanding that autonomous and unsupervised uses of free time by the unfree might endanger the social order. If uprisings of slaves and servants were unlikely in Philadelphia, autonomous recreation provided opportunities for these workers to build networks of communication and culture that might support insubordinate attitudes and shield runaways.

By the early nineteenth century, hostility to large gatherings of working people was still strong, perhaps having roots in memories of the Revolution. The city's working class pushed for radically democratic social change; several times the "lower orders" came close to seizing the Revolution from its elite leaders.[42] But new class relations, as much as memory, made crowds threatening. Ignoring the democratic heritage preserved in the people's right to assemble, some fearful commentators suggested that public gatherings be banned altogether.[43] They supported the position of employers and political leaders who opposed any manifestation of working-class radicalism, whether in the Revolutionary War's crowd violence and direct action, or in the new trade union meetings. More generally, opposition to public gatherings grew out of an awareness that workers' relationships to their superiors had changed. If employers owed workers nothing more than wages, and laborers owed masters little loyalty, where might a mass meeting lead in hard times? Under conditions of widespread poverty, growing population, and cyclical, recurring depressions, large gatherings of people were dangerous. As the riots of the 1830s, 1840s, and 1850s showed, Philadelphians could express or be manipulated to express violent hatreds. But riots were the most extreme example of problematic crowd behavior, and most Philadelphia riots were aimed at outsiders, social inferiors, and proponents of unpopular causes like abolition, rather than at factory owners.[44]

Even during peaceful times, the level of business-class suspicion remained high. Gathered in large groups, workers might recognize and examine their common interests, spread word of their discovery, and learn ways to act collectively. Fear of class recognition, more than dread of riots, prompted attacks on the working-class public presence and fed hostility toward seemingly innocent gatherings at theatres and parades.

These strains of antagonism surfaced in criticism of working-class festivity, which was becoming more explosively jubilant as the city's population boomed. Festivals were free time that the populace could structure alternatively and use collectively. As industrial capitalism transformed the uses of time in the workplace and home, festivals held appealing possibilities for autonomous recreation, something hard-pressed workers desperately needed. Autonomous uses of collective time also suggested the development of an oppositional working-class culture, a possibility that disturbed the business class. When employers and respectable citizens complained about Christmas revelry and Fourth of July street battles, they acknowledged a reordered relationship between labor and sociability, workday and holiday. The opponents of festivity, seeing older ways of life disappear before their eyes, recognized their inability to control the present and the future.

TIME AND PUBLIC CULTURE

Time and the social structuring of time codified in the calendar constituted another dimension of context for parades and ceremonies. From the city's cycle of festivals, people developed major reasons for gatherings, street dramas, and processions. Like space, festival and the uses of free or nonlaboring time had a history, particular to Philadelphia, which included conflict.

The city's growing strength in manufactures restructured collective and individual clocks and calendars. On one hand, industrial progress did not immediately destroy older urban and agrarian work rhythms. As in an agrarian culture, patterns of labor and leisure were still influenced by climate. Many industries were hand or water powered, and much work took place outdoors. New textile factories could halt for weeks at a time because of frozen or overflowing streams. The major avenues of commerce were rivers, which, when free of ice, supported longshore and ship-building trades, fishing, and oyster dredging; thus, in the coldest days of winter, whole industries dragged to a halt. Conversely, for many workers summer was a period of intense activity. For instance, construction workers often called strikes in July to put extra pressure on employers who expected high productivity in good weather. Many occupations fluctuated with the seasons, affecting everyday life and public culture as long as hand power and water power dominated work processes.[45]

New forms of industrial organization began to revolutionize the way individuals and groups sensed and used time. As Bruce Laurie has shown, a range of work processes and environments—from factories to sweatshops to hand-crafts and casual labor—could be found in the antebellum city. Each productive process placed different demands on the worker, and Laurie argues that the work experience helped shape styles of social life and ideologies. Philadelphians who worked in mechanized mills were forced to learn punctual habits and pay constant attention to a rapid and repetitive machine-driven task. This intense discipline left little room for older patterns of drinking and socializing on the job. Douglas Reid has shown that employers in nineteenth-century Sheffield stepped up this discipline and restructured the work week when they introduced expensive steam power, which they were unwilling to waste on dilatory "hands." Hard-pressed and poor, the new factory workers were especially vulnerable to the demands of evangelical piety and temperance, which stressed a guilty self-discipline and a harsh rejection of irrational habits.[46]

The majority of city workers, however, had some control over work and more relaxed attitudes toward free time. Many men toiled in small manufactories, in workshops, or at home; another large proportion were day laborers in the streets or docks, while working women plied trades at home or hired out as domestic servants. This pattern of productive organization, combining small-scale production with increasing division of labor processes, relied on the semiskilled and unskilled and was bolstered by waves of immigrant labor.

At the top of labor's hierarchy, skilled artisans and masters of small workshops had some control over their work pace and its influence on their lives. Those with greater autonomy read, argued and socialized at work, and chose their days off. Some skilled workers transmitted the radical artisanal heritage of natural rights philosophy, based on the writings of Thomas Paine, self-education, and mutual aid. These rationalists tended to oppose the rowdy, free-and-easy ways of the unskilled and uneducated, while they attacked the revivalists as irrational ranters.[47]

In the city's seasonal festivals, urban workers found a terrain in which to preserve the relaxed, if sometimes boozy, life of the workshop and tavern. As traditional liberties were assaulted in workplaces, churches, and lecture halls, time and room were found for them on days and in places freed from the dictates of time clocks and ministers. Philadelphia's festivals became the apotheosis of workers' autonomy, as men and women whose lives were constrained by harsh labor abandoned themselves to the temporary liberties of festive recreations. Those on the fringe of the work world—the unemployed, the casual laborer, the young, and the poor—joined artisans and mechanics in extending flexible labor patterns into license and revelry.[48]

FESTIVITY AND PUBLIC ORDER

Some Philadelphians who criticized local festivities complained of streets being overrun by an ethnically and racially mixed rabble who lacked decorum, deference, or restraint. Especially after 1830, three major breaks in the working year—Christmas, Muster Day, and the Fourth of July—drew complaints of outrageous, disgusting behavior.

Christmas was a time for relaxation and the reaffirmation of social bonds, but it was also an interval when urban moral order threatened to come undone. As occupations came to a halt, work made way for a week of customary recreations: drinking and dancing, sacred and secular rituals, skating parties, ox roasts, pigeon shoots, pig chases, and lotteries. Commercial theatres counted heavily on holiday audiences for special harlequinades, pantomimes, circuses, and minstrel shows during Christmas week. Militia troops, firemen, and other associations held balls and promenade concerts; ladies gave church fairs; Methodists "watched in" the New Year; and cookshops sold seasonal specialties.

Hundreds of pubs, groggeries, and taverns treated their customers "with extra liberality."[49]

For working people there was a fine line between seasonal relaxation and distress. Unemployment rose sharply in the winter city. The sense of a special, heightened time persisted from rural life, but many working people, cut off from older means of subsistence and self-sufficiency by the rise of wage labor, found the slowed pace of winter a threat to health and livelihood. To the growing alarm of observers and reformers, drink, relaxation, and despair combined with rollicking recreations to transform the Christmas streets into scenes of fighting. In the 1840s, authorities claimed that Christmas and New Year's night celebrations disgraced the city; they annually declared working-class districts out of control during the holidays.[50]

On Christmas Eve, 1833, for instance, "riot, noise and uproar prevailed uncontrolled and uninterrupted in many of our central and most orderly streets. Gangs of men and boys howled as if possessed by the demon of disorder."[51] Christmas was also marked by mob attacks on blacks, fighting among black and white gangs, firemen's riots, arson, and great throngs in the central streets and squares. City officials and middle-class observers viewed Christmas revelry as public disorder and attempted to contain it. Compared with solemn ceremonies and decorous balls, Christmas masking, noisemaking, and street performances seemed to challenge dominant ideals.

Battalion or Muster Day revelry in spring also prompted criticism. The legally required mustering and drilling of the men enrolled in public companies (theoretically, all those between eighteen and forty-five years of age) took up several days in May, during which time parades took over the city. Alongside the public companies marched the city's elite private militia, until thousands of uniformed and non-uniformed men jammed the streets and parade grounds. To city authorities Muster Day was a cumbersome, unruly holiday. Because Muster Day was required by law, it warranted a day off from work for enrollees, many of whom were mechanics, artisans, journeymen, and laborers; thus underage employees and apprentices were set free for the day. These young men swelled the crowds of ineligible blacks, children, the curious, and "criminals" who flocked to the parade grounds. In rural Pennsylvania farmers used Muster Day as a time for visiting and business, as well as drilling, celebrating it with drinking, dancing, and the selling of food and trinkets;[52] in the city, Muster Day had all these features on a grand scale.[53]

Complaints about Muster Day point to its festive tone, the suspension of work, and the extralegal activities that often accompanied it. "The jubillee of general idleness," it was despised for the "din and turmoil of reviews."[54] In 1828 a grand jury sitting at Philadelphia presented the parade ground at Bush Hill as "an ill governed and disorderly place, where all sorts of vices are practiced day and night, particularly on parade days."[55]

A welter of reasons existed for the dislike of Muster Days. Those compelled to drill resented the loss of their working time, but took the opportunity to enjoy the day—or lessen its burdens—with drink and recreation. Disorderly parade days also undermined the work discipline demanded by employers because musters encouraged absenteeism on the part of both the enrolled and nonenrolled. Employers who struggled to get men to relinquish "Saint Monday" had little enthusiasm for a legally mandated day—which could stretch into a week—of work's suspension. Reformers and Sabbatarians, who hoped to teach workers to use free time piously and rationally, viewed the informal pleasure fair as a nest of vices.

Reform of the militia system, a thorny issue through the years before 1860, turned in large part on the issue of public parade days. Raucous parade-ground activities cast doubt on the muster's value to the nation's military strength. But proposals for reform echoed manufacturers' objections as much as workingmen's dissatisfactions. In 1837, one Adjutant Small, running for the post of major in the city's Ninth Regiment, assured citizens that he "opposed all kinds of militia parades except at such times as will be least inconvenient to men of business and citizens generally."[56] Since few businessmen would have belonged to the public militia companies because of the system of exemptions, Small addressed them as concerned employers of enrollees.

Philadelphians celebrated competing versions of Independence Day. For the well-to-do and politically powerful, the Fourth of July was a temporal arena for political rhetoric and displays of partisan and civic values. Despite differences in political opinions, leaders of opposed factions shared common notions about the proper way to celebrate the anniversary—with elegance, decorum, and respectability. From the gentlemanly, enlightened culture of those who led the Revolution, along with customs of the earlier Georgian men's clubs, Freemasonry, and eighteenth-century corporate ceremony, grew an annual pattern of elite events, a mix of open and private ceremonies. Cannon and bells announced the day to everyone, and militia troops circulated through the central streets and squares. The day's political meanings found formal reconstruction and interpretation in church sermons, orations, and long, sumptuous dinners. Planned by committee and held in hotels, subscription dinners were designed for and attended by likeminded men—the Society of the Cincinnati, the Sons of Saint Tammany, Federalists, Jeffersonians, Democratic Republicans, and later Whigs and Democrats of various stripes.[57] Though these men reveled separately, they shared the same festive forms. In the vigorous political life of Philadelphia's upper reaches, men who ate and drank together on this day shared more than opinion or patriotic sentiment, for dinners were only one event in a year-round cycle of male mutuality and commensalism connecting family, business, and politics.[58]

The city's small reading public learned about these gentlemanly ceremonies through party press reports. The committee of arrangements always furnished newspaper editors with the texts of toasts and speeches.[59] Onlookers were aware of the presence of eminent diners from painted window illuminations, flags, and buntings. Most important among the techniques of self-advertisement was the dining company's parade from meeting place to hotel, announcing to spectators that the day was being commemorated with appropriate pomp by those most fit to celebrate. Processions such as those of the Society of the Cincinnati always filed from the sacred spot—the State House—to church and then to private dining rooms. Likewise, volunteer militia troops dramatically bridged the worlds of street and private club with fancy dress parades.[60] The Fourth of July created by affluent men joined together in voluntary associations presented an elegant, dignified, and patriotic face—an image projected through the combination of orderly private ceremonies and public street dramas. Dinners and orations framed the ideas about nationhood, progress, and patriotism held by all-white, all-male organizations and parties. Not surprisingly, these expressions furthered particular interests while remaining embedded in universal-sounding values.[61]

The obverse of the decorous Fourth unfolded in the streets, squares, and fields, where semicommercial popular recreations were the heart of working-class celebrations. Tavern frolics and informal excursions were popular from early in the century.[62]

With breaks in the working year crowded increasingly into the few new national holidays and the solstices as old craft holidays disappeared, the Fourth of July became less an anniversary and more a jubilantly popular festival.[63] Yet the Fourth was not observed everywhere with work's suspension. Independent artisans probably took the day off, but whether large employers granted a holiday or workers took it for themselves is unclear. One Manayunk textile operative writing in the 1830s described the Fourth as a customary day off. A study of small textile mills on Brandywine Creek, however, reports that employers tried to force workers to labor on the Fourth, and that workers took the day off by striking.[64] Customary prerogatives must have varied with the type of industry, the size of the workplace, and the needs and predilections of both employer and employee.

Complaints about working-class behavior focused on Center Square, the end point of militia company parades, where hucksters and gamblers assembled around the company tents and tavern. (*J. L. Krimmel's "Independence Day Celebration in Centre Square" among the illustrations shows just such tents and carousing.*) As with Muster Day, municipal authorities and the press found vice and corruption. A tirade published in 1822 cited the great degree of drunkenness and "bare-faced violations of the liquor laws."[65] In 1823 Mayor Robert Wharton banned stalls and booths from the site on that day.[66] Undaunted, petty entrepreneurs shifted their operations to "the hill opposite Fairmont" at the city's edge, where unlicensed liquor sales, betting, fighting, and the enticements of prostitutes persisted.

In 1839 the *Public Ledger* complained that "the licentious portion of the community have made preparations to . . . desecrate the day" and deplored "the crowds of our youth of all ages . . . reeling and staggering . . . troops of abandoned females . . . gambling, both dice and cards." [67] In 1844 the *Ledger* again called on respectable citizens to set an example and reform the Fourth of July by replacing "the saturnalia of passion" with a "jubilee of reason." [68] Class recognition continually informed criticism of Independence Day: In the 1850s, editorials denounced riots and gunfights in working-class districts. [69]

Criticism forced some changes in festive behavior, but reform from within the working class was limited to small circles. For instance, when working people tried to shape festivity for their own political causes, they often felt compelled to adopt their critics' forms and styles. Some artisans, for example, tried to mold the Fourth's popular nationalism into a temperate republicanism. Leaders of the General Trades' Union and the Workingmen's Party defended workers' rights to festivity, but they urged their brothers to mark the day with restraint and propriety. A manifesto issued in 1829 claimed the Fourth for workingmen, but urged them to accept the gentlemen's way of celebrating:

> No class of the community has so generally and constantly manifested a sense of hilarity on the Fourth of July as the Working People. While the more wealthy classes have gradually withdrawn themselves from all public display on this national holiday as *ungenteel*, the toil worn artisan has continued to set it apart with mirth and jollity, in so much as to incur sometimes the charge of exuberant levity and small discretion from those who never knew a working day. The Fourth will soon be upon us with happy auspices; for the overworked and undignified mechanic is about to take his station with the magnates of the land and boldly enter on the race for equal rights and equal intelligence. We venture therefore to suggest our friends and fellow workmen . . . adopt the most dignified and established mode of conducting *The Day*.[70]

This mode, the *Mechanics' Free Press* argued, was exemplified by the all-male subscription dinner with patriotic oratory, rather than street socializing, dancing, and gambling. Decorous toasts would dramatize the convergence of previously separate interests and establish an "interchange of sentiment and community feeling, . . . adding to our union, respectability and intelligence."[71] Respectability was the watchword: Forced to defend their right to exist at all, workers' associations framed social criticism with genteel devices. Mechanics and artisans thought that respectability would foster political development, but the gentlemanly forms of their gatherings foreclosed the possibility of a broader, more angry and moral appeal to the whole city and, thus, the creation of a larger audience. The techniques of citywide appeals to popular nationalism would be taken to their limits by more reactionary political movements, especially the nativists of the American Republican Party.[72]

The business class reacted to the explosion of rowdy and disreputable festive behavior by withdrawing from general participation and elaborating their own modes of celebration. Beginning in the 1820s, affluent Philadelphians made a custom of leaving town on the Fourth of July.[73] As for the street, proclamations attempted to contain crowds and collective recreations. Sheriffs and watchmen kept an eye on dance halls, oyster cellars, and "disorderly houses" (brothels); aldermen heard complaints against street vendors, musicians, July Fourth revelers, Muster Day brawlers, and Christmas mummers. Even before the establishment of a professional police force in 1854, ordinances attempted to limit street vendors' occupations and popular recreations. With the introduction of the police, street life and festivity could, theoretically, be brought under more uniform surveillance. It took most of the century, and concerted reform efforts begun after the Civil War, to make urban festivals safe for the city.[74]

Respectable Philadelphians countered disreputable festivity with another response: They expanded the familiar calendar to create a public ceremonial presence for themselves, and they elaborated their own styles for performance. Like ordinary citizens, well-to-do white men inherited a range of traditions for ritualizing social relations. But because these men tended (or tried) to control public spaces and techniques for making performances legitimate, they could invent their own version of the calendar and its dramas, thus fathering the city's official tradition. To state that the business class shaped festivity through processes of definition and legitimation is not to claim that they conspiratorially commandeered public culture. As previously argued, the invention of traditions took place gradually, informally, and unofficially. It was, however, predictable that men or associations who presented themselves as leaders should try to gain the foremost ceremonial place for themselves. By the late 1820s, merchants, businessmen, and governmental leaders were intent on producing edifying spectacles that highlighted their social and personal roles as leaders. Dramas sponsored by merchants and businessmen tended to represent social relations from the point of view of the business class. Whether affluent men planned street ceremonies to counter the carryings-on of their employees, servants, and other inferiors is unknown. But solemn Fourth of July parades by the Cincinnati and precise, elegant military parades on Muster Day took part of their meaning from their glaring contrast with the surrounding crowds. The tension between respectable and rowdy street theatre followed, and was understood to follow, class lines. In turn, these tensions flooded the whole of public culture with class significance.

Within the context of conflict over the uses of space, time, and dramas, parades and ceremonies flourished as important modes of communication for different classes and groups. For working people under pressure to differentiate themselves from their rowdy neighbors, street dramas could articulate claims to respectable status. During desperate times, street marches could raise angry defiance of the social order. For the poor, immigrants, and marginal workers, street performances were rites of local solidarity; they could also be used to construct images of alternative social orderings. The business class used street dramas in a variety of ways, all of which helped construct images of the rightness of its own power.

Despite all this variety and possibility, the rights to street performance were as significantly patterned by social difference as space and time. By the early decades of the century, rights to ritual self-presentation roughly traced the definition of citizenship: white manhood. This is not to say that only white males performed in the streets; rather, for all others, attempts at street performance could be physically or symbolically dangerous.

Blacks' and abolitionists' attempts at collective public display met with mockery, scorn, and violence. Abolitionists had long used their own versions of the Fourth of July for political purposes: They devoted the day to fund raising, sermons, and oratory that used the Declaration to explore the dichotomies between American principle and practice. As the sectional crisis gathered force, this oratory became a volatile countertheatre.[75] Black abolitionists moved from the pulpit to the street, inventing counter-Independence parades out of the familiar July Fourth militia march and the fife-and-drum band of black popular culture. At first, blacks marched on the fifth of July to avoid the wrath of white crowds, as well as to make a temporal and kinesic distinction underscoring their separate but unequal status. After Parliament freed the slaves of the British West Indies in 1834, an event of enormous importance to Afro-Americans, blacks had a true Independence Day to celebrate on the first of August.[76]

Parades of all kinds demonstrated blacks' unwillingness to acquiesce in their inferior status. At the same time, limitations on their street presence grew more severe as racism intensified in the 1830s and 1840s. In August 1842, for example, a black Temperance Society's Independence procession was attacked by a white mob and the melee set off days of destruction in black neighborhoods. Rumors forced the mayor to display the Society's offending banner, which depicted, not blood-thirsty slaves burning San Domingo as rioters had claimed, but a freed man with his chains at his feet. Nevertheless, city officials lost no time in claiming that the Temperance Society caused the riots by parading.[77] Other black uses of the street met with white retaliation. An early account of Christmas masking in the city describes an attack on a black fife-and-drum troop by a white gang.[78]

Whites found blacks barely acceptable when they stayed inside the circle of their own private, domestic activities, and when their social life took place in cellars, alleys, and back streets. But when the image of a unified black community with moral and political claims on the rest of society was projected into the streets, whites felt their prerogatives threatened. John Watson reflected on this challenge from a widely shared point of view: "In the olden time, dressy blacks and dandy coloured beaux and belles as we now see them issuing from their proper churches were quite unknown. . . . Now they are vain-glorious and overweaning . . . and want to be called coloured people." Watson added that he found blacks' "fondness for imitating whites in processions and banners" particularly irritating.[79]

Different limits constrained the public activities of white women. In contemporary opinion, women made themselves "public women" or "women of the streets" when they assumed performative roles outside the home. Women who mounted the speaker's platform in the cause of abolitionism or feminism were not only vilified for their ideas, but also attacked for daring to manifest them in public, a move critics interpreted as a betrayal of their gender's nature.[80] Working women, who had little choice but to participate in the life of the street, who held traditional roles as market hucksters, and who joined corner sociability with enthusiasm, thereby lost any claim to respectability. Working women became prostitutes, if only metaphorically, by their economic activity. This logic extended to female participation in street parades, so that when respectable women made their rare appearances in processions they were either escorted protectively by men or dressed as caricatures of purity. Nevertheless, not all women accepted this exclusion. In letters to newspapers, commenting on plans for great processions, women complained that they held political and patriotic concerns as deeply as men, and resented being excluded from public ceremonies.[81]

Philadelphia's large Irish Catholic immigrant population used the streets to display ethnic unity on Saint Patrick's Day, although city fathers tried to discourage parades, especially during times of intense anti-immigrant sentiment. While municipal officials were sometimes uneasy about Saint Patrick's Day, they found no reason to ban inflammatory anti-Catholic spectacles, such as the mass processions by native Americans, which called for the restriction of Irish-American civil rights. On Saint Patrick's eve, the burning of "stuffed Paddy" effigies was a venerable nativist tradition.[82]

Labor associations and striking workers often used processions, sometimes legitimating their cause—which was
considered illegal and illegitimate for most of the nineteenth century—with elaborate fraternal costumes, banners, and bands of music. Less respectably, strikers
marched to call other men away from work, announce
their grievance, and muster community solidarity behind
their cause. The representation of conflict between masters
and employees antagonized city officials. Militant strike
parades and demonstrations were contained physically,
decried by mayors and municipal authorities, and discouraged by some labor leaders.

In a variety of ways, conflict between classes and groups
gave meaning to competing definitions of public culture
and the popular uses of public space in the city. At the same
time, access to spaces and to roles for performance was
limited by race, ethnicity, gender, and class. Although city
officials and propertied citizens could not achieve full control over the uses of open spaces and free time, or which
versions of social relations might be enacted in city streets,
they tried to reshape urban culture. Slowly, they succeeded.
Through initial suppressions of street life and attacks on
festivity, through the construction of a repertoire of respectable public performances, the city's image and imageries
were recast.

The history of the patterning of public culture needs to be
drawn in more detail; it had multiple dimensions and was
shaped by several forces. Concerns over property and ideas,
customary privileges and legal prerogatives, and the tensions between material and symbolic quests for power all
interacted. As a stage for culture, the city offered a field of
places and practices useful for framing and disseminating
ideas, shaping powers and opinions, but as a human construction, this stage did not yield all residents equal time,
space, and power to perform.

CHAPTER THREE

Volunteer Militias and Urban Pageantry

In the everyday life of the city, private military clubs ranked first among street performers. Inventing special events and reinterpreting the military past in public performances, volunteer militias dominated and helped define the city's ceremonial and holiday calendar. Through this predominance, and in their frequent, elegant street appearances, these clubs of affluent young men popularized their fraternities and constructed the conventions of respectable street drama.

A Military Tribute Ceremony

The ceremonial tribute to the July 1830 French Revolution was ushered in with a blast of artillery on October 4, 1830, in a city bedecked with French and American flags and filled with uniformed soldiers.[1] At midmorning a battalion formed in Library Street; commanded by Captain James Page, it marched north on Eighth Street to the house of John M. Chapron, a French-American lawyer. The volunteers formed a line around the dwelling and prepared for a staple of military ceremony, the presentation of a flag. Two bands of musicians flanked the door, and Captain Page stepped forward to hush the crowd; then the tricolor flag was brought from the house, prompting cheers and the "Marseillaise." With customary female reticence, Miss Emilie Chapron, flanked by two gentlemen, came forward to present the flag and make an address.[2]

"With the most joyful emotion," Miss Chapron saluted the "combined sympathy and indignation" with which Americans had watched "the long protracted sufferings" of France. She hailed the "sisterly love" with which America now clasped the latest revolutionaries "to her heart." Proffering the French flag to Captain Page, she dedicated it to his men, "brave children of America, the hope and pride of your country, . . . an emblem of that friendship which should always unite" the heirs of Washington and Lafayette.

After a pause during which a "national air" was sung, Page accepted, offering his version of the import of the July Revolution and an aside on the nature of volunteer militias. "In our own tranquil republic, such a change from the extreme despotism to the full enjoyment of civil and religious liberty . . . is indeed loudly hailed by millions of freemen." Page praised the "prudence" of the Parisians in not pushing the revolution too far, and singled out the "forebearance" of the National Guard. "Thus it is always with the soldiers of freedom," Page declared, "they can never be other than friends to their country."

Page closed his speech with an interpretation of the tricolor as a symbol. For his men, it was

> an object with which every inspiring sentiment is associated —reminding them as it will, not only of *patriotism* but of the *innocence* and *beauty* which it is their happiness to admire—their duty to protect. . . . Its folds shall harmoniously unite with those of the "Stars and Stripes" and while they gently mingle in the breeze, sacred emblems of "*liberty and order*," the names of WASHINGTON and LAFAYETTE, immortal champions of both, shall be wafted to heaven with the purest aspiration.[3]

After this dramatic conclusion, Page issued marching orders. His State Fencibles and the Washington Greys joined the rest of their division in Arch Street, forming a massive procession led by Major General Cadwalader and Brigadier General Patterson. Several troops of fine horsemen, including the First Troop City Cavalry, headed the First Pennsylvania Volunteers, who were joined for the festivities by well-dressed companies from Chester and Montgomery counties. The Second Brigade, expanded by visitors from Norristown, followed under General Goodwin. Bringing up the rear came rural companies, cavalries from

New Jersey, and several hundred nonuniformed citizens mounted and formed into a file, with a tri-colored flag.[4] Heading east and south toward the State House, the parade passed through streets shaded with overarching banners and flags. Ladies crowded the second-storey windows; spectators of both sexes jammed the sidewalks for a glimpse of the musicians and marching soldiers.

THE ROLE OF VOLUNTEER COMPANIES IN PHILADELPHIA'S PUBLIC CULTURE

Volunteer companies such as the First Troop City Cavalry, the State Fencibles, and Washington Greys were the private clubs of aspiring professionals and young men from Philadelphia's most prominent families. These vigorous soldiers of freedom also claimed a public role as preservers of peace and order in the city. Captain Page and Miss Chapron had expressed views often asserted by friends of the militia volunteers, that their social origins and respectable status made them the natural defenders of the country, the true heirs of Washington and Lafayette, the "hope and pride" of America. Such rhetoric ornamented volunteers' public performances from the end of the Revolution until after the Civil War, but enthusiasm for militias and militia duty was not held by all. Indeed, extravagant praise for the volunteers was designed not only to encourage them, but also to fend off public suspicion and criticism of military reformers.

The ongoing controversy over the effectiveness of volunteer militias and the structure of militia duties was a critical part of the context framing militia parades and ceremonies. The private, elite companies formed the upper tier of Pennsylvania's semiprivate, semipublic militia system, the state's federally sponsored peace-keeping force. Below the volunteers in prestige and legal status ranked the public militias, in which all eligible white men unable to afford private company membership were required to enroll. Unlike the volunteers, public companies had neither money nor leisure to practice being soldiers or to stage elaborate ceremonies.

The structure of the militia system and the relationship between public and private companies engaged critics of all political persuasions. The eloquent Miss Chapron notwithstanding, both militias elicited charges of ill-preparedness, amateurism, and ineptitude. Even more serious, the distinction between public and private companies raised the question of social and economic equality, an explosive issue in Jacksonian America.[5]

The story of how the volunteers made themselves the city's ceremonial specialists is, in part, the story of Pennsylvania's militia controversy. The social and political implications of volunteer membership suffused the meanings of military street performances. Viewed in the light of contestation over the militia laws and the larger question of social inequality, the volunteers' struttings and their proponents' bombast emerge as a central part of the dialogue over public culture.

The militia controversy was deeply rooted in the history of militia duties in Pennsylvania. As a result of peaceful colonial relations with the Indians, the Quaker proprietorship, and distance from the French, militias for local defense were organized much later in Pennsylvania than elsewhere. During the crisis of 1775, Philadelphians formed citywide public militias, which fought in several important Revolutionary War battles and played a critical role in forming the new state government.[6]

The militia organizers, the Committees of Association, drew heavily on Philadelphia's artisans, workers, and the poor. Although the Committees made defense duty the responsibility of all capable men, from the beginning the militias were organized along class lines. Most Philadelphians drilled in companies recruited from their neighborhoods, but other troops were privately organized, usually by a few well-to-do gentlemen who enlisted friends and relatives and paid for equipment, uniforms, and supplies. Although some of the "middling sort"—small merchants and artisans—formed companies, from 1775 flashy display and exclusive membership marked the top of the militia hierarchy. Several prominent cavalry troops were known as "silk-stocking companies" because of the wealth of their members.[7]

Despite their segregation from the elite companies, the regiments drawn from poor neighborhoods became a new form of organization for men previously excluded from politics. Militias forwarded petitions to the Pennsylvania Assembly demanding equality of duties and reasonable pay for service. The involvement of increasingly radical workers, artisans, and small merchants in practical democracy resulted in universal militia service requirements and the popular election of officers.[8]

After the war, militia service bore memories of the political awakening the Revolution had stirred among the city's lower orders, connecting the agency of ordinary men with the concrete achievement of unprecedented political rights.[9] In addition to the experience of wresting liberation for the colony, fighting in the Revolution won ordinary men the right to bear arms. Immigrants from the British Isles and Europe cherished this right because it gave every citizen the power to resist an oppressive or intrusive government. The federally mandated universal militia service enacted in 1792 secured for the citizenry the right to be its own soldiery, never again to have a centrally controlled standing army garrisoned among them.[10]

INEQUITIES IN THE MILITIA SYSTEM

Contradictions riddled the militia system from its inception. Congress authorized universal militia duty but made little provision for regulating it and appropriated inadequate funds; thus responsibility for organization, revenues, oversight, and enforcement fell to individual states. Although the federal government provided ordnance and supplies, the power to raise, train, and equip men was used in ways which varied from state to state.[11]

In Philadelphia, militia duty weighed unevenly on rich and poor. Pennsylvania required service by men between eighteen and forty-five years of age, but allowed a long list of exemptions. The state recognized the distinction between private companies of affluent young men and public regiments of all others. Volunteer companies such as the First and Second City cavalries remained social clubs after the war's end and kept close ties with elite fraternities such as the Society of the Cincinnati. These cavalries placed themselves at the state's disposal in putting down postwar revolts against taxation in the hinterland.[12] Since legislators often belonged to volunteer companies, the state was unwilling to discourage such loyal and well-organized troops; therefore, the law came to allow militia duty to be filled by membership in privately raised companies. All others were required to attend two annual training days, and roll-keeping and fines enforced participation. Fines could exceed one dollar a day, beyond the reach of workingmen, but merchants and professionals who had more profitable uses for their time usually paid the fines for non-attendance. Exemptions could also be bought.[13]

The dual militia system not only reflected but also extended existing social inequities. Men with time, money, and military interests could fulfill the law's requirements by joining clubs with their friends. Private companies also served as political organizations for professionals, merchants, businessmen, and master artisans.[14]

By the third decade of the nineteenth century, it was clear that state support for the private militias contradicted the leveling ideology of the Revolution. Membership was based on the ability to afford equipment and the free time to participate in activities. The leisure to drill on weekday afternoons and the money required to pay for the uniform, finery, weapons, and ammunition limited volunteer membership to men of comfortable circumstances. The most celebrated volunteers, the cavalries, had the highest expenses: They provided and cared for horses as well as decorative tack.[15] Affluence and ceremonial visibility went hand in hand.

Friendship, family, and business connections—and in some cases, ethnicity—allowed entry into the volunteers. Unlike public companies, private militias exercised discretion over admission to their fraternities. These cliques were devoted to the careers of their officers: Some commanders assured their elections by buying uniforms for their men, and they helped maintain their position with frequent dinners and treats charged to the state.[16]

Companies introduced young volunteers to a busy social life, a fraternity away from workplace and home. Training might take place once a month or once a week, or only the mandatory two times a year, depending on the company's enthusiasm and ambition. Tavern parties were a common pastime. The 1814 diary of Thomas Franklin Pleasants, a rising young lawyer and captain in the Washington Guards, reveals that men who drilled together also drank, visited, courted, and did business together.[17]

An essay advocating volunteer membership, written in 1830, reveals that the average Philadelphian found volunteering and its paraphernalia beyond his means. The main cost of what the author called a "pleasing, instructive and rational amusement" was the uniform. A blue suit, including materials, labor, trim, a cap, feather, cartridge box, and knapsack added up to $23.50. For artisans and mechanics who rarely made more than $2 a day before the Civil War, the uniform alone represented a formidable sacrifice. Furthermore, the shoulder weapon cost about $14. Frequent drills meant loss of time and money. For a workingman, volunteer company membership could easily cost more than one month's wages.[18]

Volunteer ceremonies were expressions of affluence, displays of the social life available to those with money and time. The volunteers themselves were arrayed in a well-known hierarchy of social prestige, affluence, and style. In 1830—the same year Captain Page's Fencibles celebrated the July Revolution—four companies, totaling about 125 men, were cavalries. Seven artillery companies shared 247 enrollees, and 717 men made up the 24 companies of volunteer infantry. Thus, among the leisured upper classes, wealth differentiated volunteers' appearance and duties and distinguished them from public companies. The wealthy rode matched horses; men of middling resources worked with fancy arms, rifles, and fieldpieces. Infantry volunteers drilled with bayonets, and public companies went on foot in their work clothes, often with no muskets.[19]

Most workingmen belonged to public companies organized by city street boundaries.[20] For them, the militia system imposed an increasingly onerous burden, and some saw the militia laws as a corruption of the Revolutionary War inheritance of military service. There were immediate and material reasons for complaint. At a time when most forms of labor were irregular and wages low, a man who missed work for Muster Day risked pushing his family closer to poverty.[21] With no unemployment insurance or other compensation to buffer joblessness, low wages, or illness, workingmen rightly viewed time as a resource that ought not to be arbitrarily taken from them without compensation. The requirement that each public company member provide his own uniform and weapon added to the burden. Some men simply paid fines, but the average urban worker could no more afford a fine than a day's labor lost.[22] If the fine went unpaid, the adjutant could threaten prosecution or the confiscation of property; thus most public company members took part in desultory drills, or tried to avoid the fine collector.[23]

MILITIA REFORM CONTROVERSIES

Revisions of the law were made piecemeal. In 1818, to bolster volunteer memberships, the Pennsylvania Legislature exempted any man who had belonged to a private company for seven years from further service, thus creating a powerful incentive to leave the public companies and start new volunteer corps. At the same time, lawmakers refused to abolish general training days for public companies, stiffened fines, and stepped up fine collections.[24] In 1824, in the face of passive resistance from the public companies, the Legislature restructured the system's funding. Revenues from fines were channeled into volunteer coffers, ostensibly to encourage the only part of the system that seemed to work.[25] With these new incentives, a plethora of private companies sprang up, many of them existing only on paper; their careers followed the social ups and downs of their officers.

The militia system drew stinging fire from many directions, and despite legal bolstering, the private companies were not immune from attack. Complaints ranged from mild to outraged; some thought an inept system better than none, others urged the law's abolition.[26] Advocates of militia reform deplored the disarray of the public companies but asserted that the volunteers were too interested in tavern parties and fancy dress, an assessment later supported by military historians.[27] Critics rightly asserted that volunteer company membership was a social climber's technique. One of the most important advantages of volunteer membership, besides friendships and business connections, was acquiring a title. The designation "captain" or "colonel" could serve as a useful entrance into "good society" and an aid to election to public office.[28] Since many men joined the volunteers to retire after seven years with titles, companies frequently dissolved in wranglings over officerships.[29] Volunteer companies, critics charged, were top-heavy with officers and short on privates.[30]

Volunteer membership afforded chances at political power as well as social clout. Although they have never been studied as political organizations, militia companies were closely connected to local factions and parties. Several Philadelphia mayors held prominent positions in the volunteers during the first half of the nineteenth century. Justices of the peace, sheriffs, aldermen, city councilmen, and state representatives also wore officers' uniforms.[31] On the one hand, private militia membership could open the way into councils of government; on the other, volunteer companies served as privileged adjuncts to local government, much as private men's clubs and businessmen's associations do today. In short, these exclusive organizations provided privileged access to the sources and exercise of public power.

For workingmen, militia laws raised the explosive issue of social and political inequality. Radical artisans and the Workingmen's Party took their attacks beyond charges of ineptitude; the laws stood for corruption, and public displays of unearned power and private influence were attempts to extend inequality. Social climbing, tokens of distinction, such as costumes, and prestige won in closed elections all smacked of aristocracy, which radical artisans had accused merchants and bankers of trying to impose.[32] Some workers proposed abolition of the system, while others propounded a thoroughly democratic restructuring. Some voluntarists thought the solution lay in abolition of public trainings and the support of private companies. The Workingmen's Party, and later the Jacksonian Democratic Party worked for reform, using the septennial election of field officers to try to replace elite commanders with workers.[33] Reformers within the public militias hoped to reduce fines and change training schedules to fit the needs of laboring men. These reforms were continually thwarted, and public militiamen found more dramatic means of attack and resistance.

With criticism coming from all sides, the volunteers were faced with a dilemma. The law that made volunteer companies possible engendered social hostility toward them and the militia system in general. Designed to be public and universal, the militia system gave selective support to men who were already society's privileged members; the field officers' performance of their duties at Muster Day fed class antagonism and hostility. Reformers' critiques and popular resentment posed the problem of legitimacy for the volunteers: They had continually to create a rationale for their existence. To do this, the volunteers had to appear popular, recruiting new members with money and free time. Most of all, the private companies needed to forestall any reform of the militia laws that would undercut their funding and titles, or limit their ability to function as political associations. To these ends, the volunteers held conventions to foster their associations, built connections with volunteer troops and officers in other states, sponsored military magazines, and recommended reforms that strengthened their own position.[34]

A critical part of the volunteer offensive was the creation of a worthy and expert public image. Parades, displays, and ceremonies that depicted volunteers as universal defenders of the public good were ideal tools with which to attack the problem of legitimacy. Elegant performances graphically distinguished the volunteers from the "poor, pelted standing companies," and distanced them from the unpopular militia laws.[35]

A Year of Militia Ceremonies

The elite volunteers built a distinctive tradition of military ceremonies around an annual cycle of public displays. The calendar of ceremony and socializing knit young men together, giving them a chance to appear before the city as uniformed comrades. On the most prominent days, Washington's Birthday, Muster Day, and Christmas, the volunteer parades drew the attention of invited guests, street crowds, and the press.

From the Revolutionary War's end, the volunteers annually honored Washington's Birthday. Although Washington, a kingly symbol of patriotism and selflessness, was seen as neutral and aloof from what contemporaries called "the spirit of party," the earliest celebrants of February 22 were unquestionably elite. Affluent citizens copied the essentials and details of Georgian royal birthday celebrations during Washington's postwar residence in Philadelphia. Church services, dinners, balls, and receptions at the president's house marked the day in the 1790s. Militia officers and "all persons of consequence" had audiences with the hero, and the paying of birthday respects could last into the early hours of the morning.[36] In 1791 the city "saw every demonstration of public joy, the Artillery and Light Infantry were paraded and at 12 O'clock a federal salute was fired."[37]

> [In 1793] Capt. Fisher's company of Volunteer Artillery and three companies of light artillery paraded to the State House, from whence they marched to the Artillery Ground and proceeded to the Corner of Ninth and Market Streets, where they fired fifteen rounds and gave three cheers; afterwards they marched down Market Street and gave a salute as they passed the President's house. . . . All the shipping in the harbour had their colors hoisted and the bells of Christ Church rang peals.[38]

The forms of militia parades and ceremonies for Washington's Birthday changed little between the 1790s and 1860, but February 22 became a more popular and generally celebrated holiday after 1815. The day's core remained distinctly martial and elite. The morning always featured assemblies of volunteer troops, according to the officers' published orders, and a procession by the troops with patriotic and beneficial society members to a church to hear an oration. In streets and squares, individual troops performed drills and maneuvers, fired salutes, and marched to the music of hired bands. Bitter weather and slushy streets notwithstanding, crowds always formed to watch. Then a march to dining rooms advertised that troop members would spend the evening enjoying a lengthy dinner punctuated by speeches and toasts.[39]

The Washington's Birthday parade of 1821 typified the kind of processions organized by the Cincinnati and the Washington Benevolent Association after the War of 1812. The line of march included the First and Second Troops City Cavalry, two companies of Washington's Guards, the Washington Blues, the National Guards, and several suburban companies, followed by the Cincinnati and Benevolent Association officers, the committees of arrangement, and Association members ranked two by two. The line formed at Benevolent Hall in Third Street, and moved to the Grand Saloon of the American Museum to hear a patriotic oration.[40]

In 1832 Washington's Centennial Birthday was "very generally celebrated by processions, orations, social and convivial meetings," by "the firing of cannon, ringing of bells, display of flags, by civil, religious and military ceremonies." City Councils helped fund a civic procession that was planned by volunteer leaders and featured a huge mustering of militias. The following February, the volunteers and the Society of the Cincinnati organized a one-hundred-first birthday parade to revive the previous year's glory. Ceremonies included a prayer, orations, and a cornerstone-laying in newly christened Washington Square.[41]

During May Musters, the largest of the annual parade days required by law, the private and public companies drilled together, once in battalion formation and again in regiments.[42] Because the May drills immediately preceded elections for officers, they marked a critical point in a company's year. Private company commanders had time and resources to run for field or division offices; such rank gave them command over private and public companies alike and reflected honor on their own troops. Thus, May Muster drills were performances to convince voters of a captain's or colonel's skill and worth. A company's stylish and correct showing on the parade ground directly influenced its leader's chances for elevation through the militia ranks, which could influence his personal career and those of his martial comrades.[43]

May Musters exceeded one day, and just as there were two distinct militias, there were two kinds of parades. For most of the first half of the century, on General Muster or Parade Day all companies turned out together in battalions for inspection or review. On a second regimental parade day, companies were inspected individually. Volunteers' performances in both drills received notice in the newspapers because editors were often closely involved with volunteer companies.[44]

Press reviews convey reporters' approval of volunteers. In 1825 the *Saturday Evening Post* noted the volunteers' "showy appearance" and commented on the pleasure inspired by the "dazzling glare and pageantry of military scenes."[45] The *Democratic Press* compared the amateur soldiers' accomplishments with those of professionals, saluting the "high degree of precision" in their movements

and their discipline.[46] Muster Day in 1826 was a "grand
Gala Day for the Military," announced the *United States
Gazette*, citing the volunteers' "very imposing and military
appearance."[47] In 1836, "Colonel Peter Fritz's company had
a fine band of music; Colonel Worrell's Washington Greys
had Johnson's Band and a huge display of cavalry was out.
The Regiment marched to a delightful parade ground and
was industriously drilled."[48] The next year "Captain Hol-
liday's company, the Hibernian Greens" attracted attention
from the *Public Ledger*, which pronounced them a "credit
to themselves and their country, Eire," although the members were Americans.[49] That a parade in 1850 of the First
Brigade of the Pennsylvania Volunteers "attracted the attention of thousands" shows the unabated popularity of
volunteer displays.[50]

Parade days served as a forum for the presentation, inspection, and evaluation of company attributes. If the standards for volunteer appearance and behavior were not fully
shared by street audiences, their description in the press
gives clues to how Philadelphians appreciated military
parades and the effects companies aimed to achieve. In
1821, one correspondent, using the pen name "Lafayette,"
praised a drill by the Washington Guards and the State
Fencibles. "Lafayette's" accolade is typical of dozens of
similar newspaper reports.

> The general appearance of the men . . . among whom I
> recognized some of the most prominent young men of the
> city, was truly military; their dresses being perfectly clean
> and neat and not an article . . . appeared to be neglected. . . .
> Skill in manual exercise, the regularity of firing . . . the order
> and precision displayed in various evolutions . . . did honor
> to themselves and would by no means have been discredit-
> able to the veterans of a standing army.[51]

The press regularly praised the young men's "neat and elegant appearance," their "perfect order and regularity," the
"high degree of precision" in their movements, their "in-
dustrious" and "disciplined character," and their "prominent" family origins.

Stylish dress received much attention, and uniform was
a subject for evaluation by the press and street audiences. A
large part of company resources went into fancy costumes,
which companies used (and updated) to expand their repu-

tations and differentiate themselves. In 1835 *Niles' Weekly Register* announced the auspicious debut of a new cavalry corps, the Philadelphia Lancer Guards, whose costume was "a coat of rich maroon cloth, faced with buff . . . crimson pants with a stripe of buff . . . a lancer's helmet with a skull of beaten brass and a crest of crimson." The *Register* considered this the "most elegant and fanciful costume we have seen," and thought the troop would "add greatly to the splendor of our parades." [52]

The volunteers amplified their imposing presence with brass bands. Accompaniment by one of the city's famous cotillion orchestras, such as Frank Johnson's all-black ensemble, denoted great expense.[53] The dressy uniforms of the fifteen marching musicians were a well-received improvement over those worn by the old-fashioned militia staple, the black fife-and-drum team. The band's music was complex, varied, and rich: Its volume announced a troop's presence from far away.[54]

In regimental or battalion musters, the public companies appeared much less elegant than the volunteers. On Battalion Day the spectacle of the huge mass of uniformed and nonuniformed men—most on foot, carrying brooms and shovels instead of muskets, and commanded by hoarsely shouting officers—drew crowds to the parade ground. Although the unpracticed public militias did poorly in drills, the festive atmosphere of Battalion Day made up for their lackluster performances. The muster drew enrollees and many others away from factory and workshop to the Bush Hill fair. Amateur soldiers drank at musters; hucksters, liquor vendors, gingerbread sellers, and lottery proprietors seized the chance to cater to onlookers as well as soldiers. Drunkenness, extralegal activities, and general license provoked complaints about the moral effects of parade day. The *Mechanics' Free Press* called Battalion Day "the festival of folly and dissipation," a blot on the state's reputation.[55]

Without doubt, volunteers resented their forced public appearance with ill-trained, ragged companies and heartily wished they were not required to go through insultingly basic maneuvers with men who had reluctantly left work under threat of a fine. Volunteers argued that the untrained nonuniformed companies brought disrepute to the entire system, and they found other opportunities to display their skills.[56]

After Muster Day, the volunteers prepared for their biggest parade day, July Fourth. From early in the century, private companies marked Independence Day with dress parades through principal streets, performed precise maneuvers, and fired guns and cannons for spectators. On July Fourth the city was the scene of dozens of small military parades, which began at hotels and squares, wound past the State House, and moved down Market or Chestnut Street to the open ground at Center Square. Here artillery companies issued first a federal salute (one shot for each state in the Union) and then a ripping *feu de joie*, in which all guns fired simultaneously along a line, creating a wave of sound.[57]

Troops were met at the Square by crowds out to see the uniformed show, along with gamblers and gangs of hucksters selling food, drink, and trinkets. The downtown fair grew so large that the mayor banned it in 1823, but resourceful booth-owners moved their disreputable enterprises to Fairmount outside the city, where they attracted ever-growing numbers of patrons and volunteers.[58]

Individual troops might spend the rest of the day firing cannons from Fort Mifflin, cruising on the river, dining at their hotel, or shooting at targets. Troops often attended church services and dinners with political allies, much as they did on Washington's Birthday. Whatever the political alignment of a volunteer company, the day was spent in rededication to their version of patriotism. Food and drink, toast and song knit male bonds of belief, opinion, and conviviality.[59]

The transportation revolution of the 1820s allowed the volunteers to expand their activities and turn July Fourth into their premier outing. Some companies left the city for a week, marching out of town in high style and traveling to Baltimore, Camden, or Newark by fashionable steamboat or railway. At their destination, the volunteers were met by their host company; then they paraded through town and were installed in camp. Philadelphians participated in drills and contests and enjoyed dinners and theatrical entertainments in their honor. Because Fourth of July tours were covered by the press, the volunteers always returned in a blaze of glory. Elite troops like the State Fencibles returned the hospitality with imposing receptions and parades for visitors from as far away as Boston.[60]

Volunteers kept special anniversaries of their own, which were nearly always connected with the Revolutionary past. From the late 1820s, prominent militiamen traveled across the Delaware to Camden every October 22 to reenact the Battle of Red Bank,[61] a Continental victory over the Hessians in 1777. On a typical anniversary, eight Philadelphia companies enacted important tactical maneuvers (including a Continental landing by steamboat). The rest of the day included military drills performed for newspaper reporters, an oration by their commander, and a salute to the "handsome grey marble" monument they commissioned. The commemoration of the Battle of Red Bank remained an important militiaman's outing during the antebellum period.[62]

Such anniversaries were by no means purely historical. Jacksonian holidays and commemorations featured what commentators called "economical motives," and many militia ceremonies had commercial ties and sponsors. Commercial advances were bound to and legitimated by the Revolutionary War in military performance, as military displays themselves became a kind of popular entertainment. July Fourth was regularly used by canal and railroad financiers as a day for ribbon-cutting and grand openings; militia volunteers provided music, banners, and a marching spectacle to frame the commercial ceremony.[63] In 1832, on the anniversary of the massacre of Wayne's troops by the British at Paoli (September 20, 1777), militia performances celebrated the construction of a monument to the dead and the completion of rail lines linking Philadelphia, Paoli, and West Chester. Heralded by booming cannon, the inaugural cars arrived from West Chester and Philadelphia at noon.

> As the two sets of cars moved gracefully and majestically towards each other, the two companies respectfully waved their hats. . . . The military were in full view, . . . the banners of the soldiery floating richly in the air, the dazzling brilliancy of their arms, their regular and soldier-like aspect and the magnificent appearance of the railroad carriages combined to make that moment one of universal joy.[64]

After their return to the field, the volunteers testified "more particularly to their respect" for the fallen "by moving to the solemn notes of the dead march by the monument which is consecrated to their memory."[65]

NATIONAL EVENTS AND LOCAL SPECTACLES

A private company member expected that if any important person visited Philadelphia, the customary military reception and parade would give his company yet another opportunity to appear at its best. The arrival of a dignitary might be noted by a ceremony as simple as a fired salute of welcome and an escort into town, or as elaborate as the combined military review and procession that greeted the Marquis de Lafayette.

Dignitaries honored in municipally sponsored or informally organized ceremonies were met and escorted by volunteer militiamen who introduced them to the city. The most famous early guests were Washington and Lafayette, who stopped in the city during national tours in 1789 and 1824, respectively. Conducted on a grand scale, these pilgrimages to the people received generous coverage by the press. The republican, antimonarchical symbolism of each reception, presentation, and speech was carefully dissected for an attentive readership.[66] When Washington passed through Philadelphia on his way to New York, he was brought into the city by a procession of fashionable cavalry and met at Gray's Ferry by an enormous concourse of militiamen and ordinary citizens who gathered around a Roman triumphal arch and crowned the hero with a laurel wreath. Infantry and artillery joined the procession escorting Washington to the City Tavern, and the next day troops of light horse paraded before him.[67]

Similarly, an advance guard of cavalry met Lafayette in New Jersey, escorting him to a field on the Frankford Road, north of town. A massive gathering of volunteer soldiers, including some companies formed especially for the occasion, assembled for review. An anonymous lithographer who attended the reception for Lafayette at Independence Hall has left the only contemporary graphic record of the enormous spectacle. (See "The Arrival of General Lafayette . . ." among the illustrations.) During his stay in Philadelphia in 1824, Lafayette received numerous military delegations, watched parades from his window, inspected companies and witnessed displays of martial skills and art.[68]

Less spectacularly, when a president or a presidential candidate arrived in the city, volunteer companies paraded in his honor, although the man's politics frequently influenced the turnout of troops. A man of Whiggish persuasion, gentle background, or ties to Philadelphia's mercantile and financial community might be greeted and hosted by the prestigious cavalries. If, like Andrew Jackson, he sub-scribed to newer, more populist strains in American poli-tics, the guest would be met by throngs of working people as well as some of the less fancy volunteer troops.[69]

In February 1819, the hero of the Battle of New Orleans on a national tour stopped in Philadelphia and was enter-tained by militia officers. In 1833 President Jackson met a large cavalcade of volunteer militias and an enormous gathering of citizens. For several days elaborate proces-sions escorted Jackson around the city with barouches, trumpeters, banners, and delegations of high-ranking offi-cers from the city and outlying counties.[70] Many other foreign dignitaries, presidents, and patriots were welcomed by militia parades.

Events of critical national or local interest also provided reasons for military display. The ratification of the Consti-tution in 1788 prompted Federalist leaders and manufac-turers to organize an impressive processional pageant made up of military, allegorical, and crafts displays.[71] Perry's vic-tory on the Great Lakes in 1813 gave cause for citywide illuminations and elaborate militia parades.[72]

The death of a great American, even if he were not a Philadelphian or to be buried in the city, could prompt a peculiarly nineteenth-century event, the military "sham funeral."[73] Washington and Lafayette were honored with the largest of these, but Presidents Jackson, John Quincy Adams, Harrison, and Taylor were also saluted in this way.[74] Sham obsequies consisted of a parade of volunteers leading a riderless horse, accompanying an empty, flag-draped coffin to a church where a funeral service was con-ducted. The long funeral train, joined by municipal officers, patriotic societies, and firemen, wound a zigzag path through the city, as much a spectacle for the citizens as an expression of local mourning.

Lafayette's death ten years after his famous visit re-awakened memories of Philadelphia's sober display of re-publican pride and gratitude. The officers of the Philadel-phia and county volunteers moved to the forefront to plan the funeral. Leading the procession, the uniformed city volunteers and their major general marched "with side arms and standards dressed in crape." A riderless white horse bedecked in black ribbons followed them, as city and county officials, firemen in mourning, and craftsmen brought up the rear.[75]

Volunteers held uniformed funeral processions for their own officers and members. The church service was only a preliminary to the solemn but glorious display of finery and precision in the march from church to cemetery. In 1846, for example, the Washington Greys turned out to bury a brother "in considerable numbers with an unrivalled band to which a gong had been added.... At the grave, the firing of the Greys was very exact." [76] Like beneficial society and Masonic funerals, military funerals advertised the advantages of fraternal membership. An elegant and dignified line of attendants would see their comrade to his final rest.

THE SHAPING OF PUBLIC CULTURE

Through a wide variety of events, volunteer militias developed powerful, positive images for the city at large. In turn, their performances helped shape the character and meaning of public events in Philadelphia. The meanings volunteers gave to public culture can be understood by examining the dominant patterns of context for and content in their ceremonies.

Festivity was the most powerful, recurrent context for volunteer self-presentation. Private companies shaped the context for their performances by selecting festive times and presenting themselves to the city on days like July Fourth and Washington's Birthday. Elite companies helped build the very "specialness" of these holidays, whose distinct natures were by no means obvious, known, or accepted in the late eighteenth century. The volunteers helped define patriotism as they made themselves its chief interpreters, taking charge of national symbols (especially flags) and firing the salvos that made all residents inescapably aware of a great day's importance. Skilled demonstrations in the streets, colorful parades, speeches, and toasts published in the press reminded readers and onlookers that the volunteers were "the bulwark of our nation," and tied them to the origins of American freedoms.

Parades and battle reenactments made volunteers look

like real soldiers. Since they were under attack on several flanks for being overdressed and underprepared, acting out battles helped the private companies persuade audiences that they were fighters, carrying on a tradition of just rebellion. Reenactments also dramatized links to actual events and to the Continental Army, establishing a direct lineage for the volunteers.[77]

On days they promoted as militia holidays, the private companies highlighted a proprietary version of patriotism, one connected to voluntarism, private association, and martial display. Such patriotism drew heavily on a volunteer interpretation of the Revolution. July Fourth parades, for instance, connected private companies to the mythologically central event of the rebellion in Philadelphia, the reading aloud of the Declaration of Independence at the State House. The 1830 ceremonies for the July Revolution in France reveal what the volunteers valued in revolutions and what they meant by freedom. The private companies celebrated the July days precisely because the (nevermentioned) workers of Paris overthrew a tyrant but backed away from a radical social reordering, allowing the bourgeoisie to install a constitutional monarch with the "forebearance" of the National Guard. This was exactly the sort of revolution the volunteers imagined themselves part of, one that dislodged illegitimate authority but preserved peace and property from that other illegitimate authority, "the crowd."[78]

Likewise, historical commemorations sponsored by volunteers presented a highly selective version of local Revolutionary history and their role in it, not least because they made themselves the center of historical narrative. In reenactments militiamen proposed that the leading actors in the American Revolution were men just like themselves: cavalrymen, artillerymen, and bravely outfitted infantrymen. Of course, most veterans of the Revolution were ordinary men, who nevertheless felt themselves transformed by the extraordinary events in which they had taken part.[79] By the 1830s, the most senior "revolutioners" were long departed, but some younger participants survived to be treated as hoary relics, drawn through the streets in a carriage on the Fourth of July.[80] This was the only public recognition these men received, although the scandal over veterans' pensions kept the modest origins of most of the

Continental soldiers in public memory, and this memory
sometimes cast a harsh light on the volunteers.

One "Enoch Timbertoes" wrote of a July Fourth march
by "old Revolutioners,"

> Afterwards when I saw them voluntary companies tram-
> poosing through the streets and dressed up so fine[,] what a
> difference there was atween them and the old seventysixers.
> They looked like men who didn't fear snakes nor gunpowder,
> t'others like milliners gals all show and would run at their
> own shadders.[81]

In the events they chose to memorialize, the volunteers
focused on victories and martyrdoms and ignored debâcles.
At the same time, they helped erase the memory of the poor
people's battles of the Revolution. Neither the disastrous
Battle of Germantown nor the revolt of the Pennsylvania
Line were deemed appropriate subjects for reenactment, although both were important in Philadelphians' experience
of the war. The radical Associators' street wars against
profiteering and collaboration by Philadelphia's Loyalist
elites were written out of this version of military history.
Could it have been because the Associators met defeat at
the hands of silk-stocking companies? From the volunteers'
point of view, it was important that the war had been won
and could be interpreted in terms of the gains, progress,
and plenty of the present.[82] Conflict and dissent within the
ranks held no more legitimate place in a version of the past
than they did in the present.

The volunteer version of history unfolded unproblemati-
cally toward the present.[83] Militia dramas embodied the
point of view, the general class outlook of young merchants,
master artisans, bankers, lawyers, and doctors: The Revolution began an era of human progress, which happened to
include economic progress, studded with railways, canals,
and factories and evolving toward plenty. Not all Philadelphians viewed the present so positively; many workingmen and artisans interpreted the direction of the nation's
economy and politics as a betrayal of their fathers' struggles.[84] Perhaps they interpreted local history differently, in
oral and other traditions.[85]

Just as the volunteers claimed that men like themselves
were at the center of history, they affiliated themselves with
prominent historical and contemporary figures. By usher-

ing in and paying honor to nearly every great man who visited the city, by marking birthdays and deaths of patriot heroes, and by presenting themselves for approval by the eminent, the volunteers linked themselves to men whose names and faces constantly circulated before the public via the press, theatre, popular literature, and patriotic ephemera. Conversely, the volunteers played a key role in popularizing the patriot heroes. The majority of volunteer troops favored Washington and Lafayette as icons. In their troop names and banner images, volunteer companies continually placed the French aristocrat and the Virginia gentleman before their audiences. Celebrating these heroes, the volunteers gathered under the mantle of America's gods, sharing their qualities of bravery, honesty, and military genius.[86] But because they were the custodians of popular history, the volunteers themselves defined the pantheon. The radically democratic strains of the Revolution were left out of this iconography, since volunteer troops never claimed names like "Tom Paine's Guards." Jefferson's and Jackson's name graced only short-lived reformist troops.[87]

Volunteer displays of all kinds focused on present-day social problems, most immediately those of the militia system and the relation between private and public companies. Volunteers' elaborate and colorful uniforms, fancy equipment, and horses overshadowed the public militias' bleak disarray. The private companies' affluent, orderly appearance made them seem the natural military and social superiors of raggedly clad men who were unable to form a straight line.[88] Highly structured group movements and carefully timed "evolutions" showed the benefits of regular practice. Every volunteer ceremony, from precise gun firing to the reverent handling of banners and flags was a short discourse on the theme that good families and private companies produced efficient, dutiful soldiers.

Because they took place in the holiday streets, volunteer parades and ceremonies addressed the larger issue of public behavior at a time of sharp and growing concern over working-class festivity. Exercises and drills, small dramas repeating the values of order and deference to authority, stood out in the surrounding plebeian uproar. "Discipline," "order," and "regularity" defined volunteer performances. While men in public companies chafed at being ordered around "by some fool in a uniform" on Muster Day,[89] volunteers enthusiastically "paid respects," "saluted," and "did honor to" immediate superiors and visiting dignitaries in a manner "old revolutioners" would have called groveling. Manners and gentility were also constructed in ritualized courtesies, such as escort in and out of the city. While public presentations of standards, badges, and chalices from troops to officers or among officers dramatized fraternal mutuality, they also outlined the bounds of deferential respect.[90]

Volunteer parades challenged the holiday customs of the urban crowd. Conversely, the connections among the public, militias, general musters, and disorderly festivity were explicitly drawn in the press.[91] Embodying discipline in action, militia parades contrasted with rowdy license, carving order out of disorder and asserting respectability and elegance over irrationality and poverty. Small dramas on military worthiness were also lessons about what should take place in public and how men should act.

Philadelphia's public culture was thus infused with an image of social good for which volunteers were the chief models, just as they made a history in which they were the central actors. A brilliantly dressed, well-disciplined, obedient network of young men from good families, held together by ties of service and patriotic reverence, the volunteers exemplified all a male citizen should hope to be. This image commented on and stood opposed to working-class social style, while it implied that good families contributed the best citizens. In this antithesis, the volunteers' version of social good was linked to other attempts to reform working people's customs and habits, including Sabbatarianism and the Sunday School Movement, temperance, moral reform, public education, and the movement for rational recreation.[92] The uniqueness of the volunteers' contribution was that they personified and performed this social criticism. As voluntary associations with governmental support, they were a living, marching alternative to the lower orders' ragged recreations. Private companies on parade embodied both criticism and model.

Because of the volunteers' enthusiasm and popularity, the conventions of military display came to dominate Philadelphia's parade repertoire. Military respectability infused parade making until parade making itself became a respectable act, an evolution made possible by the social power of its sponsors and propelled by their need for self-legitimation. Although Philadelphia had no official ceremonial planners or directors (as most twentieth-century cities do), the volunteers, as ceremonial specialists, in fact occupied this position. Since private militia officers often held municipal offices, the volunteers had privileged access to city approval and occasional funding of their demonstrations, commemorations, and receptions. Private ceremonialism thus had a governmental stamp, and the city's few forays into civic ceremony were proposed, planned, and led by public officials acting in a private military capacity.[93] In this way, the volunteers' popularity increased among the general public, and respectable families dictated definitions of values and legitimate public performances.

As the next chapter explores, other unsanctioned street traditions existed in the city and persisted despite complaints of the respectable and the good examples of the private companies. As for the volunteers, they won at least part of their battle for legitimacy, triumphing in their campaign to become the state's sole militia. In 1858 Pennsylvania abolished compulsory training and effectively abandoned the attempt to maintain public companies.[94] While this legislation was a victory for some reformers, through it the leisured and privileged had arrogated to themselves the political responsibility claimed for all men in universal militia service. By asserting their role as the exclusive domestic peacekeepers, and by stressing private organizations, the volunteers assured business-class dominance over the handling and outcome of strikes, riots, and other upheavals. Indeed, after the Great Strike of 1877, Pennsylvania's volunteers became the state's National Guard and embarked on a long career of protecting private property from the public.[95] The volunteers presented themselves as proficient, creditable, and respectable; they also held a monopoly over the use of force in urban disturbances. Thus, they helped define—as well as defend—an early-nineteenth-century version of public order useful to the business class. Combined with the recurrent manipulation of patriotic symbols and a selective version of the Revolutionary past, the social basis of this carefully developed legitimacy seemed impervious to challenge.

CHAPTER FOUR

"Confusion Worse Confounded"

Burlesque Parade Traditions

While affluent Philadelphians developed elegant public ceremonies, poor and working-class Philadelphians created other varieties of street theatre. Mockeries and maskings provided a distinctive mode of political expression for the city's poor and working peoples, who used irreverent spectacles to make political demands, propose alternatives to affluent Philadelphians' social styles, and identify antagonists. Burlesque street parades were linked to the history of folk drama. But while laughter, disguise, and burlesque often jibed at social injustice, their uses were not inherently just. Poor people's techniques of political folk drama could be freely borrowed for racist and nativist purposes, and techniques for criticizing social inequality could be used to harass other weaker Philadelphians. Part of the story of the political uses of folk dramas, then, is the story of their dilution.

ORIGINS OF URBAN FOLK DRAMAS

The history of the city's folk dramas reflects the changing uses of the street and the transformation of older forms of plebeian protest—both urban and rural—in the nineteenth century. Far from meaningless foolery, these much-enjoyed burlesque parades had coherence and meaning for their performers. To untangle and trace these meanings, we need to connect mockeries and maskings to the larger context of the city's politics and culture.[1]

The history of folk dramas also clarifies the relationship between culture and class relations. If maskers thought their performances significant, even political, street maskings and parodies were often perceived by representatives of the propertied—the party press, reformers, and local governmental authorities—as wild and irrational, a problem of working-class conduct in general and festive behavior in particular. Masked burlesques took place in the context of festivity, riot, and disorder in the streets, but behind concern over disorder lay that over the uses of public communication. As alternative traditions of street performance, burlesques also posed the problem of the relation between the political and the theatrical, of which meanings might be enacted in public and by whom. In some cases, burlesque performers were censured, even arrested and prosecuted; in other cases, they were seen as harmless.

The origins of parodies, maskings, and burlesques are part of the history of public culture, and not just an antiquarian concern. The origins of folk dramas, however, are elusive; evidence is scattered, and documentation of North American popular culture was usually random or accidental in the eighteenth century. Burlesque, parody, and folk drama were deeply rooted in Philadelphia and the surrounding countryside. A variety of folk dramatic traditions came to the city with migrants from the hinterland and immigrants from overseas who crowded the city's neighborhoods after 1800. Other sources influenced local vernacular culture. After 1800, older folk traditions interacted dynamically with the commercial culture of the stage and the penny press.

The best-known eighteenth-century uses of street theatre were the stylized, ritualized actions of crowds and mobs during the Revolution. Philadelphians and other colonial city dwellers relied on dramatized actions to voice disaffection, defend popular prerogatives, or threaten justice to wrongdoers. As Alfred Young has shown, colonial traditions of public political ritual were drawn from several sources. Some techniques of crowd justice—for example, hangings in effigy—borrowed from and played with the theatrical conventions of the official exercises of state power: public whippings, humiliations, and executions. Others were elaborated from the customs of occupational groups, for example, tarring and feathering. In this case, Anglo-American sailors recast a maritime punishment into a publicly visible mode of justice, applying it to landlubbers and adding it to America's Revolutionary political language.[2] As the Revolution began in Philadelphia, the lower orders employed techniques of folk justice against Tories, sympathizers, engrossers, and forestallers, merchants who aimed to profit from wartime shortages. Hangings in effigy, burnings of "Stamp Men," mock funerals for the loss of liberty, and ritualized public humiliations of Crown officers were part of local Revolutionary mobilization.[3]

In many cases, these street dramas were produced with the acquiescence, assent, or collaboration of local elites and the leaders of the Revolution. Many crowd actions drew economic and political leaders and the "lower orders" together in revolt. A vivid account of the 1780 procession in "honor" of Benedict Arnold shows the cross-class nature of these street dramas. The traitor's effigy, borne along on a cart,

> was dressed in regimentals, had two faces, emblematic of his traitorous conduct, a mask in his left hand and a letter in his right from Beelzebub. . . . At the back of the figure of the general was the figure of the Devil shaking a purse of money in the General's left ear, and in his right hand a pitchfork ready to drive him into hell as the reward due for the many crimes which his thirst for gold had made him commit.[4]

The manikin was surrounded by didactic transparencies, explaining Arnold's crime and declaring his treachery "held up to public view, for the exposure of his infamy . . . his effigy hanged (for want of his body) as a traitor to his native country and as a Betrayer of the laws of honour." The procession was led by several gentlemen mounted on horseback, "a line of Continental officers," "sundry gentlemen in the line," but also by a "Guard of the City Infantry," drawn from among the "lower orders" and "attended by a numerous concourse of people, who after expressing their abhorrence of the Treason and the Traitor, committed him to the flames."[5] (See "Mock Execution of Benedict Arnold" in the illustrations section.)

The crowd could also act autonomously, aiming dramatic techniques—and violence—at local elites and national policies. In these cases, direct action and symbolic communication were sometimes suppressed. Rioting broke out in the city in 1779 over the Loyalist sympathies of local leaders; later, some among the lower orders used riots and dramas to demonstrate support for the French Revolution and antagonism to the Jay Treaty and tò postwar tax policies.[6] The political uses of impersonation, ridicule, and direct action by the crowd continued in the nineteenth century, but these uses were shaped by changes in social relations. On one hand, where there had been elite support for direct action against illegitimate authority, this support waned as local property owners consolidated their own power. At the same time, the public theatrical exercise of state authority in punishments and executions came under attack, was modified, and finally withdrawn from the theatre of the streets. Floggings were stopped, the stocks were torn down, and public hangings were moved inside prison walls.[7]

The official display of power was more and more removed from public view, but political and economic leaders reorganized public ceremonial roles for themselves. Through patriotic and military ceremony, affluent young men cast themselves in the roles of defenders of the peace and the preservers of historical memory. At the same time, those with economic and political power withdrew from participation in plebeian cultural traditions. Despite Quaker suppression of popular culture, affluent Philadelphians had probably understood—if they did not patronize—folk dramatic practices (for example, Christmas customs such as "shooting in" the New Year). Eighteenth-century urban elites elsewhere, for example, had tolerated the traditional Pope's Day brawls and effigy burnings in Boston and Negro Election Days in New Haven and Albany.[8] By the early nineteenth century, the educated and propertied classes viewed plebeian dramas and customs as rude and quaint at best; when elites took customs more seriously, they called them barbarous, irrational evidence of the degeneration of the lower orders.[9] Samuel Breck, recalling a late-eighteenth-century Christmas mummers play in Boston, commented on this changed attitude. Breck saw the mummers burst from the nighttime street into the rich household, to perform their antic play and beg a treat in honor of the season. What, Breck wondered, "should we say to such intruders now? Our manners would not brook such usage a moment."[10]

While elites withdrew their tolerance for the old customs, folk, political, and street dramas were given new life by the flowering of commercial theatre and printing. Conversely, media entrepreneurs drew on the older genres and street culture to popularize their products. As Raymond Williams has pointed out with regard to press history, in the early nineteenth century an unprecedented fluidity characterized media genres. Generic boundaries between kinds of media—for example, the lines separating theatre and magazines—were permeable, and content moved easily between communication modes the twentieth century treats as isolable and discrete. The commercial media found novel uses for the street's oral traditions, old stereotypes, and familiar ideas, continuing and amplifying them in ways calculated to garner ever-larger audiences. At the forefront of these developments, media historians argue, were crime news, sensation, and the elaboration of racial and ethnic stereotypes.[11]

Burlesque, the humorous or mocking exaggeration of traits, burgeoned in Philadelphia's popular theatre and street literature, beginning at least as early as John Durang's imitations of Pennsylvania German dialect and manners in his traveling theatricals.[12] Early-nineteenth-century caricatures and stereotypes, as well as stock characters, moved easily between stage and street; thus heroes of urban working-class life—the most famous being Mose, the Bowery B'Hoy—played on stages in every northeastern city.[13] At the same time, minstrelsy's characters, Shakespearean staples, and the theatre circuit's favored stereotypes all appeared in street parades.

MILITARY BURLESQUES

Two major, interrelated uses of street burlesque flourished in Philadelphia before the Civil War: costumed political parades mocking the militia system and masked Christmas revelry.[14] The tradition of military mockery, a political use of the British and European charivari, lent its styles and devices to Christmastide masking, which grew quickly in the nineteenth century. Young men from working-class neighborhoods combined house-visiting and noise-making customs with the political charivari to make full-blown, costumed Christmas uproars in the city's downtown.

Parades parodying musters opposed the militia system and laws in general and questioned forced participation in the public militia. This widely felt hostility toward militia laws, which spread and deepened from the 1820s through the 1840s, was articulated in party platforms after 1828. Philadelphia's antimilitia activists not only tried to effect changes in militia laws, but also employed a dramatic strategy. In burlesques, they hailed ridicule on the system of duties and the militia officers, trying to end an unjust institution, as they put it, by laughing it out of existence.

The best-recorded burlesque of a militia muster took place in 1825 in Philadelphia's Northern Liberties. A poor working-class district clustered around boatyards and docks and pocked with small workrooms, the Northern Liberties had a long history of resistance to unjust authority. Many of the crowd actions against Loyalists had drawn personnel from this neighborhood; in the 1820s and 1830s, the Adjutant General's militia fines collectors who ventured in the Liberties risked a pelting with rotten eggs, at the very least.[15]

One day in May 1825, at the militia officers' election, the Liberties' obscure foot regiment, the Eighty-Fourth, nominated and elected John Pluck, "a poor, ignorant, stupid fellow," an ostler at a tavern stable, their colonel.[16] Although the division officers execrated the Eighty-Fourth's choice and tried to invalidate the election, Pluck was approved by a vast majority.[17]

John Pluck's election was a joke, a slap at the division officers. The *Saturday Evening Post* announced, "Pluck has been elected, Governor Schultze [sic] not withstanding, and there can be no question but that the gentleman will answer all honest and honorable anticipations. . . . True, it is a little out of his ordinary sphere, but what of that?"[18] That a colonelcy was indeed above Pluck's station was the crux of the joke. As a laborer who cleaned stalls for a living, the new colonel ranked among the lowest of local society, especially compared to the other officers, most of whom were lawyers, merchants, and bankers. Because Pluck's job was a filthy one and he owned no tools and took part of his pay in lodging, he was considered to be a servant or retainer. He was not even an independent workingman. To elect him regimental colonel was to invert all protocol, bringing honor to the ground and the smell of the stables into the officers' quarters. The *Post* explicated the pranksters' point: "'Honor and Shame from no condition rise: Act well your part and there the honor lies.' . . . If this be the case, Colonel Pluck is to all intents and purposes a right honorable man. . . . He acts as well his part whether it is in cleaning out a stable or rubbing down a pony."[19]

The ostler's comrades elected him to make the point that even one of his low station was a better man with a clearer sense of honor than titled and careerist officers, appointed adjutants, and elected officials who time and again thwarted attempts at militia reform.

The men of the Eighty-Fourth chose Pluck for more than his occupation and his brave last name. He was severely deformed and, according to several press reports, he may have been mentally deficient. "Napoleon is low in stature — Pluck is lower still!" crowed a reporter. "I estimate him at five feet bare."[20] Extremely bowlegged and hunchbacked, Pluck, with his bulging eyes and huge head, had suffered neighborhood taunts for years.[21]

In electing Pluck, the Eighty-Fourth Regiment followed a familiar pattern of social inversion for symbolic purposes. Ritual elevation of the deformed and deficient was common in European folklore, found in the Feast of Fools of medieval England and the Abbey of Boys of early modern France,[22] but a more recent precedent had suggested the mock election. At Garrat, near London, an annual election spectacle drew both city gentry and rural people to see the investiture of a dwarf or hunchback as mayor amid a week of festive license. During the political repression of the late eighteenth century, the Garrat election found its way into the literature of the London stage as part of a radical and comic critique of Parliament's politics and personalities. The implication that the raucous Garrat election was more valid than the serious and corrupt system of parliamentary representation, in which every principal of law could be violated with impunity, connected neatly with the Wilkesite agitations in support of the rights of electors to democratic representation.[23] Even the phrase "a Garrat election" moved into popular speech and glossed a travesty of fair play and established procedure. More broadly, the Garrat election stood as a muffled but unmistakable denunciation of a political system determined to trample the natural rights of ordinary men.[24] Philadelphia's natives and immigrants were aware of the Garrat spectacle, and it was thus one possible source of burlesque.

The Eighty-Fourth had devised a variation on the Garrat theme, with specific local meanings and effects. Pluck had been chosen not for a day of reverse role playing, but to hold office legally for seven years. His electors accurately aimed to make their point through inconvenience and embarrassment, as well as through laughter.

The Eighty-Fourth pushed militia burlesque beyond mock elections. To the division officers' chagrin, Pluck's duties included leading his troops through the city streets to muster at the Bush Hill parade ground. As officers could be criticized through the election, so battalion drills, "those vexatious parades," would be lampooned by a comic procession.[25] The *Post* described an addled Pluck amid cheering supporters at the spectacle:

> On Wednesday last [May 18] was enacted the Grand Military farce, in which the redoubtable John Pluck made his debut in the character of colonel of the Merry 84th. The sport was not so great as was anticipated by the lovers of frolic and fun, and from the complete indifference with which the Colonel went through his part, apparently unconscious of everything around him, staring with stupid indifference and scarce possessing the spirit to answer occasional questions . . . which, the more plausibly to carry on the joke were put to him by his officers. It is said he once mustered sufficient Pluck to say "he did not know where they were going to march him but would tell them all about it when he got back, if he could remember the way . . ." which was much applauded as a brave speech by his friends and clamorously encored by the great crowd which had gathered around his quarters.[26]

In the parade, the Eighty-Fourth used two strategies for attacking the militia laws, simultaneously parodying public battalion days and the officers' uniforms. The colonel made an outrageous officer, mounted on a spavined white nag and wearing a huge *chapeau-de-bras*, a shoulder-covering woman's bonnet with a bow knotted under his chin. A belt with an enormous buckle cinched up his baggy burlap pants. A giant sword and spurs half a yard long with murderous rowels parodied ceremonial military dress while making Pluck appear dwarfish. The *Post* reported that on taking command he shouted, "Well, at least I ain't afraid to fight, and that's more than most of them can say!"

The mock muster was purposefully disorderly and topsy-turvy, a perversion of military discipline. With hurrahs, the regiment surged through the streets to Bush Hill,

> with the Colonel at their head but so encompassed by horse-men as to be out of sight of those on foot, who were only now and then favored with a glimpse of the little fellow's plume or his long rusty sword as it rose from its extreme length above his cap and served to show the zig-zag course he pur-sued. His regiment did not wear their uniforms but bore sticks and cornstalks . . . and huddled together in such un-governable merry mood withall as baffles description, and was in reality "confusion worse confounded."[27]

The parade ground soon exhibited "as motley a collection of figures and as grotesque" as reporters could recall, yet the scene was "more numerously and fashionably attended than any parade of that kind ever witnessed."[28] Militiamen with cornstalks and brooms were a familiar sight to Phila-delphians: Poor men had to carry mock weapons at Muster Day because they rarely owned shoulder arms. But men who objected to militia duties elaborated on this disadvan-tage, parodying themselves.[29]

Pluck's fame spread quickly. "No one talks of anything else," wrote the *Democratic Press*.[30] A few days later, theatre crowds were shouting for Pluck and he was in demand at the circus. For weeks, editorialists groused about the spectacle and decried its effects. Letter writers defended Pluck in the papers, poetasters composed odes to his bravery, amateur historians proposed biographies, col-lectors saved "Pluckiana," and the lettered linked his name with Butler's Hudibras and Jonson's Bobadil. New York and Boston papers, taking up the strains of popular an-tagonism to the militia system, reprinted sarcastic descrip-tions of Pluck's activities, to the delight of their readers. The ostler had become, to everyone's surprise, a phenome-non in commercial popular culture.[31]

During the following spring, Pluck led the "Bloody 84th" through the Liberties, around the city's center, and throughout the district of Southwark. He was joined by "fantastical corn toppers" and hailed by crowds of thousands. At the solicitation of Colonel William Stone and Major Mordecai Noah, New York newspaper editors, Pluck began a grand tour, after the fashion of Washington, Lafayette, and Jackson. At New York City, he was "introduced" "armed and equipped in most ludicrous manner." Drunk, he "exhibited himself in his hotel room for 12½ cents to each visitor." [32] Now a national sensation, thanks to publicity by Stone and Noah, Pluck visited Albany, where he was "nominated for vice-president"; toured Providence and Boston, where the police offered to arrest him as a vagabond; and moved on to Richmond, where he became the toast of the town. [33] By October 1826 he was back in Philadelphia for a court-martial to attempt to end the farce. Pluck was pronounced incapable of holding office for seven years and cashiered. [34]

The hilarity that met Pluck's meteoric rise and his abrupt fall might tempt us to dismiss him as an amusing oddity of popular culture. Pluck's career deserves to be taken seriously, however, and not only because his contemporaries took the joke seriously enough to court-martial him. Militia advocates argued that the burlesque exposed the system to contempt, but contempt had been long simmering and was widely shared among workingmen. Pluck's transformation into an icon of popular culture concentrated this contempt, made a joke of it, and presented it publicly. The militia burlesque did not give the state a bad reputation: It made that reputation impossible to deny.

The press responded to the offense taken by military leaders; outraged correspondents declared that Pluck had shamed the entire state and dealt the system "a death blow." Some officers suggested legislation to make parading in a borrowed uniform a misdemeanor in office. [35] The *Democratic Press* reported that irreverence for military authority attracted "many of the depraved part of the crowd," seeing "everywhere surrounding us something filthy or debasing." [36] For others, Pluck's election and parades were "a declaration of public opinion" about the militia law and how it operated. As the *Saturday Evening Post* wrote of his election, "The friends of free suffrage and republican simplicity have eminent cause for congratulation. . . . And as to throwing up the commissions of the militia and the reputation of the state, why, who cares?" [37] A working-class public had made Pluck their symbol of thick-headedness in high places.

But corruption, more than ignorance, characterized Pennsylvania's officeholders; the burlesque stood for "the recent election of the most illiterate and unfit candidates" and "the disrepute into which the system has sunk." [38] One "Colonel Washington" wrote:

> It is the disgust with which I have seen so many of our offices filled by ignorance and imbecility that induces me to intrude. . . . Why should Pluck be the butt of aspersion when he is only the latest of a long list? . . . The question has long since ceased to be whether the candidate for an epaullette is acquainted with the duty to which he aspires, and the man who would propose such an enquiry on the election ground in Pennsylvania would be looked upon as a mere novice. . . . [39]

In fact, "Washington" alleged, the burlesque's message applied to political realms beyond the militia. Corruption had seeped into every state office.

> Those gentlemen who are so tender of the reputation of our state [might] open their eyes a little wider. . . . [They] may open a much more important field of inquiry about our civil department. . . . They may commence at the very head and also through every branch. . . . Their investigation will afford them numerous and much more interesting opportunities to complain that merit and qualification are not guarantees of office in Pennsylvania. . . . Some of their objects would not be able to defend themselves as well as John Pluck who called himself an "honest man." [40]

Pluck's burlesque drew knowing nods as well as laughter. Using inversion, the elevation of the low and the investiture of responsibility with one who seemed an idiot, the men of the Eighty-Fourth pointed the accusation of stupidity, self-interest, and dishonesty at public officials.

Pluck's popularity, achieved through street performance, media accounts, and his tour, rested on widespread antagonism to the militia system and laws, an antagonism that sprang from the city's class divisions. Workingmen clearly had reasons to resent the law and harass the officers. Workers' hostility toward the unequal burden of militia service and the rise of "distinction" gave the joke its bite and force. Yet some among the propertied and respectable saw the burlesque's humor for different reasons and from different points of view. Colonel Pluck and his crew gave militia advocates and reformers a chance to laugh at the martial performance of the "poor, pelted" public companies, whom they disdained. Only the high division officers, charged by law with maintaining the unwieldy, unpopular system, found it hard to laugh.

Another source of Pluck's wild popularity may be located in Jacksonian social change and the anxieties it elicited among elites and the city's traditional leaders. Some Philadelphians, accustomed to their power, found that the election of a booby symbolized all that they feared from the widening of electoral participation and new forms of political activity. Other elites could enjoy Pluck's election because it seemed to label ordinary democratically elected men unqualified and illegitimate. Indeed, such carping was at the heart of "Washington's" letter.

The Spread of Militia Burlesque

Philadelphia's drama, cycled through commercial culture and popularized by Pluck's grand tour, was taken up in the countryside and in other cities. "Corntoppers" became familiar at annual battalion drills in rural Pennsylvania, New York, and New England. In the spring of 1829, men at Pennsylvania training days substituted canes and cornstalks for muskets, prompting an editor to observe that "*ordinary* musterings are absurd"; "they only give a parcel of silly ones high titles" and "a little brief authority and a chance to strut their hour in regimentals."[41]

Albany and then New York City witnessed large fantastical processions in 1831 and again in 1833. In Albany, "fusileers" and "invincibles" dressed in wild costumes, women's curls, and enormous whiskers protested the state law. One newspaper took up the theme typographically, printing its account of the "Grand Fantastical Procession" in jumbled, mismatched typefaces.[42]

"General Lafayette's Arrival at Independence Hall," September 28, 1824, lithograph. Between 100,000 and 200,000 people witnessed Lafayette's triumphal entry into the city. FREE LIBRARY OF PHILADELPHIA

"Grand Fantastical Parade, New-York," December 2, 1833, engraving by "Hassan Straightshanks." In this rare visual record of a militia burlesque, many traditional elements appear—antimilitia banners, men in blackface (or perhaps blacks), wild costumes, and a Pluck-like commander. LIBRARY OF CONGRESS

"Mock Execution of Benedict Arnold," wood engraving from Steiner and Cist's 1781 Almanac. Nineteenth-century Philadelphians drew on eighteenth-century urban traditions of symbolic punishment and protest like the burning of effigies. THE HISTORICAL SOCIETY OF PENNSYLVANIA

"The Nation's Bulwark: A Well-Disciplined Militia," etching by Edward Clay, 1829. A popular Philadelphia caricaturist, Clay was one of several artists who helped record and expand hostility toward the militia laws. LIBRARY COMPANY OF PHILADELPHIA

Members of the City Troop and Other Philadelphia Soldiery," watercolor by touring Russian artist Pavel Petrovich Svinin, 1811–1813. Philadelphia's most elite cavalry taking its ease on Muster Day. THE METROPOLITAN MUSEUM OF ART, ROGERS FUND, 1942. [42.95.21]

COL. PLUCK'S

TOAST AT MORSE'S HOTEL NEW YORK 1826.

May the enemies of our Country have a long
Journey to Ride, a hard trotting horse a por-
cupine Saddle & a cobweb pair of breeches.

COL. PLUCK Mounted on the Eclipse Colt!!!

presented to him by COL. STONE & MJO:NOAH!!!!

"Col. Pluck's Toast at Morse's Hotel," a caricature of c. 1828. This
anonymous representation of Pluck parodied contemporary heroic
images of Andrew Jackson. THE NEW-YORK HISTORICAL SOCIETY,
NEW YORK CITY

"Procession of Victuallers of Philadelphia," 1821, aquatint and etching with watercolor by Joseph Yeager after J. L. Krimmel. Many traditional craft images appear here: rolling ships, workshops, occupational costumes, and banners with trade devices. PHILADELPHIA MUSEUM OF ART, GIVEN BY THE ESTATE OF CHARLES M. B. CADWALADER

"The Gold & Silver Artificers of Phila. in Civic Procession," lithograph by M. E. D. Brown, 1832. Spectators gathered on the steps of the Second Bank, crowds jammed Chestnut Street, and women and children leaned from windows to see the trades go by

"Independence Day Celebration in Centre Square," watercolor by John Lewis Krimmel, 1819. Krimmel shows us a placid, respectable Fourth of July, enhanced with food, drink, and music. THE HISTORI-CAL SOCIETY OF PENNSYLVANIA

"Riot in Philadelphia, July 7th, 1844," lithograph by J. Baillie, New York. By the 1840s, Independence Day had become hard to romanti-cize. This print reports the Protestant attack, prompted by the Fourth of July Nativist procession, on St. Philip Neri Catholic Church in Southwark. THE HISTORICAL SOCIETY OF PENNSYLVANIA

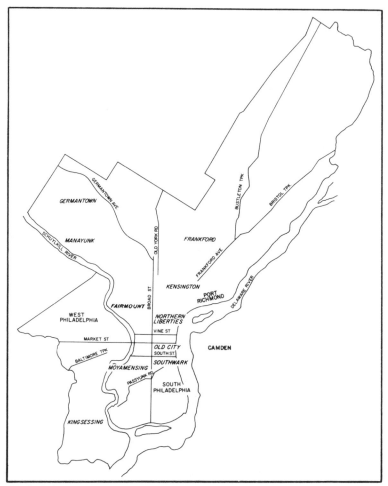

Philadelphia in 1854. Reproduced from Allen F. Davis and Mark H. Haller, eds., *The Peoples of Philadelphia: A History of Ethnic Groups and Lower-Class Life, 1790–1940.* TEMPLE UNIVERSITY PRESS, 1973

As the Workingmen's and the Democratic parties took up the cause of militia reform, burlesquers continued their performances.[43] In May 1833 the men of the Northern Liberties revitalized the memory of Pluck. Colonel Peter Albright, a young man active in the Democratic Party, allowed his company of the Eighty-Fourth to appear in "fantastical dress" calling themselves the "Hollow Guards." Albright's men marched

> to the music of a penny whistle . . . in no uniformity of uniform. . . . [Each] had endeavored to exceed the other in grotesqueness, and every variety of apparel and decoration was brought into this requisition. . . . The orderly sergeant bore on his right hand a wooden staff shaped like a sword on which was painted "defender of the laws." . . . The adjutant was . . . most ludicrously decorated with ribbons and patches of red flannel . . . his cap measured at least five feet in circumference. The standard bearer had one leg of his pantaloons red, the other white, and wore for covering an old fire bucket, with a painted rice fan for a cockade. . . . On the seat of honor was lashed a knapsack with "The Bloody 84th" painted upon it. . . . The banner he carried bore on one side—Life Guards of Pennsylvania Senators. On the other, a sketch of Senator Rodgers [sic] of Bucks County. . . . Some of the privates were in calico frocks and some in small clothes [knee breeches]. One carried a fish for a weapon, another an old broom . . . a fourth was embellished with the figure of a heart placed conspicuously on his back [a walking target dummy].[44]

After this detachment came another,

> still more singularly attired . . . preceded by wheels drawn by horses, an old and rusty two pounder, upon which a small boy in Indian costume was astride, flourishing a matchrope. . . . There followed two banners: "Hollow Guards, the Terror of the World" and "The Nation's Bulwark—The Bloody 84th." . . . One artillerist wore a weird sister's cap . . . [another] had his head stuck in a possum skin, a third tied up in a blanket. . . . [A fourth wore] a moon and stars on his back . . . [and a fifth] was bulged up as large as two Falstaffs.

Albright addressed them "with martial words" and as the column of men took up march, "they were followed promiscuously by ununiformed members with umbrellas, broomhandles and sticks." These men trooped helter-skelter through the principal streets, to the amusement of the downtown crowds. "At every street corner they gained additional force," and the "thousands who followed entirely blocked up the streets." [45]

Again the press pointed to the explicitly political purposes of the enactment:

> To all intents and purposes they looked as ridiculous as ridiculous could be and the object in view—that of establishing the folly and absurdity of our ordinary militia parades was most fully obtained. . . . Since the militia laws are clearly a farce, none should complain about this . . . therefore, let [the militia system] be ridiculed until those in authority either amend it or abolish it altogether.[46]

The militia officers, themselves experts at creating imagery through street ritual, did not appreciate being made the butt of public jokes. Rather than allow the farce to become a spectacle, they arrested Peter Albright and prepared to court-martial him "for permitting unsoldier-like conduct." Although some newspapers favored Albright as "a martyr in the cause of the picturesque," [47] he and his company had trod on important toes. Senator Rogers, whose portrait adorned the banner, was a militia general and chair of the state legislature's committee on the militia. Albright's parade was a response to the rejection by Rogers's committee of a report recommending abolition of public trainings and restructuring of fines. The committee, the press claimed, reported against the bill despite vigorous efforts by city delegates and unanimous support in the Pennsylvania House of Representatives, because Rogers and his friends were unwilling to abolish their own titles and commands.[48] As embarrassing as the use of the general's portrait in a tatterdemalion street display, the burlesque preceded an election for brigadier general by only a few weeks. Resurrecting the memory of Pluck and drawing on all the strains of antagonistic laughter aimed at the pretensions of officers and uniformed militiamen, the Hollow Guards threatened the legitimacy of command at a crucial moment, the time of the transfer and confirmation of power.

Far from dampening the Guards' enthusiasm, Albright's arrest spurred them on. In the fall, they celebrated the colonel's release from jail with still more theatrical and incongruous costumes and music. Again, they used anti-uniformity—"no two dresses bore the least resemblance to each other"—and borrowed images and costumes from the popular theatre—"knights clad in armor, a cavalier clad in a bearskin with an iron charm around his middle, Indians, clowns etc." Beards and paint hid faces, and exaggeration had free rein. "Swords under the length of six feet in the blade were 'quite despiseable.' Twelve feet was the regulation length of their muskets." In a jab at the serious ceremonialism of the volunteer militias, banners displayed random slogans like "Dinners baked here at the shortest notice." Banners also reminded the audience of the problematic relation between office, merit, and authority, making use of slogans such as "Honor to whom honor is due." [49]

The burlesques continued, celebrating the Guards' moral victory and opposing Albright's persecution. Each "exceeded in splendor all former exhibitions," and featured "three to five hundred men . . . fully accoutred." [50] In late October, Albright appeared as a Revolutionary War officer. In a powdered wig, his face floured white and his nose generously smeared with brown shoe polish, he bowed graciously to the crowd. Albright had lost none of his nerve. His costume pointed to the disgrace brought on the militia system by the inequality of burdens and the machinations of self-interested leaders; his makeup called the officers a lot of "brown noses." Personal and political antagonism also blended as an effigy of William Hurlick, the city's despised fines collector, swung from a pole.[51]

Antimilitia protests continued in Pennsylvania and New England. In New Haven an "awful battalion" formed under the command of "Timothy Tremendous," to "shame all scarecrows." Their standard showed "a bull rampant," with a Revolutionary War veteran "in reverse order [seated backwards] on his back and holding on by the tail," surmounted with the motto "The Bull-Work of Our Country." "Music was by callithumpian masters," a band wreaking havoc with broken pots and pans: "The very cats were dumfounded by it." A working-class ward in Easton, Pennsylvania, about sixty miles north of Philadelphia, celebrated Jackson Day in 1834 with the election of a Pluck-like "Redoubtable Colonel Scheffler," and planned processions for training days. At Chambersburg, west of Harrisburg, the *Repository* recorded a vast mock battalion in June 1835 with young men in blackface and patched and scavenged clothes. Wild weapons, rough music, and deformed horses highlighted the parade. "So much for the useless militia system, which excites such indignation," and so much for training days, worse than useless "when men are trained for no other purpose than to make them weary."[52] These were only Pennsylvanian variations on the mock militias; records of similar burlesque parades can be found from Maine to Georgia, and for later dates in the midwest.[53]

In Philadelphia, burlesquers harassed militia officers for at least another decade. Colonel Thomas Duffield, long a commander in the Spring Garden district, addressed a volunteer militia convention in Harrisburg in 1842

> with a view to bringing to the notice of the officers present the extraordinary difficulties which they had to encounter in some portions of the county of Philadelphia in attempting to carry out the militia law. . . . [T]here were a large number of persons there opposed to military trainings, and they took every means in their power to bring the military into disrepute and cast ridicule upon them. . . . [They] appeared on parade grounds, dressed in fantastical dresses, and when officers attempted to make them do their duty, they raised riots and mobs.[54]

Duffield reported that resistance had spread beyond the parade ground. "When they attempted to collect fines from these persons, they would permit their property to be sold for fines and then bring suits against the officers."[55]

POLITICAL PROTEST AND THE CHARIVARI

The political use of disguise and burlesque generally, and fantastical militias in particular, was not confined to Philadelphia or Pennsylvania; the notion of comic costumed street processions was borrowed from the *charivari*, or "rough music." Violet Alford and E. P. Thompson have documented and analyzed the uses of "rough music" or "skimmington riding" in nineteenth-century England; Bryan Palmer has traced the survival and transformation of this method of folk justice in Canada and the United States.[56] The Philadelphia (and Chambersburg, Easton,

New York City, Albany, and New Haven) mock militia parades shared much with European and American charivaris. Typical devices included the use of pots, pans, chamber pots, and household utensils as musical instruments, and elements of inversion, such as backward seating on an ass, horse, goat, or bull. Singling out and mocking or threatening transgressors, whether a senator, Hurlick the fines collector, or officers in general, preserved the core of folk justice.

The charivari's earlier use was an effort at community control of sexual mores and sexual access: Newlyweds, partners in marriages deemed unnatural because of age disparity or the recent death of a spouse, adulterers, wife beaters, husband beaters, or others who overstepped the usual bounds of relations between the sexes and generations became targets of cacophonous, sometimes violent processions. Both Palmer and Thompson argue that the charivari found its way into social criticism in the nineteenth century. In England, the "rough music" or "skimmington" became a community weapon against speculating landlords and other disrupters of older economic relations. Palmer cites an early-nineteenth-century American "shivaree" aimed at a wedding celebration, not to tease the bride and groom, but to upbraid the family for using the party to distinguish themselves from their neighbors. The rough musicians directed their scorn at "d—d aristocratical and powerful grand big-bug doins." [57] Political uses of the charivari were thus local, and aimed at known violators of social relations, which, while not egalitarian, were seen as protected by the shared mores and expectations Thompson has called "moral economy." [58] Contempt for new sources of law and order, or hostility to legal and political transformation also found expression in Canadian charivaris: Rough musicians violently protested the Confederation of Canada in the 1830s.[59] There was also an earlier and continuing North American precedent: In New York State's Helderberg region, tenants opposing their landlords' encroachments used calico dresses and tin-horned masks in their nighttime raids.[60]

Links between political protest and the charivari are also found in etymological evidence. In Pennsylvania, both charivari musicians and the bands accompanying mock militias called themselves "callithumpians." This dialect word was used in the west of England to designate Jacobins, radical reformers, and "disturbers of order at Parliamentary elections."[61]

Other sources of the tradition, although the connections are difficult to prove conclusively, are the costumes and dramas of the Luddites, the secret society called the "Scotch Cattle," and the "Rebecca" rioters, in the British Isles. These protests by agricultural and rural industrial laborers relied on secret organization, disguised nighttime raids, anonymous threats, and the destruction of offending machines or of obstacles (turnpike gates in the case of the Rebecca riots, knitting frames in the case of the Luddites). Norman Simms argues that the use of folk dramatic techniques—disguises, secret cries, and mythical leaders—is evidence that the Luddites and their ilk saw themselves as defenders of community, the same community created by less antagonistic dramas such as Christmas maskings.[62] Certainly Philadelphians heard, whether through the press or by word of mouth from recent immigrants, of the panic the Luddites had caused in the English government, and of the complicity and solidarity the textile districts lent the machine-breakers.

Mock militias took a familiar form of folk justice and altered it to fit specific local purposes. That cornstalk militia parades diffused and persisted shows that the issue they addressed was salient beyond Philadelphia; the burlesques' popularity reveals the ease with which older British and European folk dramas could still express dissent, even in the different, less-repressive political climate of the United States. The charivari had been used to regulate conduct among neighbors or to attack persons who threatened community norms. In the case of the fantastical militias, offenders were also known, sometimes personally by protestors, and their transgressions both affected the economic well-being of mechanics and artisans and offended their notions of proper social relations.

Workingmen's charivaris expressed several criticisms of the militia system and social relations. The immediate source of antagonism was the odious company drill, which weighed heavily on workingmen. Urban mechanics and artisans experienced Muster Day as an arbitrary and malicious use of official authority; drills removed them from work without compensation, and the militia forced them to supply uniforms and equipment at their own expense.

In drills and officers' conduct, workingmen found something more troubling: The power over men symbolized in title and rank was being exaggerated into an unrepublican fondness for distinction, which was becoming the basis for social power. The private volunteer companies that only the most prosperous master artisans could afford to join were dominated by lawyers, bankers, merchants, and "gentlemen." The volunteers provided the militia system with most of its field and division officers. In turn, militia title and rank were concomitants of government officeholding, and acknowledged as necessary for entrance into bourgeois "good society." As the burlesquers pointed out, uniform, office, and title were hollow proofs of merit in a frankly unequal system.

In militia elections and commands, workingmen located a means by which businessmen and professionals improved their social image and tried to foist "aristocracy" on ordinary citizens. While these petty tyrants were clambering over social equals they went out of their way to deny their social origins. Military jokes abounded in newspapers and comic periodicals, pointing to the effects of "military pride." "A farmer who was elected to a corporalship in a militia company, his wife after discoursing with him for some time on the advantage which his family would derive from his exaltation, inquired in a doubting tone, 'Husband, will it be proper for us to let our children play with the neighbor's now[?].' "[63] Nastier slurs compared militia officers with drunken Negroes, and concluded that the latter were the more honorable sort of human being.[64] These insults, like Peter Albright's brown-smeared nose, pointed to the character, motivations, and morals of the officers as corrupt and self-serving.

The same attitude toward officership and the construction of social authority through appearances underlay the use of fantastical disguises and costumes. The term *fantastical* bore a derogatory implication. It meant anyone in burlesque dress, but "more in rags than ribbands."[65] Like the harlequin, whose diamond-patterned suit was an abstraction of the beggar's rags and patches, and like the

Irish or English Christmas mummers dressed in straw, rags, or paper, the fantastical may have been ragged as much in imitation of the rural poor as because of his own origins.[66] American fantasticals imitating militia troops drew on this double-edged mockery. Appearing in wild antiuniformity, they at once made fun of the militia's stress on elaborate and uniform dress, brought the officers into contempt with the crazy parodies of their costumes, and laughed at their own public company's lack of style and prestige. Antiuniformity was carried to the extreme, in varicolored pants legs, oddly formed hats, and mismatched shoes. Over and over reporters noticed that no two performers were costumed alike. Similarly, the officers' and volunteers' love of equipment was lampooned by carrying dead fish or deer's legs instead of guns, using rusty culvert pipe for field pieces, and wielding impossibly large swords and bayonets. Pride could be brought low with broken-down horses and random banners—references to the volunteer's satins and fine animals. Another edge of the same laughing mockery was blackface, which injected the raucous laughter of the popular theatre into military burlesque while it compared officers to blacks.

Commentary on the mock militias affirmed a generalized hostility to pretension and self-aggrandizement, but critics also drew parallels to concrete and immediate problems in social relations. The most important of these was the hostility among mechanics, craftsmen, and employers that resulted from the crumbling of older crafts and trades.[67] New work routines, the devaluation of skill, the disintegration of apprenticeship, gross exploitation of factory, sweatshop, and outworkers—all features of the changing urban economy—ignited personal antagonism against employers and wealthy masters. Feelings like those expressed about "military pride" found their way into descriptions of employers' social style and economic practices. The *Mechanics' Free Press* relentlessly jabbed at the growing tendency to judge men by external attributes, yet angrily acknowledged that, in the modern world, money makes the man. The *Press* saw the use of carriages, fine clothes, and titles and the elegance and exclusivity of social events as tools in the construction of inequality.

Radical artisans argued that "[t]he many opportunities that gave men the means and ready access to fortune . . .

have pushed men into good society who positively disgrace bad. . . . [S]uch men . . . are now dictating monarchical principles to us . . . and little kingly notions have crept into our institutions." Part of this project was the creation of "visible lines of distinction."[68]

New inequalities arose from economic practices, but social style was being used to legitimate injustice. The columnist "Peter Single," wrote that men in power "who originally were without character and of course without friends . . . succeeded by nefarious means in amassing a small sum, by speculating in human misery, grinding down some poor illiterate being . . . and now ride in their carriage, give balls and act the rich nabob." "Single" specified men who rose to the status of master artisans and then denied responsibility for their fellows. "When they drain all they can from his labor [they] despise [the workingman] as much as they do the reptile which crawls upon the ground."[69]

For critics like "Single" and the men of the Eighty-Fourth, militia musters and the militia system were part of this process of exploitation and legitimation. The *Mechanics' Free Press* described musters as "worse than useless military show" because they forced men to "submit to the degradation of being an instrument for transforming men into peacocks."[70] That is, they provided yet another occasion for men who thought they were better than workingmen to "accumulate popularity" by dressing up, mounting a horse, and ordering a regiment around. The tone of such criticism of the militia system shows that many workingmen viewed regimental officers and employers as the same kind of accumulating person, if in fact they were not actually the same person.

The mock election and burlesque militia parades combined general social criticism, specific political protest, and personal satire of known individuals. Their flexibility in accomplishing all these tasks at once, and in accommodating a variety of understandings of social relations testifies to the vibrancy of folk-dramatic traditions in the early nineteenth century. That militia burlesques provoked complaint, denunciation, and courts-martial shows that they hit their mark, and that mockery could not be shrugged off easily. What Mikhail Bakhtin has called the subverting power of laughter was, in these cases, a way to tug hard at one corner of the emperor's cloak.[71]

INDEPENDENCE DAY BURLESQUES

Parodies of military dress and style combined with other familiar forms of masking and disguise and spread beyond Muster Day. Some uses of masking moved away from mockery as protest. Independence Day, the year's most important forum for ceremonious patriotic ritual, also had room for fantastical militia marches. In the late 1830s, groups of young men devoted the Fourth of July to making elaborate costumed processions through the city and suburbs. These clubs, like fire companies and serious militia troops, had meeting places or clubhouses, hired bands, and rehearsed their marches. More organized, and apparently more affluent than the "Bloody 84th," they advertised their meetings in the press. Their names, the Crows, the Buzzards, and the Pirates, blended strains of blackface minstrelsy and music-hall culture with militia volunteer and fire company nomenclature, such as the Independent, Washington, Jr., and Laurens, after the hero of the Revolution.

The Crows and similar clubs advertised their Fourth of July parades and excursions weeks in advance, often conducting cryptic word battles with each other in newspaper classified columns. In June 1837 the Independents described a "skirmish" with the Crows that ended in a "Horrible Calamity!"

> Ten thousand Carrion Crows or Ninney Men Frightened by the Regulars' Standard! . . . were so alarmed that their general fell wallopping in the mud, while the remainder hastened to a cannon near the Navy Yard. But I would inform them that when they usher forth again, they need not be alarmed, as the Eagle suffers small birds to sing. . . . A regular.[72]

This was parody of military convention, perhaps especially the volunteers' sham battles, in the terms of minstrel-ese.

Like serious militias, the Buzzards and Crows hired brass bands and steamboats for Independence Day excursions. The parade with the band to and from the dock was an integral part of the day's recreation and an occasion for the troops to display themselves to their neighborhoods and the city. These clubs appeared strikingly costumed in their own wild versions of military dress. In 1838 a "huge concourse" of clubs excited the downtown at midnight on July 3. A line of "old men and Indians," men in blackface "dressed in all colors," were led by a "generalissimo of the crows . . . with expanded wings and a bill several feet in length." Another member rode "a pasteboard charger, which plunged and careered like a war horse."[73]

In the 1830s the Crows and their cohorts carried parading to great lengths, giving several performances each July Fourth and taking their processions to outlying towns, such as Manayunk and Camden. Town residents were amused but not surprised by their crazy visitors, for similar hilarity was widely known on the Fourth of July. In many New England towns, Invincibles and Horribles made costumed second lines behind the traditional volunteer militia parade. Boston's Antiques and Horribles clearly parodied that city's Ancient and Honorable Artillery Company, and the practice is well recorded in Maine.[74]

Independence Day burlesques drew on the tradition of antimilitia protests, casting antagonism into a less political context and diffusing its antiaristocratic, anti–special-privilege thrust. Because the parading clubs had more organized, more affluent origins—possibly including militia clubs—their mock marches were less devastating in their parody, less hostile in their tone. Their marches were approvingly, laughingly, reported with none of the uneasiness that greeted Pluck's and Albright's troops. No one threatened to arrest the generalissimo of the Crows. Nevertheless, the July Fourth burlesques were part of a significant alternative tradition; Independence Day, for all its interminable speeches and florid rhetoric, had a persistent underside of parody and burlesque in many parts of the country. Crazy, disguised parades gathered up the Fourth's rowdy strains, countering prominent Philadelphians' solemn processions with laughter that broke down the restraint of precision and pomposity.

CHRISTMAS MASKINGS AND MUMMINGS

Street performers borrowed parodies of military dress and style and grafted them on to older seasonal folk dramas. Fantasticals and callithumpians performed in Christmas streets; their burlesques retained antimilitia, anti-authority

resonances, even as the meanings of mock-militia performances shifted. Several points are significant for the history of Christmas disguising. First, Christmas disguising
and house-visiting traditions were brought to Pennsylvania from Europe, the British Isles, and Africa via the South
and the Caribbean. Calendrical festivals in addition to
Christmas were marked by dramatic disguising traditions
in Ireland, Scotland, many parts of England, Scandinavia,
Germany, Newfoundland, Jamaica, the Georgia Sea Is-
lands, and the Carolinas. All these areas sent migrants to
Pennsylvania. Although folk dramas were often rural traditions, they were also known in cities. On one hand, the
widely shared familiarity with folk drama kept masking
traditions lively in the city and perhaps ensured the survival of customs. On the other hand, the flowering of maskings after 1800 must have had distinctly foreign and immigrant associations.[75]

By the nineteenth century these customs were considered
the property of the poor and ignorant. As Samuel Breck
revealed, the wealthy and respectable, to whose doors
maskers sometimes came to exchange a performance for a
treat, felt increasing distance between themselves and the
maskers. In turn, the customs seemed increasingly strange
and obnoxious to the well-to-do.

Christmas disguising is not well recorded in the city until
the 1830s, when the mock militias flourished and the penny
press began to reprint complaints and charges from the
mayor's and aldermen's courts. A few early descriptions—
one a record of an arrest for holiday transvestism in the
early eighteenth century, another a proclamation against
masked balls during the War of 1812—do not add up to a
clear picture of festive folk dramas in the city before 1820.[76]
Much more is known about the political uses of ritual by
and for crowds.

We can make some assumptions about early festive traditions based on what we know about the Pennsylvania countryside. In the hinterland, Christmas customs of gun-firing
and drumbeating were mingled with house visits in disguise. One well-known folk dramatic form, "belsnickling,"
was imported to the city from the German-speaking
countryside. The *peltsnickle* or *belsnickle* ("hairy Saint
Nicholas" or "Nicholas in his skins"), an adult disguised in

a hairy costume with a pack of gifts on his back, visited houses and interrogated children about their behavior over the past year, terrifying them by simultaneously scattering gifts and cracking a whip.[77] After the 1830s, the term *belsnickle* declined, as dialect German, once Philadelphia's second language, became less common. The *belsnickle* was supplanted in print culture by "Kris Kindle" and later by Saint Nicholas. As a custom, belsnickling survived into the twentieth century in rural Pennsylvania and in Palatinate German settlements elsewhere. Herbert Halpert notes that urban Christmas maskers and rowdies called themselves *belsnickles* in Saint John's, Newfoundland, although they did not keep the familial child-visiting custom.[78]

The English terms *fantasticals* and *callithumpians* replaced *belsnickles* to describe Christmas Eve revelers in Philadelphia. Their masked processions with mock instruments were recognizable from the antimilitia movement, but seem, from the fragmentary historical record, to have been novel for Christmas nights. Young men roved in bands and stopped at taverns, making rough music and uproarious noise. On Christmas Eve in 1833, "riot, noise and uproar prevailed, uncontrolled and uninterrupted in many of our central and most orderly streets. Gangs of boys howled as if possessed by the demon of disorder."[79] The "possessed" were up to something besides howling, and for this reason observers applied the names "fantasticals" and "callithumpians" to them. The troops of young men wore exaggerated costumes, often women's dresses, and played the familiar instruments of the kitchen, washhouse, and outhouse.

In 1844 knots of young men "succeeded in most beautifully fooling themselves" in fashionable Chestnut Street. "Some, more fantastic in their taste and extravagant in their expression . . . tricked out in burlesque garb and whimsical costumes, while musical costumes from the trumpet to the pennywhistle enlivened the ear with sound, if not melody and harmony."[80] Revelers clearly borrowed the charivari's conventions. On New Year's Eve in 1847, a "callithumpian band . . . accoutred grotesquely and with blackened faces . . . with rams horns, bells and kettles . . . shocked the very moon with their enactments.[81]

Mock-militia troops made frequent Christmas appearances. In 1854 the " 'Strut-Some Guards' marched, preceded by a fine band. No two of the company were dressed alike, the costume being of the oddest description. The officers carried wooden swords and some of the men most terrible broomsticks."[82] The "Shanghai Guards" made their debut in 1855, "numbering about thirty, costumed in the most ridiculous fashions and preceded by a one horse band."[83] The next year the "Ampudia Guards" and the "Santa Anna Cavalry" made "quite a sensation with their absurd appearance." Many more fantastical companies of young men were noted but only summarily described.[84]

Simpler disguises appeared among Christmas Eve maskers. Women's dress provided an easy and familiar costume, with a radically altered appearance. Young men were sometimes arrested for transvestism, as a description from 1846 indicates: "Three nice young men put forth with some twenty or thirty of their jolly companions to have a grand promenade. Their habits were in such bad taste they were caught foul and with all their trappings, flounces, bustles and all, politely gallanted to the watch house."[85] In court the judge imposed a staggering fine of $300 each, pointing out that "nothing is more offensive in the eye of the law . . . than the assumption of that which by nature and art we are not, and cannot be."[86] Although authorities viewed Christmas masking with uneasiness, penalties were not usually so severe. Transvestism, though common on holidays, elicited fear and outrage.

Some maskers reinterpreted the rural *belsnickle*. In 1845 William Haines of Spring Garden "mounted a huge shaggy cap and with mask and flowing beard had drawn a great crowd around him in Chestnut Street." Haines was "seized upon and carried captive to the lockup."[87]

The most common disguise, familiar from folk tradition and the minstrel stage, was blackface, which had also been used in mock-militia protests, antiblack riots, and July Fourth burlesques. The best-known sources of blackface as a style of impersonation was the wildly popular minstrel show that played to packed audiences from the 1830s. Names like the "Strut-Some Guards" played with minstrelsy's mocking reconstruction of black English, just as "Crows" and "Buzzards" were derogatory racial epithets comparing blacks to blackbirds and "Jim Crows."[88] Christmas masking was infused with popular theatrical imagery, and when maskers sought new identities for Christmas Eve, they seized upon racial stereotypes.

The Christmas "fantasticals" and "callithumpians," like the mock militiamen, had close ties with neighborhood life, especially the tavern. Maskers built processions around tours of drinking establishments; going from door to door, they stopped to offer a rough serenade and collect a treat in honor of the season. If treats were denied, maskers retaliated by starting a "broil"; Christmas newspapers overflowed with descriptions of ransacked taverns and injured barkeeps.[89] Some tavernkeepers went so far as to shoot at unwelcome fantasticals, although most probably saw their antics as customary fun. More tavern fights were caused by the crossing of neighborhood boundaries than by hostility to masked visitors. Tavernkeepers sometimes preferred callithumpian performances to interference by authorities. In 1854, when the night watch arrived to intervene in a rough serenade at William Myers's tavern on Ridge Road, the owner, the clientele, and the band joined forces to thrash and drive them away. When the diligent officers returned a second time, they were badly beaten.[90]

In the 1840s and 1850s, fantastical processions and callithumpian concerts were very rough sports. The fragmentary evidence about Christmas maskings is biased in favor of violence; riotous Christmas revels and assaults by disguised men received more newspaper coverage than peaceful door-to-door performances. Nevertheless, the violence in Christmas disguising traditions was connected to the city's serious youth-gang problem, which had become a full-blown crisis by the 1840s. Some bands of young visitors shared names with notorious gangs; some pushed custom beyond its limits, past petty violence, to murder. In 1850 the refusal of New Year's Day hospitality to the Schuylkill Rangers, a tough gang from the Moyamensing district, ended in the death of the host.[91]

Fantasticals fought each other, challenging rival troops or more sober serenaders to fights with their huge wooden swords. A melee in 1857 resulted in the stabbing death of a young German workman. Witnesses at the inquest related that the fantasticals wore white costumes, plumes and hats, blackface, and gold earrings. When the troops' members, calling themselves the "Ruggers," decided to fight a band of German serenaders, they put down wooden swords for brickbats and knives, throwing the neighborhood into a turmoil, and murdering Andrew Beiche.[92] This was a dramatic and well-recorded incident, but it was not unusual for Christmas disguising to result in injury to persons or property, or even death. Little wonder authorities and respectable Philadelphians came to dread the approach of Christmas.

Christmas disguising traditions had a volatile, violent side that could transform a festive masked procession into a nighttime riot in the blink of an eye. Individually or collectively, masking could be used to express violent racial, ethnic, and personal antagonisms. While most bands of young men engaged in nothing more serious than street fighting and petty vandalism, their constant battling was directed against "outsiders" and "others," blacks and immigrants. As costumes and disguises used racial stereotypes to mock and emphasize differences between kinds of people, Christmas brawling served to define and protect neighborhood boundaries and territory. Masking, performed at night and oriented toward neighborhood audiences, could blend custom with the city's pattern of increasing antiblack, anti-immigrant hostility. Disguise conveniently served young men who made sport by attacking the watch, ganging up on blacks, chasing German immigrants, and disrupting services in black churches.[93]

Riotous disorder, racial violence, and jolly foolery for neighbors and audiences existed side by side, part of the same festival, for decades. Fantastical troops strutted their dances to wild music for crowds in Chestnut and Eighth streets, the busy theatre district, while disguised rioters made street war in Southwark. Municipal authorities disliked masked parades in the city center because they exacerbated an already uneasy situation. Christmas Eve and Night were always marked by throngings of theatre-goers, promenaders, and sightseers; workingmen and boys in these crowds celebrated the holiday with abandon. Customary Christmas license combined with seasonal unemployment made the winter holiday a noisy, drunken, threatening period in the eyes of the respectable.

In the midst of looming general disorder, fantasticals, no matter how controlled their burlesque marches, could only seem ominously irrational to propertied observers. Owners of downtown shops and bow windows were especially anxious at Christmas and pressured the city for police protection.[94] Newspapers connected fantasticals with intemperance; the *North American* compared masked procession to the artisan's Sunday drinking, noting that "the holiday which succeeds such a night must be depressingly blue."[95] After the city gained a consolidated, professional police force in 1854, it stepped up attempts to discourage hornblowing, gun-firing, fantasticals, and callithumpian masquerades. Increased concern was also prompted by growing working-class enthusiasm for a wild Christmas. After the Civil War, Christmas remained a problem of public order, and civic authorities tried a variety of strategies for suppression and control. Suppression proved impossible, but a combination of licensing performers and massive police presence eventually succeeded in turning the wild night into a popular, city-sponsored pageant.[96]

Continuity and Change in Urban Folk Drama

Parodic, burlesque, and rough musical traditions enlivened Philadelphia's festive calendar; they spread and persisted, opposing and undermining Philadelphia's serious ceremonies. Impersonation, transvestism, blackface, and other ways of being "crazy" in the streets continued, although their specific meanings and uses shifted over the antebellum period. The flow of mock-military imagery from the antimilitia movement's burlesques into Christmas revelry, exemplified both continuity and change in urban folk drama. The Eighty-Fourth Regiment and men like them borrowed from older traditions of political protest, folk justice, and festive disguise; they elaborated new dramatic conventions for the street to suit their antimilitia and antiaristocratic purposes. At the same time, the influx of immigrants from the British Isles after 1820 and the inmigration of rural Pennsylvanians refreshed the city's memories of older Philadelphia Christmas traditions and poor peoples' struggles. The custom of holiday street performances grew in neighborhoods where mock militias were still lively; this blend of urban political drama and rural folk culture helped shape working-class alternative traditions of street drama.

The predilection for ridiculing the pompous and decorous, focused by the mock militias' attacks on unfairness and inequality, persisted in working-class culture and in Christmas mummings. Mockery lost some of its explicitly republican edge, as the strain that identified aristocracy with capitalist speculation "in human misery" receded. When burlesquers lampooned exploitative militia laws, pompous volunteers, and ambitious officers, they aimed laughter at their social betters and questioned the basis of distinction. Fantastical militia processions on Christmas thus kept a strong element of class criticism, as long as the militia system remained a grievance and mechanics and artisans understood why it was unjust.

The commentary in masking and burlesques also aimed downward on the social scale. Although the general tone of Christmas revelry and disguising was irreverent and rough, maskers' impersonations increasingly depicted social "inferiors" or "others" like blacks, immigrants, and outsiders. As much as these neighborhood bands of young male peers created sensations of solidarity for themselves by dressing up, drinking, and visiting, they also defined who belonged in their groups and who did not. By creating hilarity through the delineation of deviant characteristics (blackface, women's dress), young men laughingly drew their social circle tighter. Blended with ethnic and racial antagonisms, hostility toward authority still persisted: Those who asserted authority over working-class youth (usually the night watch) could become victims of violence. Fantasticals had few compunctions about attacking the Christmas Eve patrol, and they usually got away with it.

Masking clearly borrowed from the nasty stereotypes of the stage and popular print; the street performance of these stereotypes fit larger social processes. By the 1840s, Philadelphians focused on blacks and immigrants when they sought causes for discontent and economic distress.[97] The gangs' and fire companies' practice of neighborhood definition and defense through violence, and the older traditions of crowd action, gathered new strength in antiblack and anti-Irish street wars, irrevocably splitting older cross-ethnic alliances. It is no surprise that maskings in black-face flourished during the city's era of violent white race riots: The two types of street action were very different manifestations of the same process, the intensification of racism and nativism. When masking burst into violence, the two phenomena became one, and definition of who was an insider and who was an outsider became even clearer. In Christmas masking, white male prerogatives found a homely, friendly, neighborhood-oriented expression.

The earlier uses of masking and "rough music" to point to unequal privilege and unjust power seem to have been eroded and pushed to the periphery of street drama. With political burlesque weakened, where was working-class political criticism expressed? Social criticism persisted in the street, certainly, in demonstrations and strike parades, and mockery of unequal social relations sometimes flickered. After the Civil War, municipal officials trying to deal with irrepressible maskers regulated the content of parades, making it illegal to impersonate police officers and local politicians; clearly, Christmas masking still had local political uses, for impersonations of dogcatchers, policemen, and mounted policemen were popular. Maskers sometimes used their marches to present grievances to the mayor in comic songs.[98] But compared to the wide-ranging implications of the 1830s burlesques, mocking intrusive city employees was a weaker form of social commentary. This use of parody only pointed to the local representative of power, while Pluck and his men had questioned the very legitimacy of power and the purity of its sources.

CHAPTER FIVE

Class Dramas
Workers' Parades

The ceremonial life of Philadelphia's workers was largely
shaped by their roles as the city's producers and by their
experiences as laborers. Out of the city's several working-
class cultures, laboring men developed a variety of uses
for parades and a range of ceremonial styles.[1] They used
parades and ceremonies to define their problems and to
address citywide and national social issues, reinventing
traditional practices while creating new techniques to promote their own institutions and goals. At the same time,
their parades were defined from without and above, by
social pressure and attempts at suppression. As workers
strove for a legitimate public presence and political power,
they were forced to adopt techniques of display and legitimation that they had not designed. Workingmen were pressured to appear in public, not as workers, but as respectable,
classless citizens.

Because parades in hard times were part of labor's fight
for survival, the very use of street dramas was contested
by the propertied and their representative authorities. The
more disputed the social issue—for example, a strike or
unemployment—the more hostility businessmen and employers expressed toward parades and demonstrations. One
response available to the business class was its participation in the creation of labor's public image: Throughout the
nineteenth century employers sponsored, controlled, and
injected themselves into labor's pageantry wherever they
could.

While members of the working class sometimes accepted this attempt at control, they often rejected it and designed their own repertoire for public performance. While propertied observers contested the meanings and uses of parades and ceremonies, working-class leaders and followers often disagreed among themselves about the uses of display. These cross-cutting tensions underlay the development of competing working-class styles of representation.

VARIETIES OF CEREMONIAL LIFE

Three notable patterns marked workers' participation in public ceremony. The first, which contemporaries termed *civic ceremony*, incorporated older English and European uses of procession and display—in which guild customs had played an important part—into Philadelphia's rare city-sponsored rituals. Few guilds had survived the Atlantic crossing, but colonial companies of craftsmen had selectively retained some customs. Scattered mottoes, banner motifs, devices, arms, costumes, holidays, and work practices survived to be held up as ancient and honored traditions.[2]

A second and more newly visible use of display and parade sprang from Philadelphia's nascent labor movement, in which men not only organized craft and trade unions but also built a citywide general union and a labor party.[3] By the late 1820s, life in Philadelphia was decisively shaped by these political innovations. Unions and workers' parties responded to the destruction of older work patterns and challenged the exploitative relations between masters and men. In some cases, workers' organizations proposed far-reaching and pragmatic social changes. At the same time, employers and their political allies disputed the right of working-class organizations to exist and forced unions and parties to fight for their legal identity. Trade unions and parties used parades and public ceremonies to assert their right to political recognition in the face of strong opposition, as well as to spread their ideas. The parade, the public meeting, the festive celebration, and the mass demonstration became tools for popularizing positions and visions.

The strike, and the strike parade especially, found increasing use as working people were harder pressed by the cyclical economic crises between 1820 and 1860. Connecting the parade with the demonstration, the strike parade served to recruit members, gather moral force, propagate a point of view, and threaten retribution to opponents and betrayers.

Third, workingmen took part in the displays of fraternal and voluntary associations and reform movements. This participation reflected the ambiguous cross-class nature of urban associational life, at least below the elite levels of society. Propertied, professional, and working-class citizens came together in voluntary associations in the early nineteenth century, but whether participation by members of different social backgrounds was equal is not clear. The displays of voluntary associations expressed both working- and business-class values, sometimes entwined and sometimes in conflict.

Two important voluntary groups that incorporated working-class members and used parades vigorously were fire companies and temperance organizations. Early hailed as exemplars of voluntary service, fire companies tried to appear selflessly devoted to the public and attractively sociable. Examination of firemen's activities, however, shows that they met the needs of working-class male peers much more than they met the expectations of affluent citizens or the municipal government. By the 1840s these rowdy fraternities appalled their municipal sponsors; tightly connected to working-class gangs, fire companies were the city's leading recreational brawlers and arsonists.

Temperance associations received reformers' approval for their staunch assaults on working-class patterns of recreation and sociability. Stressing hard work, piety, and self-restraint, temperance societies strove to inoculate young men and women against the city's evils and give them a social base from which to build a more "rational" life. Both temperance associations and fire companies used processions to invent and present favorable images of themselves and their programs. Placed beside unions, they exemplify the possibilities and directions of working-class organization: Their parades disclose the tensions between working-class ways of life and the reformers' attempts to save the lower orders from themselves.

The picture of shifting strains and varieties within working-class cultures is complicated by the lack of sources on workers' lives outside the workplace. Little is known about the membership and activities of early unions that created street displays, and only a little more is known about temperance associations and fire companies. The press is the main source for parades and ceremonies of these least-documented Philadelphians. Philadelphia's news-papers, with the exception of the short-lived labor press, were as explicitly hostile toward labor organizations as they were to working-class street culture. Reports treated workers' political activities with derision, often distorting events and outcomes. For example, the contrast between reports of parades by the militia and those by the trade unions reveals antagonism toward labor. Accounts of mili-tary displays were detailed and approving; reports of trade union demonstrations, terse and hostile. Fire companies and temperance associations received more positive notice, and civic ceremonies with manufacturers' and employers' participation were covered extensively. Given the strength and continuity of labor agitation during this period, it is safe to assume that much of what happened went unre-corded; furthermore, the perceptions of workers involved in the recorded strikes, meetings, and demonstrations proba-bly differed from those of reporters. Philadelphia's union-ists were treated unfairly in the press—except when at the height of their power in the general strike of 1835—and were often described as mobs of men unwilling to work.[4]

THE CORPORATE IMAGERY OF LABOR

The tradition of public craft and trade displays in America descended from English and European guild customs. Guilds sponsored London's Lord Mayor's Day, a major ur-ban spectacle in the early eighteenth century.[5] Elaborate processions and allegorical dramas were commissioned by the newly elected mayor's craft brotherhood. But American craft associations did not bear direct connections to their early modern ancestors, nor did they develop active inde-pendent ceremonial roles. Labor in the Colonies was scarce, and the import market for European goods undermined the development of skills requiring long periods of training and kept alive by tightly organized bodies of men. Colonial labor was also highly mobile.[6] Many of the skilled craftsmen who migrated to North America after the Revolution did so precisely because their skills, techniques, and standards of living were breaking down in their home cities.[7] For these men, public guild and craft traditions were already a fading memory, and their performance in America must have been a conscious act of revival. After the Revolution, occasions for the display of occupational symbols as "traditional" were usually patriotic events. In parades saluting events in local or national history, craftsmen led by their masters presented themselves as members of a corporate body, as contributors to the social good through their practice of a useful, productive skill. Craftsmen and tradesmen represented this identity by enacting their occupations for street audiences.

The Grand Federal Procession

Philadelphia's first and most elaborate display of corporate craft imagery unfolded in the Grand Federal Procession of July 4, 1788. This pageant celebrated the ratification of the United States Constitution, after long years of struggle and hard sacrifice. Although three states had yet to adopt the document, approval by ten brought the nation into official existence. This huge display not only memorialized a momentous event, but also set a precedent for Philadelphia's later civic ceremonies. The Grand Federal Procession hovered in local memory—heralding the end of the eighteenth-century world and symbolizing the beginning of a new order. Yet while the Grand Procession's devices were frequently borrowed and copied, Philadelphians waited a century to reenact the pageant.

The Grand Federal Procession was planned and supported by the highest levels of Philadelphia society. Scripted by Francis Hopkinson, an artist, poet, wit, judge of the navy, signer of the Declaration of Independence, and a prominent Federalist, the procession was an educated man's street extravaganza, a carefully crafted play.[8] The result of weeks of committee work and much stitching, sawing, painting, and nailing, the jubilee of allegory treated

both the country's recent past and its future in arts, industries, and manufactures—with a brief nod to agrarian interests. Dramaturgically, the procession was divided into
two parts: a chronological pageant of governmental progress since 1776 enacted by local leaders, with an extensive
display by the elite city and county cavalries, and a huge
mustering of the city's crafts and trades.

The prominence of crafts and trades in the procession
acknowledged their importance as the city's producers and
hopes for economic growth under the new government. The
wealthy and powerful trade companies were best represented; they went to great lengths to contribute elaborate
allegorical floats. The city's most famous brotherhood of
craftsmen, the Carpenters' Company was made up of the
city's wealthy and powerful master builders and architects.
The Company displayed the power of its knowledge and
expertise by constructing a "new roof or grand federal edifice" symbolizing the Union. "Begun and finished in the
short space of four days, by Mr. William Williams and Co.,"
the edifice featured a "dome supported by thirteen Corin-
thian columns raised on pedestals proper to that order . . .
ten columns complete and three left unfinished," and "a
frieze decorated with thirteen stars." Atop the dome, a
cupola supported the goddess Plenty with her cornucopia.
Seated on the edifice were ten gentlemen "representatives
of the citizens at large, to whom the constitution was committed previous to ratification." Behind the edifice walked
"architects and house carpenters in number four hundred
and fifty" under their standard, and the saw cutters and
file makers headed by their masters "carrying a flag with a
hand saw and a saw mill saw, gilt on a pink field." [9]

In addition to sponsoring allegories, prominent craftsmen cast themselves in ceremonial roles as the leaders
of their men or as workers. The wealthy Samuel Powel,
Esquire, led his Agricultural Society under a banner of the
goddess Plenty with a sickle and cornucopia. Enacting
agricultural labor were Richard Willing, Esquire, "in a
farmer's dress," directing four oxen pulling a plough and
young Mr. Charles Willing "in the character of a ploughboy." A sower casting seeds, a horse-drawn plough, and a
company of farmers and millers brought up the rear. [10]

A group of prominent merchants and financiers, the Manufacturing Society, heralded Philadelphia's future as a center of factory-organized textile production. Just a year earlier the society had launched modern textile arts in the city by establishing a House of Industry where poor women might card, spin, and weave for their keep as they learned to use new machinery.[11] Mr. Gallaudet led the investors of the society under a blue flag, "the device of which was a beehive standing in the rays of the rising sun."[12]

On the rolling platform were arrayed specimens of the latest textile machinery and newly trained workers who demonstrated the remarkable gains in production made possible by technology. One woman worked 80 spindles at once "drawing cotton suitable for fine jeans [stout cotton fabrics] or federal rib"; two men at a carding machine processed cotton at the rate of 50 pounds per day. Another workman wove "rich scarlet and white livery lace," and at a large loom with a fly shuttle a weaver made wide jean.[13]

According to the Manufacturing Society's display, the future of the new nation was tied to the success of independent American industries. Industrial progress and independence were linked by Mr. Hewson who printed "muslins of an elegant chintz pattern" on his new apparatus, proving domestic goods could be as fashionable as imports. Likewise, Mrs. Hewson and her daughters penciled a "piece of very neat sprigged chintz" while wearing "cottons of their own manufacture." Waving spectacularly over this mini-manufactory was a newly designed calico printers' flag, the stars and stripes bordered by patches of "thirty-seven different prints of various colors . . . specimens of printing done at Philadelphia."[14]

In less spectacular array, the textile industry's rank and file, the handloom weavers, and cotton carders marched behind the rolling workshop under a weavers' flag: "a rampant lion in a green field, a shuttle in his dexter paw—motto —'May Government Protect Us.'"[15] These men worked in their own home workshops; thus the textile industry segment of the procession presented a condensed picture of productive relations in the city. The manufacturer, preceded by his investors, displayed his astonishing new machinery. He was followed on foot by his own employees and by the independent artisans of the trade who would soon be, if they were not already, displaced by his innovations. The patchwork Old Glory advertised the range and quality of goods local manufacture could offer. The old British weavers' standard could still share parade space with the new flag, adopting a note of confidence in the government's protective benevolence.

Enactments by the shipping and shipbuilding trades of the Delaware docks displayed the power of the port, its shippers, and its master craftsmen. Eighty-nine members of the Marine Society of sea captains and merchant traders marched "six abreast, with trumpets, spy-glasses, charts... wearing badges in their hats representing a ship." The society guided an elaborate float through the streets. "The Federal Ship *Union*," 30 feet long and "mounting twenty guns," made a stage for Commander John Green, Esquire, and his crew of 25, including "four young boys in uniform as midshipmen." On this "masterpiece of elegant workmanship . . . decorated with emblematical carving" an occupational drama was staged. Her crew rehearsed "setting sail, trimming her sails to the wind . . . throwing the lead and casting anchor . . . with the strictest maritime propriety." [16]

In the wake of the *Union* came the master shipbuilders and their men, bearing a "draft of a ship . . . and cases of instruments in their hands," and the flag showing a ship on the stocks, the huge wooden framework that supported a vessel during construction. Behind the builders walked "mast makers, caulkers and workmen, to the amount of 330, all wearing a badge in their hats representing a ship on the stocks and a green sprig of white oak." Representation of the shipyard and port trades continued with a "frame representing a boat builder's shop, eighteen feet long . . . mounted on a carriage." On a platform underneath, seven hands built a boat that "was nearly completed during the procession. . . . The whole machine was contrived with great skill and drawn by four bright bay horses and followed by boat builders . . . led by Messrs. Brooke and Warwick Hale." [17]

Shipyard workers who did not enact their labors on rolling stages represented their craft by carrying tools or sometimes the materials of their trade. The master ship's joiners carried the company arms, "a binnacle, and a hencoop, crooked planes and other tools," with the motto, "By These We Support Our Families." Rope makers and ship chandlers were led by their senior members who carried pieces of rope and hemp in their hands. The journeymen and apprentice rope makers marched "with hemp around their waists" in direct reference to the rope-walking process "and spinning clouts in their hands."[18] Many more merchants, trades, clerks, and apprentices whose livelihoods bound them together held up their flags, compasses, and ledgers, symbols of individual trades and the collective vitality of the port.

Next, a cavalcade of individual trades and professions filed in front of crowds of silent respectful watchers. On rolling workshops bedecked with ribbons, men acted out their jobs, stressing the useful value of their products. Distributing their goods, they made usefulness manifest. For example, cordwainers laboring under the standard of St. Crispin made boots and shoes, then flung them into the crowd. Stationers, bookbinders, and printers handed out copies of a "Federal Ode." Coppersmiths fixed holes in old kettles and blacksmiths beat rusty swords into sickles. Painters prepared window sashes, and tinsmiths snipped tin.[19] Flags and mottoes pointed to use value: "May Our Manufacture Be Equal in Its Consumption to Its Usefulness" read the breeches-makers' standard. Trades supplying foodstuffs vividly depicted their product's life-sustaining role. The victualers and butchers, marching under the motto, "The Death of Anarchy and Confusion: We Feed the Poor and Hungry," led stately oxen to be slaughtered and distributed the meat as alms. Porters and draymen hauled barrels of "Federal Flour" and presented them to the overseers of the poor.[20]

Luxury figured as prominently as use value in the pageant, and craftsmen producing finery for the carriage trade marched proudly. These master craftsmen displayed fine chintzes, watches, clocks, carriages, jewelry, saddles, and even a "cabriole sopha" on their workshop floats.

Master craftsmen, journeymen, makers of luxuries, and the suppliers of everyday needs expressed the same hope in federal governmental policies. The central theme of the crafts and trades portion of the procession was support for the development of American manufactures. If the United

States encouraged its own industries and protected producers from unfair competition in Britain's remaining colonial markets, domestic consumption would grow, bringing prosperity. On this, craftsmen of all kinds and statuses agreed. "May the Federal Government Revive our Trade" on the biscuit-makers' standard emphasized how bad times had been in the city since the beginning of the War. The gunsmiths looked forward to the commissions of a federal armory, the brewers proclaimed "Home Brewed is Best," and carriage builders demanded no taxes on their locally made wares.[21]

For the ordinary artisan and journeyman, support for the development of manufactures was more than self-interest: Enthusiasm for economic progress was tied to their notion of labor's place in the new society. Skilled workers had strongly supported the Constitution, and artisans saw themselves as builders of a republic made up of small producers.[22] Banners, standards, and displays announced that since the government was the creation of workingmen, it should benefit them first and foremost. The bricklayers' banner, for instance, depicted workmen erecting a "federal city" in the wilderness. Some literally connected their work techniques to the labor of making a new nation. The tailors' white flag read "By Union Our Strength Increases," comparing piecing seams to binding states together. The smiths' motto, "By Hammer and Hand All Arts Do Stand," announced that labor underlay all human activity and gave legitimacy to political institutions. Likewise, the bricklayers stated "Both Buildings and Rulers Are the Work of Our Hands."[23]

The independent producers saw their role as a moral one, predicting that the values of hard and honest industry, simplicity, and usefulness would nurture the political system built by artisans and farmers. In the procession the imagery of work made this moral claim through old craft symbols. This claim was put most succinctly by the plane-makers' standard, which showed a plane simply labeled "Truth." Thus carpentry's most basic action—straightening—became a metaphor for the maintenance of fundamental values. Work itself was portrayed as a source of political strength and social good. In this metaphorical linking, artisans and craftsmen declared that their ability

—and their right—to define and test social virtue rested in their skill and honesty as laborers.

In the Federal Procession, artisans differentiated themselves from other workers even as they declared themselves the base of the body politic. Skilled manual work was by definition honest and good; artisans were the "honorable" workers, as contemporary usage put it. As opposed to men who toiled for others, the upper level of artisans owned their own tools and workplaces in this period. Independence at work meant that the artisan controlled his own labor; it also meant that in hard times he was less likely to migrate in search of work or apply to the overseers of the poor. But many of the city's workers had less "honor" than this. Artisans' prominence in the procession contrasted with the total absence of casual and day laborers. Aside from a few sailors (played by young boys), the stevedores, sawyers, vendors, caterers, domestics, and women who toiled in their homes found no representation in the street drama. Or, to be precise, the working poor's representation was as the invisible object of the charity of the butchers and carters, as recipients of gifts to the masters of the almshouse. Although everyday life in the city depended on those without self-sufficiency, the procession's depiction of social relations had room only for the respectable trades.

Within the procession's images of the honorable trades, lines of power and status were clearly drawn. Masters and senior craftsmen came first and took the honor of bearing the company flag. Behind them came their journeymen, and young apprentices brought up the rear. Masters and employers appeared paternally responsible for the integrity of the trade and for their men; they enacted their supervising, instructing roles, carried the banners, and led the rank and file. In some cases the dramatic action demanded that gentlemen, owners, and masters be cast in the parts of workmen, while many workers dressed "up" to the role of honorable independent craftsmen, eschewing work clothes for silk sashes, ceremonial aprons, badges, and hats. Farmers marched unnamed while the gentleman agriculturalist, distinguished by the title "Esquire," appeared in farmer's dress, and his son in the character of a ploughboy.

In theory, a master owed nearly familial care to his employees, especially the apprentices. Because he bore the responsibility for skill and knowledge, as well as the behavior of his men, the quality of the goods and the appearance of the company reflected credit on the man who ran the workshop. The depiction of an occupation as morally good and useful was bound up with the master's personal reputation as much as with the artisan's image of his role in society.

Master artisans enhanced their reputations by planning and sponsoring the gilded and beribboned crafts displays. For instance, the brass founders' display was wholly "executed by Mr. Daniel King," a master founder, "at his own expense." King had provided a car drawn by four horses, the emblematic colors, and "a blast furnace in full blast during the whole procession," as well as a "three inch howitzer, which was mounted and fired with the artillery on Union Green." [24] The Federal Edifice and the ship *Union* were provided by the Carpenters' Company and the master shipbuilders, respectively. Many others, as individuals or members of groups, likely paid for the silks, devices, and floats that enlivened the long train.[25]

In the Federal Procession, artisans' ideas about their status, independence, and political role mingled with the self-promotion of the master craftsmen. The ideal of the craft as a whole, binding men together in the production of socially useful goods and contributing moral strength to the nation was still intact—at least as an ideal. But in real life, the independence of the artisan was threatened. The war had eroded the well-being of many craftworkers and the "legitimation of self interest" weakened ties of dependence between urban masters and men.[26] The market economy, in which the small producer became less secure, had begun to penetrate Philadelphia by the 1780s. As some masters became entrepreneurs and speculators, they tried to reorganize work in the crafts and dilute their responsibilities to their apprentices. Relationships between masters and men would soon belie the familial trade unity presented by the procession.

In 1788 the spectacle of craft regalia and work processes could bring together men of different status, giving them a way to present themselves as worthy producers. In general, however, important Philadelphians took the leading parts in planning and performing the Grand Federal Procession and its depiction of labor and work. This leadership by influential citizens would characterize the dominant strain of processions by workers and about work during the nineteenth century. Employers came first, displaying their affluence and paternal power through props and ceremonial primacy. In the late 1780s this emphasis on hierarchical relations seems to have been acceptable to journeymen and apprentices. This was partly because artisanal status itself remained honorable in the late eighteenth century, and the image of the craft as a corporate body still made sense in ways it could not on the eve of the Civil War. The Manufacturing Society's display foreshadowed what would become common. Craftsmen made up a significant proportion of the city's work force, perhaps as much as 50 percent in 1788, and few felt that mechanization or new productive processes threatened their livelihoods; most artisans were not yet wage workers.[27]

Vast, elaborate, and widely hailed, the Grand Federal Procession provided an important ceremonial precedent for nineteenth-century Philadelphians. The procession moved into memory as a great success, to be recalled later as the time when the whole city (or so it was claimed) united in orderly performance. A tavernkeeper preserved the floats of the *Union* and the Carpenters' Company's "Federal Edifice" to display in his pleasure garden on Independence Day. The old flags, devices, and symbols of artisan republicanism were passed along, to appear again and again in nineteenth-century streets.

As a ceremonial resource and precedent, the Federal Procession proved useful, especially to employers and industrialists. The procession's expense and finery would remain associated with popular patriotism, and patriotism's links to industry were strengthened in reenactments of parts of the pageant. Philadelphians would not reenact the Grand Federal Procession until the Constitution's Centennial, but they would borrow from it in a highly selective manner.

NINETEENTH-CENTURY CRAFT CEREMONIES

The most important use of the memory of the Federal Procession was the refitting of the old imagery of labor to help define the shifted and conflicting new relations between

masters and men. These relations between master craftsmen and journeymen, employers and employees changed
irrevocably after 1788; the ideal of the craft as corporate
body became irrelevant. Yet masters and manufacturers
continued to sponsor some uses of labor's corporate imagery. When the old crafts symbols appeared in the streets,
they were often being manipulated by men who had ceased
to be workers. At the same time, as the sons of honorable
artisans became wage laborers, they invented new modes
of representing their relation to society.

The Lafayette Reception

Philadelphia's reception for the Marquis de Lafayette in
1824 showed conflicting ways of representing labor. Part of
the national self-congratulation on republican virtue, the
procession to greet Lafayette both drew on the memory of
1788 and became a memorable event in its own right. (*See
the illustrations.*) The reception was organized by Committees of Arrangement linked to the City Councils; it was
planned in a formally democratic manner. Participants
chose places in line in a lottery, and were urged by the
committees to appear in plain "citizen's dress" as opposed
to fraternal regalia or occupational costume. Exempt from
these provisions were the volunteer militias, who led the
reception in uniform and ranked themselves according to
their own military protocol.[28]

In 1788 style, some trades mounted workshop displays.
Ship masters, officers, and seamen not only got up a "suitable banner," but also "resolved to make a ship for the
occasion and to make her sail through the streets with our
own hands." [29] Printers again bore their press through the
streets, striking off copies of an ode to the nation's guest
and tossing them into the crowd. Like the ship masters, the
manufacturers and weavers of the city, led by factory owners, held a meeting and resolved that they "might justly be
charged with ingratitude . . . or of undervaluing their own
importance as citizens or as members of the great national
family should they be backward about participating" as
representatives of industry. They recommended that those
in their employ wear "Wash or Wilm [*sic*] striped pants,
long cloth coats, black or blue [and a] black hat with Revolutionary cockade and Lafayette Badge." The manufac-

turers' advertisement for "two or three good bagpipers" completes a picture of the factory owners and weavers on parade.[30]

Most trades, however, adopted a different mode of republican ritual. Plainly dressed cordwainers, rope makers, ship carpenters, wagoners, carters, and farmers limited themselves to displaying their banners. Putting even more distance between themselves and well-to-do masters, some workingmen chose to march separately, identified as a discrete segment of the trade. Journeymen paraded apart from master printers, as did groups of apothecaries and mechanics, announcing that they were the "young men" of their trades. A division of "Young Men Apprentices of the City and County" similarly underlined differences in status.

By 1824 new divisions had arrived in the work world, and the lower ranks were not shy about enacting them publicly.[31] By the 1830s, craft spectacle and the plain conventions of republican ceremony would diverge until they constituted separate conventions for performance. Black or blue coats, hats, and a badge were the mode for independent workingmen who understood that the simple values of laborers and farmers should define the nation. In displays by owners of large-scale manufactories the old idea of employees enacting work processes was retained, embedded in bright colors and fine textures, surrounded by new, exotic motifs. Employers used "economical spectacles," as contemporaries termed them, to hail canal and railway openings, mark the completion of buildings, or simply display their strength and importance in the city's economy.[32]

The Washington Centennial

A full-blown example of popular patriotism grafted onto economic spectacle was the Washington Centennial Procession of 1832. This gaudy display of consumer goods and new machinery was as much a salute to manufacturers' influence as a commemoration of the patriot hero. Trades and occupations were loosely grouped by occupational sector, but their enactments had grown more lavish. Instead of one rolling workshop, many trades now had two or three, and all flew elaborate banners, ribbons, and streamers. Three hundred hatters, "gentlemen in every respect creditable to the procession," wore white silk aprons with portraits of Washington and marched before two cars outlining the process of hat making. Six horses led by "a well looking black man habited as a Turk" pulled the first car, which bore a cargo of furs attended by a boy dressed as an Indian; the second car, with men at work, preceded two hatters dressed as trappers. From another "moving manufactory," tobacconists dispensed "a goodly quantity of segars to the multitude." Bakers, from "a car as an oven at work," distributed small hot loaves beneath their "Wheat Sheaf" and a banner reading "May Our Country Never Want." A long line of brickmakers "wore white aprons on which were painted portraits of their working materials" and accompanied two large cars, one with a brick-making operation, the other bearing a working kiln.

On the float of the tanners, morocco dressers, and curriers, men were "hard at it, fleshing and working hides, shaving leather, coloring and polishing morocco," amid a beautiful array of finished products. Shipwrights, rope makers, riggers, sail makers, tin-plate workers, factory spinners and weavers, dyers, bookbinders, copper-plate printers, coopers, and blacksmiths showed themselves at toil. And in familiar style, the printers struck off a special ode and "Washington's Farewell Address" as souvenirs for the crowd.[33]

The Washington Centennial Procession hailed the well-off, powerful masters through the organized displays, spectacularly ornamented cars, and finely dressed men. The printers, for instance, were led by "the venerable Matthew Carey and other gentlemen in a carriage"; "Messrs. Bury and Redmon's apparatus" was in use in the dyers' display, and Mr. McCauley surrounded his carpet weavers with an array of fine rugs. Once again, the master shipwrights, the ship captains, and sea-going merchants produced rolling ships and barges. The largest of these, the *Pennsylvania*, was manned by a cast of captains playing parts from commander to cabin boy.[34]

Members of many crafts and trades, mounted on horseback and wearing matching sashes, badges, and uniforms, emphasized a decorous, affluent image. Red, green, and blue silks and satins predominated, and workmen wore white kid gloves, as if to distance themselves from manual labor.

Richly painted images of Washington complemented Mr. Sully's bank window illuminations. Copper-plate engravers tossed fringed squares of satin bearing the general's portrait to the crowd. Even the victualers' "two famous fat oxen" had Washington's face painted on their foreheads.

Manufacturers saw the pageant as a form of advertising. Using the imagery of work and presenting themselves as Washington's loyal heirs, they hoped to promote Philadelphia's industrial prominence. The press declared that the procession would be noticed in other parts of the country; indeed, tourists flocked from other towns to see it.[35]

This mode of promotion was related to national politics. Coming as it did during the nullification crisis, Washington's Centennial parade was overlaid with immediate political references. Workers joined masters and employers in supporting national unity over the political goals of the southern states, and banners and standards stressed this theme. The blacksmiths' and whitesmiths' banner read "Behold the Union as it Stands," subtended by a painted chain; "The Territories Yet Remain" was made graphic with open links. The coopers likewise showed a hoop and staves labeled "United Thus."[36]

Local meanings could also be found in the concept of unity. The cordwainers marched as a "Union" with their officers as parade marshals. Led by William English, they bore a banner given them by the cordwainers of New York especially for the occasion in a gesture of fraternal solidarity. With a badge on each breast and blue sashes and white ceremonial aprons, the shoemakers, instead of enacting their craft, presented themselves as a new kind of political organization joined by ties of self-interest and opposition to masters.[37]

Two years later, in 1834, Lafayette's death prompted a "sham funeral" parade of citizens and militia. The trades joined to make a separate section of the parade, marching in citizen's dress of dark pants, coat, and hat with mourning badges and sashes, and journeymen differentiated themselves from their masters. This time, separate performance was prefaced by debate and controversy over labor's role in the parade; the Lafayette obsequies occurred in the midst of the gathering battle for the ten-hour day. William

English claimed the parade's committee of arrangements had purposefully excluded workingmen and trade associations from their plans. The committee's long-delayed invitation to the trades failed to reassure the city's General Trades' Union, which canceled its plans to march.[38]

Honors to Jackson and the "Bank War"

By the early 1830s, economic fluctuations and changes in the organization of work forced a new perception on workers and artisans. Those who had earlier seen themselves as society's central producers now found themselves oppressed, embattled, and discriminated against, not only by their employers but by "combinations," private corporations, monopolies, and banks. Parades and demonstrations during the "Bank War" illustrate both the heightened conflict between employers and workers, and the changing uses for the imagery of labor. Workers used the newer resource of citizen's dress to express support for President Andrew Jackson in his attempts to bring the Bank of the United States under closer federal supervision, while employers used old craft images to rally their men in opposition to Jackson. When President Jackson visited Philadelphia, downtown residents and artisanal Southwark staged a citizens' reception. The ceremony's date, June 10, 1833, marked the anniversary of Jackson's veto of the bank's federal re-charter. At the State House, "thousands of people of all ages and sexes entered [and] bowed to the President," in plain republican style. Philadelphians of antibank persuasion then walked in a procession, presenting themselves not as members of occupations or associations, but as citizens.[39]

Next spring, when Jackson was deeply embroiled in his conflict with bank president Nicholas Biddle, Philadelphia's merchants and businessmen mounted a unique demonstration. Jackson had removed federal deposits from the bank, and the outrage of the business and manufacturing community poured out in mass meetings with processions and speeches in State House Square. Whig and conservative democratic leaders railed against "executive usurpation" and violation of the Constitution. It is not within the scope of this study to untangle the complexities of pro-and anti-Jackson sentiment in Philadelphia's working class during the Bank War, a subject about which historians still disagree. Clearly, some workers could be persuaded that the economic collapse was Jackson's fault, whereas it now seems clear that Biddle manipulated the economic situation to pressure Jackson.[40]

A large anti-Jackson gathering in Independence Square on March 20, 1834, was led by militia generals and prominent merchants, and swelled by trades processions from several parts of town. While the meeting was ostensibly packed with "the bone and sinew," its style contrasted markedly with the plain republican approval of the previous July. Demonstrators' occupational banners and symbols made the point that manufacturers and trades suffered equally from Jackson's attempt to control the bank. This support from artisans and mechanics urged political leaders to force Jackson to back down. Gay banners with craft emblems expressed unstinting support for the "Constitution." Citizens from the young textile district of Manayunk bore a stuffed eagle shrouded in crepe; the Moyamensing weavers marched behind a loom out of gear with a placard stating "No Work." Resolutions were presented by painters, goldsmiths, hatters, and builders. Nearly five hundred merchants and traders of the county filed in, "and certainly a more respectable body never made their appearance in our streets—their motto was neatly inscribed on a flag, 'supporting the Constitution and the laws.'" Tailors, cabinetmakers, coal dealers, boatmen, painters, glaziers, hatters, cordwainers, and hundreds of builders joined the rally with trade emblems.[41]

This demonstration seemed to show that some workingmen had ceased to support Jackson over the bank issue; in times of crisis some workers could be persuaded that their interests lay close to those of their employers and the bankers who financed industrial ventures. In public displays, the case for this unity of interest was expressed in old-fashioned emblematic style, using old-fashioned symbols and paraphernalia.

As the press noted at the time, the demonstration was not a spontaneous outpouring of antiexecutive sentiment. The rally was one of a series of Whig experiments with mass demonstrations, which featured free public banquets and the prominent display of older patriotic devices, such as rolling miniature ships.[42] Furthermore, Samuel Hazard's *Register of Pennsylvania* noted that, as "all the shipping in the port had their flags at half-mast, the occasion may be said to have been sanctioned by the entire body of our merchants."[43] The anti-Jackson employers had made "unparalleled extertions" to turn out huge crowds, shutting their factories for the day and paying to have employees transported to the city center. Shops and stores closed so clerks could attend, but the prolabor *Pennsylvanian* alleged that "the trades did not muster strongly."[44] By offering time off to attend a demonstration, employers used their powerful discretion to create political opinion. What looked like a laboring men's demonstration was in fact a partisan rally to build support for the anti-Jacksonians. The use of craft symbols at once attempted to garner labor's backing and impress the city with unanimous support for the cause.

The uses of craft symbolism were linked to the paternalism and prerogatives of employers; the ambiguities of the symbols' uses stemmed from the increasing distance between masters and men. Workers, rejecting older conventions of occupational display and enactment, developed their own ways of presenting themselves in street parades. There were no patriotic, multicraft spectacles after the 1830s, although employers continued to use the corporate imagery of labor for their own purposes. Eventually, the enactment of work processes was located in industrial exhibitions and museums.[45] Workers, meanwhile, found it useful to present themselves not as employees but as members of brotherhoods bound by ties of solidarity, not dependence. This unity was expressed in a love of the republican anniversaries, such as the Fourth of July and Jackson Day. Trades and political organizations marked holidays and founding days with dinners and speeches. Sometimes orations were given by men explicitly called "ordinary," in rejection of the employer's customary address to his men.[46]

STRIKE PARADES, MILITANT AND RESPECTABLE

Throughout the early nineteenth century, Philadelphia's laborers, craftsmen, and artisans struggled against erosion of wages and working conditions. As new methods of industrial organization split journeymen from their masters and turned them into mere "hands," as the value of apprenticeship depreciated, and as more men and women faced the prospect of a lifetime's labor for low wages, workers responded with a variety of political actions. One of their chief tools, the strike, frequently included parades.[47]

The history of strikes and the use of processions to enjoin unity in the trade or the community dates back at least to the great eighteenth-century labor struggles, such as the seamen's strike of the Port of London and the mass demonstrations of the Spitalfields weavers.[48] The word "strike," while it carries the sense of a violent blow, seems to have come from seagoing workers who halted labor by "striking," or lowering, the sails.[49] The history of strike techniques and traditions remains obscure.

In the United States, strikers used processions from the beginning of the labor movement to make public their stance on the disputed issue. The etymological connection between "strike" and "parade" is very close. Another early meaning of strike is "to set out on foot," or "to walk out." In the early nineteenth century, the words "turn out" were synonymous with parade and strike; thus striking and parading were closely connected concepts and activities.

In Albany in 1826, a journeymen carpenters' society had "what is inaptly termed a turn out."[50] One hundred and twenty-five to one hundred fifty men assembled opposite newly erected buildings in Beaver Street, which they doubtless had worked on, "thence they traversed the whole city, calling at several workshops, each carrying a piece of a pine sash staff as an emblem of their profession and marching two and two in a peaceable and orderly manner."[51] In the afternoon the journeymen reassembled, renewed their resolution, and forwarded a proposal for a shilling-a-day increase.

A similar use of a parade was seen in New Orleans in 1825 when "a promiscuous crowd of black and white sailors" spent the day "parading through our streets, bearing the National Flag" and "huzzahing." The sailors "united for the purpose of raising wages from 14 to 15 dollars [per month] to twenty." The New Orleans paper, asserting that such demonstrations would never be tolerated in the North, asked police to curb the "rioters who are certainly very prejudicial to the tranquility of our city."[52] Thus in 1825, strikers who made their demands in the open space of the street were charged with disturbing the peace.

Philadelphia's most dramatic labor uprising, the 1835 movement for the ten-hour day, used strike parades extensively. A legal limit to working hours was labor's most pressing cause at a time when employers required people to work from sunup to sundown, often as long as thirteen hours in the summer. The increased pace of water-driven machinery, the growing concentration of some kinds of workers in large manufactories, and the rationale of wage labor had begun to dissolve customary restraints on the exploitation of workers' time. When workers resisted, employers used the language of morality and religion against them.[53]

Ten-hour-day advocates, led by the citywide General Trades' Union, organized a general strike. With employers, the party press, municipal authorities, and evangelical preachers ranged against them, unions needed a way to establish the morality of their cause before the city. The labor press was one way to reach the public; the "card" or poster placed in shop windows was another.[54] Committees of vigilance organized their neighborhoods, but the uses of public space played a central role. Parades, demonstrations, and mass meetings presented the strikers as a strong, unified community linked to a moral undertaking and made the city aware of the issue.

The general strike began in late May when coal heavers at the Schuylkill docks walked off their jobs to protest long hours.[55] A few days later, when they paraded the streets, cordwainers, carpenters, and other tradesmen stopped work and joined them. The press reported "A large body of men, whom we understand to be the journeymen shoemakers and the Schuylkill laborers paraded the streets with fife and drum and flags" with the inscription "6 to 6." They entered the Merchants' Exchange at Third and Walnut streets, and when they filled it, found more room and a hustings in State House Square.[56] By the end of the week, many trades and occupations had "turned out" on strike and many of these marked their decision with parades, until the downtown area came to resemble Muster Day with marchers passing each other in the streets.

Workers both black and white and from all levels of skill joined the general strike. In the press, a derogatory reception met the parades of the unskilled. On June 12, the *United States Gazette* ingenuously reported:

a procession of persons calling themselves stevedores — some eight or ten white persons bearing banners, which we suppose rather belonged to the ships' carpenters. These were followed by about twenty blacks. One of them had a long pole in his hand, from which floated a pennon, probably the signal of some ship. "A drum and a wry necked file [fife]" were played for the benefit of the parade. The persons of the company were not noisy and did not make known the object of their movements.[57]

The *Gazette* further underlined its disapproval of black-white collaborations in an item headed "Turn Out, Extra (Wood Sawyers)." "The cullings of a lot of blacks and a few whites marched from the drawbridge to Walnut Street and after half an hour and a lot of noise, marched back." The newspaper, uncertain whether the procession was for higher wages or an inferior imitation of a legitimate parade, concluded, "It behooves the class to make less noise."[58]

In the same tone, the *Gazette* described a "recent exhibition of seamen in the streets . . . [who] struck on Tuesday last for higher wages and marched through the streets in procession bearing a banner with the following fierce motto . . . 'Eighteen Dollars per Month and Small Stores or Death!'" (Small stores were rum rations, a customary part of the seaman's wages.) The paper accused the sailors of being drunk while parading, adding sourly that "the turning out for wages is sanctioned by custom, but the turning out for rum will not do in these temperance times."[59]

Other observers reported strike parades more sympathetically, noting details such as banners and uniforms. On June 13, four to five hundred members of the carters' union demanded an increase in their wages and fares, appearing "on horse back, riding in pairs with flags and banners and two bands of music pealing forth" in a procession that took up three blocks.[60] On the same day, seamen marched down several of the main streets in a "numerous and respectable display . . . in uniform, blue jackets, blue silk badges and white trowsers. A handsome miniature ship was drawn in front of the procession, followed by a band of music and flags and streamers in profusion."[61] On June 17, journey-men bakers renewed their strike resolve with a procession of more than one hundred men, with music and flags, and stated that they especially resented being required to work on Sunday.[62]

Newspaper editors were impressed when strikers turned out in large numbers. The difference between a favorable and unfavorable report was tied to the marchers' appear-ance and their use of popular parade conventions. In neat and colorful musical processions, striking seamen, carters, and bakers appeared much as they had at Lafayette's re-ception, as an orderly community of republican citizens demanding no more than what the republic owed them. In contrast, the stevedores and sawyers—racially mixed, un-skilled, and lacking the colorful sashes and hired bands—were described by the press as rabble.

As the general strike spread, the city took on a festive tone. Bruce Laurie estimates that as many as twenty thou-sand workers left their jobs in the first weeks of June.[63] Although parades and demonstrations could seem celebra-tory, unionists, branded with a variety of moral sins by employers and the press, knew the standout was serious. General Trades' Union leader Israel Young, speaking at a rally at Independence Square, urged strikers to stand with the wharf and coal workers "against insults and lies" and the attempts of "merchants to brand them liars and drunkards."[64]

Trade unionists used the memory of the Revolution and the powerful symbolism of Independence Square to frame their claims to justice and the right to strike. As a parade terminus and the site of mass meetings, the Square infused leaders' demands with the Revolution's moral force. "What have we lately seen?" queried the *Pennsylvanian*: "Free-men compelled to assemble in thousands near our great hall of Liberty, day after day, and there declare as our fathers did their independence."[65]

Radical artisans frequently compared their fathers' struggle against royalty to a strike against an employer's tyranny. At a Mechanics' and Workingmen's Temperance Society July Fourth dinner an artisan offered the following toast: "Our forefathers: theirs was a glorious strike for lib-erty. Full pay and extra allowances to the survivors!"[66]

Conversely, the labor movement was described in terms of the Revolution. Strikers were "standouts for rights" gained in their fathers' war. One "Ires" wrote, "Journeymen bricklayers, why do ye not come out, one and all, and support the cause of equality and justice, as our forefathers did on the 4th of July, 1776."[67] Memories and symbols of the Revolutionary War pervaded strikers' efforts: Grocers' clerks, cordwainers, and printers announced their intention to begin keeping shorter hours despite their employers—effective on Independence Day.[68]

The general strike of 1835 was a mixed success. Because parades and demonstrations had convinced some local leaders of the justice of the cause, City Councils voted a mandatory ten-hour day for all public works projects. Many private employers went along reluctantly, increasing hours as soon as economic conditions made it possible to compel their employees. Support for the ten-hour day and solidarity between skilled and unskilled, and even male and female, workers, continued in 1836.[69] The spectacular economic collapse of 1837 fractured this unity and devastated the General Trades' Union and its component unions. Although the city's workingmen would not be organized across craft and skill boundaries again for decades, strikes continued, and with them the problems of trade unions' legitimacy, the right to concerted action, and the unionists' need to make their case freely and clearly to the widest audience.[70]

The strike parade had even more direct uses. Parades could show force, warn off strikebreakers, and threaten violence to "blacklegs" or scabs. Weavers and textile operatives used parades in this way for decades to resist wage reductions and the introduction of new machinery. Desperation made Philadelphia's weavers militant. Handloom weavers were often poor British Isles immigrants who owned little property and were hard hit by economic downturns.[71] In 1839 weavers in Moyamensing, a southern district of the city, published a notice describing the relation between their wages and their costs of living. They earned about 81 cents a day, or $4.86 a week, with 75 cents deducted for preparation of the yarn, or "winding." The weavers opposed a reduction that would allow a family of five $1.63 a week with nothing left over for medical care or periods of unemployment. "Are we not justified" the weavers demanded, "in using all lawful means of resistance?"[72]

In the summer of 1842, a time of severe unemployment, Kensington weavers began a long, bitter strike. In order to win their strike, they needed to recruit all the city's weavers; thus they used meetings, petitions, and parades. The press interpreted attempts to achieve unity as attacks on the rights of other workers. "For the last two days," the *Public Ledger* reported, "a large number of Kensington weavers have been on turn out against all and every of their fellow craftsmen."[73] In fact, the weavers opposed only those who worked below their set rate. "On last Wednesday night they held a fife and drum parade" in an attempt to ensure unity.[74] The strikers stripped the looms of working weavers and sent the material back to employers. Alternatively, they poured vitriol on the web and forwarded money for the damage to the employer. The Kensingtonians did not want to rob their masters of profits, but would not tolerate working below set wages.

On August 25, 250 weavers paraded past the *Public Ledger* office, taking their parades from Kensington into the city's center to reach a larger audience.[75] The following Saturday they marched to Moyamensing and "paraded the streets together" with sympathetic weavers and "compelled several persons there who were disposed to . . . work to join in their movement." A man weaving in Moyamensing was driven from his house, "his web taken and carried to the manufacturer."[76] A warrant for the arrest of these "rioters" was issued, and the *Ledger* commented that the law should "protect those disposed to work" against "petty criminals" and "the material of mobs."

More loom strippings heralded by fifes and drums took place in early September. Then strikers extended their confrontations with blacklegs into the factories. On September 6, strikers entered William Baird's mill in Kensington and "with great violence" forced a hand to leave off weaving and spoiled his material. They traveled to Mr. Floyd's factory and did the same. When owners took out warrants against the strikers, the arresting officers were chased out of the neighborhood.[77] Guards responded to rumors that strikers planned to tear down another factory housing new machinery, but the action never occurred.[78] Even at the end of October, fife and drum corps continued to visit the homes of strikebreakers.[79] New machinery and the huge numbers of Philadelphia's hungry poor gave employers the edge. The weavers lost their strike, but dramatically enforced their community morality.

In the harsh winter of 1846, a tenacious and angry group of handloom weavers from Moyamensing used parades in a fight against piecework wage reductions. Many in Moyamensing were unemployed and starving due to an economic slump. Every morning the strikers ended their tactical meetings with a procession through the neighborhood and into the city. Processions served to rally community support and declare their intention to succeed. Moyamensing bolstered the strike with soup kitchens and moral support, but the longer the weavers stayed out, the more difficulty they had with blacklegs defying their ban on piecework weaving. From early in the strike, Moyamensing weavers used parades to threaten retribution to men weaving under police protection.[80] The possibility of a protest parade on Washington's Birthday led the mayor to place extra watchmen on duty in the textile districts,[81] but the meetings continued. On March 9, a "parade with music and banners created some excitement in the southwest part of the city. . . . Some working weavers thought they were being attacked and prepared to defend themselves."[82] The next day the weavers again paraded with fife and drums, but this time they were forced to stay inside a police cordon set up at the city boundary. Like the loom strippings of 1842, the fife and drum parades of 1846 threatened retribution to strikebreakers. Strikers also threatened to pull down houses. On one occasion, the strikers "were only prevented from destroying the premises [of a man at work] because he was old."[83] The threat of dismantling a house was a favored working-class mode of direct action, of which the most famous instance was the attack on Governor Thomas Hutchinson's house by Boston's South End crowd in 1775.[84] Significantly, this sort of action was usually reserved for use against traitors, betrayers of the community's definition of its own interest. In the strike of 1846, a working weaver had clearly placed self-interest ahead of community interest, and he was fortunate that working-class traditions usually stopped short of personal injury.

Forced by hunger to agree to a new price list, the Moya-mensing strikers passed a resolution to select two manu-facturers by lot for whom no striker would work without an advance. Again, they mounted a procession and attempted to march to Fairmount to gather support there. The sheriff threatened them with arrest if they crossed into the city, so they spent several hours parading around Moyamensing in a tough display of moral rectitude. Within their district, with their neighbors' support, the weavers won the strike, but the city's grinding poverty and the employers' ability to draw on labor from elsewhere in the city prevented mobili-zation of all handloom workers.[85]

Workingmen's uses of parades in strikes ranged from spontaneous to planned, in forms from simple to highly structured. Strikes were festive and warlike, rowdy and re-spectable.[86] The city's whole parade repertoire was reflected in strikers' marches. Some unions looked like the decorous uniformed militias with their bands, the dignified Free-masons, or the gay and colorful firemen. On the other hand, strikers' parades bore close ties to redressive folk dramas and the ritualized street actions of the "mob," well known in the American Revolution and in rural England.[87] The militialike style of the fife and drum procession her-alded retribution to blacklegs and called up memories of war—whether in Ireland, England, or America—and of the agency men found in military service and the necessity of choosing sides. The fife and drum procession communi-cated a central truth of all labor struggles: "There are no neutrals here."[88] At the same time, fifes and drums called other uses to mind. One familiar tune, "The Rogues' March," announced the crowd's favored method of extralegal jus-tice, tarring and feathering. In Manayunk, striking mill operatives threatened their despised boss spinner with a ride on a rail.[89]

Trade union leaders, city officials, press observers, and workingmen were sensitive to the implications of these dif-ferent uses for parades. At several mass meetings, workers debated whether to have processions protesting unemploy-ment, and conflict surfaced over whether processions were an appropriate means. Those against parades argued that they alienated the otherwise sympathetic "respectable" of the community. In 1835, for example, journeymen carpenters stated that their "usual plan of forming themselves into processions and marching through the streets when on strike has had a pernicious tendency, by causing undue excitement and thereby incurring the disapprobation of that part of the public who are otherwise favorable to our proceedings." They resolved, "We strenuously disapprove of processions and all undue excitement." [90] In "undue excitement" the carpenters recognized the unusual festive state of the city that summer, when thousands of workers went not to work but to rallies in Independence Square. By the "otherwise favorable" part of the public they meant the small masters, shopkeepers, and merchants who decorated their windows with "6 to 6" placards. While merchants supported strikers' goals, they may have worried about the effects of large crowds gathered downtown. Similarly, at meetings in 1842, when workmen declared they were "starving on free trade," leaders argued against mass processions of the unemployed because "such a display of strength by the working classes" would have an "undue and alienating effect on their [legislative] representatives." [91]

Uneasiness over the use of parades surfaced in the comments of one leader, James Logan, at a "bread meeting" during the Panic of 1857. When three men bearing black and white flags appeared in the crowd of "upwards of five thousand" hungry people, Logan and other speakers took the banners as an incitement to riot. Disparaging "raw head and bloody bone work," Logan insisted that if workingmen wished to succeed in their demands for relief they must first prove themselves worthy. If deference and politeness failed, "God will hold the rich accountable," Logan argued. Parades, the traditional display of collective unity and moral force, were among the impolite means he condemned, along with "incendiary motives [mottoes]," banners, devices, and music. Not everyone at the demonstration agreed: Broadsides urging "Bread or Battle" and "Force the Usurers to Disgorge!" circulated through the crowd. [92]

Beneath cautions and complaints lay the recognition that strike parades expressed collective working-class power and a new way of looking at relations between masters and men. In the strike parade, the mustering of moral force implied the threat of physical force, and the uses of physical force were well known in labor disputes of the 1820s and

1830s. Whether implied or directly threatened, force and the display of group strength called to mind the oppositions —economic and cultural—between the lives of the propertied and the lives of workers. Strike parades expressed anger at those who betrayed the community; at the same time, they expressed rage at those who profited unequally and unjustly.

Strikers extended the symbolic differentiations made by workingmen in civic ceremonials and manufacturers' pageantry. While artisans and mechanics chose to separate themselves from their masters in patriotic ceremonies, strike parades took this distinction beyond separation. In their processions, strikers declared that their lives and interests were radically opposed to those of their employers. Strike parades, then, took distance to its furthest limit, making public and undeniable the existence of class conflict. Unlike mercantile pageants and the corporate imagery of work, strike parades attempted to destroy the superficial gloss of paternalism.

Because it communicated this unified opposition, the strike parade could not fail to offend and frighten businessmen and their allies in the press. For this reason, in the 1846 weavers' strike, authorities imposed spatial boundaries on parades. Employers and the mayor hoped to contain the strike's moral message as well as its contagion.

Strikers often felt forced to contain the threat of their marches, to disguise or downplay the open representation of class conflict. Perhaps because their positions were often weak, perhaps because they felt compelled to plead for support from their "betters," parade organizers were caught in a bind. To strike was to express the recognition of power, the only power workers had: to withdraw their labor. Without classwide solidarity, public enactments of this power could be belittled, dismissed, or suppressed, so strikers turned to the devices of legitimate parading.

The desire to appear nonthreatening, "creditable," "worthy," and "respectable" to those in power and to the city at large shaped parades by trade unionists less obsequious than James Logan. In 1850, for example, striking cordwainers gave a procession so much like a militia parade that a newspaper reporter only identified their purpose when he got close enough to read their "beautiful, white satin banner." More than four hundred "boss and journeymen cordwainers . . . mostly dressed in black with a badge of red white and blue ribbon, [were] preceded by a grand marshal, mounted, and the Washington Brass Band." [93] The parade, thoroughly outlining respectability, elicited admiration. Not only were the men dressed uniformly and somberly, with patriotic symbols, but also they had rented a brass band and were led by a man on horseback. Here again the parade was a display of collective resources, made possible in part because the strikers could muster material support. The striking cordwainers were far removed in appearance and intention from ragged hand-loom weavers.

Finally, respectability in strike parades may have been defined in relation to the ethnic identities of militant strikers. Weavers and textile operatives in Philadelphia were heavily Irish. The journeymen carpenters' denunciation of parades, in 1835, as "undue excitement" may have been based on the association of the fife and drum processions with these least respectable of the city's workers. The militance of Philadelphia's poor Irish was well known: The mere hoisting of a green weaver's banner could sometimes bring out the watch.[94] After the Kensington weavers' riots of 1844, when "native Americans" violently denied the civil rights of "foreigners," Irish workers, like blacks, were viewed as a subspecies. Reiterated in popular culture and on the stage, the division between the poor and respectable in the working class was firmly maintained in street parades. Militant-styled strike marches may have seemed like "acting Irish" to some trade unionists.[95]

SPECTACLES IN PROFUSION: VOLUNTARY SOCIETY PROCESSIONS

Workingmen also appeared in the parades of voluntary societies. Fire companies and moral and political reform associations made marches in which workers displayed themselves not as laborers but as communities dedicated to the social good. Voluntary society activities and processions commented on and related to working-class neighborhood life, yet they involved a limited range of working people, and as organizations they attacked cultural issues, not the problems of work and wages. Early-nineteenth-century voluntary associations drew members from the edges of social-class boundaries: In general, men who joined benevolent and reform associations tended to belong to the upper ranks of the working class or the lower edges of the property owners. Typical male voluntarists were skilled artisans, petty professionals, small merchants, and clerical workers. While class boundaries might be bridged in such associations, there is little evidence of equality of influence and participation. Men on their way to wealth and power tended to lead voluntary societies; men with meager prospects and resources were frequently the followers. It seems likely that the parades of voluntary associations shared this mix of business-class leadership and working-class membership.

Fire Companies

The venerable Philadelphia fire companies were among the most popular fraternities in the city. In the eighteenth century, the companies had been founded and manned by well-to-do artisans; the class make-up of fire companies in the nineteenth century is less clear. Because they were neighborhood organizations and Philadelphia's neighborhoods were becoming increasingly differentiated, the hose and engine companies had diverse occupational, ethnic, and political party ties. Bruce Laurie argues that, in the early decades of the century, skilled craftsmen and small property owners organized and led the fire fighters, but that, by the late 1830s and early 1840s, the proliferating companies became more solidly working class. From the 1830s until the department was organized in 1871, fire companies could be either respectable or rowdy, depending on neighborhood context and the uses members found for their fraternity. In artisanal Southwark, the social life of skilled craftsmen centered in the engine house. In nearby Moyamensing, petty and professional criminals used the companies as part of their neighborhood machine.[96]

By the 1840s fire companies were perceived as a major social problem. One source of concern was the fraternities' appeal to young men and apprentices. Many companies had groups of young followers or "runners" who socialized at the engine house and tagged along to fires. The runners, unemployed or absent from work, sometimes took part in petty crime such as theft, lounging, or loitering, prompting charges that fire companies corrupted youth. At the same time, adult rivalries between fire companies and associated gangs often burst into brawls and riots. As much as they fought among themselves, fire companies would also turn against unpopular outsiders. They were well known for attacks on blacks, immigrants, abolitionists, and the city watch.

Under attack by reformers and municipal officials, rowdy and respectable firemen used processions to present themselves as public-spirited citizens dedicated to service. The year's central event was the annual procession of the entire fire department, for which scores of companies vied to contribute a grand marshal. Each company hoped to create a striking impression and no expense was spared. Elaborate hose and engine carriages, painted and embroidered coats, tall leather buckets and hats, silver fire horns, and heavy emblematic banners were standard accoutrements. Wealthy companies added matching horses, brass harnesses, and runners costumed as footmen.[97]

The annual parade demanded impersonations and spectacles. A member of the William Penn Company usually turned out as "The Founder" accompanied by dancing "Indians." Neptune Hose featured a hoary water god astride its carriage, and many more companies dressed their postillions as foreign oddities: "Turks," "pashas," and "Asiatic dwarves."[98] Companies lacking horses dramatically harnessed themselves to a pumping machine and drew it through the streets. Trains of men enacted bucket brigades, lugged huge lengths of hose, or pulled wooden cenotaphs dedicated to members killed in the line of duty.

In their names and iconography, fire companies on parade identified themselves as belonging to and serving neighborhoods. On March 27, 1834, thirty-nine companies representing all parts of the city made a two-mile-long train. Ten called themselves after city locations, such as Northern Liberties, Kensington, Schuylkill, and Southwark. The names of patriot and local heroes distinguished others, while mythological and allegorical figures—such as Neptune, Fame, and Columbia—blended national imagery with godlike virtue.[99]

Company names and emblems revealed that firemen wished to present themselves as devoted and morally worthy. Mottoes like "Good Intent" and "Liberty or the Wishes of the People" combined patriotism with selfless sacrifice. Similarly, flags and banners, garlands, and uniforms were predominantly light blue and white, which commentators interpreted as symbolizing pure motives and fidelity.[100]

Themes of worth and utility were repeated on carriages and banners, and on firemen's elaborately painted hats and coats. The Washington Hose carriage had a portrait of the hero on every panel, including a rendering of the crossing of the Delaware; their motto declared, "All private duties are subordinated for those we owe to the public." The Lafayette Hose banner proclaimed, "Like Lafayette, we assist in time of need." Southwark Engine stuck to a simple device: "Southwark—Always Ready." Many more emblems and slogans on themes of devotion and purity contrasted ironically with firemen's everyday image and outrageous activities.[101]

The parades' imagery of service reconstructed the older stress on utility presented in occupational enactments, as paintings and banners referred to the value of firefighting. At the same time, the claim of selflessness echoed the calls for justice, mutuality, and solidarity embodied in strike parades. In this sense firemen's parades drew on values and experiences embedded in their working-class neighborhoods. But the working-class ethic of mutuality codified in trade unions and upheld by strikes was split away from the workplace and cast into a vision of public service organized voluntarily and across class boundaries. This split took place not only because small merchants and property owners belonged to and led fire companies, but also because the companies needed to appear "worthy in the eyes of the thousands who watched."[102] Fighting reform and reorganization, firemen needed to appear respectable, not raucously working class.

For fire companies, the gorgeous display of resources could mitigate their working-class identity. But despite the stress on selflessness, the emphasis on silver fire horns and matching uniforms resulted in worthiness and wealth becoming closely intertwined. The expense of fire-fighting paraphernalia and displays indicates that, while the city funded the fire department, affluent members helped fill company coffers. Prominent militiamen were company presidents, and they were regularly chosen to act as parade grand marshals.[103] Whereas other workingmen had rejected the use of finery to show morality—for instance, in the convention of citizen's dress—most firemen were sincerely devoted, if not to service, at least to fine machinery. The reliance on novelty and decoration—huge bronze statues of firemen, lavishly painted cars, and the lace, gilt, and velveteen of the postillions—showed that the conventions of gorgeous display had won out.

Temperance Associations

Temperance associations presented working-class images starkly opposed to the gaudy firemen and angry striking workers. The temperance movement in Philadelphia drew on both affluent and poor citizens. Early organizers had been wealthy merchants, small property owners, and skilled artisans. During the depression of the late 1830s, evangelical Protestantism gathered thousands of poor people into its fold and gave new life to the temperance crusade. Temperance and beneficial societies branched out through networks of churches, offering moral support and social welfare services to converts. The cause of abstinence became the nineteenth century's first mass reform movement; advocates claimed it would strengthen society by binding the middle and working classes together. But although affluent center-city residents and poor suburbanites joined the crusade, temperance leadership was distinctly respectable and upwardly mobile. Petty professionals, skilled workers, and small merchants figured prominently in temperance ranks and evangelical congregations.[104]

The temperance movement was a struggle for purity at the individual and societal level, but its overt aim was the reform of the degraded among the working class, whose moral flaws the depression of the late 1830s had made frighteningly evident. Preachers explained the workers' misery in terms of character flaws: Irreligion, drink, and the free-and-easy male social life of poor neighborhoods caused poverty and hardship. Sophisticated and vigorous organizing techniques brought this argument into every neighborhood. Through exhortation, house-to-house visiting, proselytizing, and printed propaganda, temperance leaders sought to penetrate the lives of the fallen.

To strengthen the will to abstain, temperance societies created little communities and cultivated an alternative social world. Life, temperance advocates stressed, properly revolved around chapel, hearth, and family, not the alehouse, workplace, or street corner. This message was aimed especially at young people whose habits were yet unformed. Readings, prayer meetings, hymn singing, cold-water picnics, and ladies' charity fairs bound leisure time with purpose and stood in criticism of the irrational aspects of working-class social life.[105]

Temperance leaders used popular forms, notably the procession and the festival, to criticize urban vernacular culture. Temperance Independence Day activities opposed the usual patterns of urban festivity by constructing orderly and rational meanings in street ceremonies. The finely branched structure of the district associations enabled leaders to muster hundreds, and later thousands, of members into the streets. Organized by wards and sometimes by blocks, the marchers made parades so vast that they seemed to take over the city.

Elaborate routes were published well before July Fourth, a standard method of gathering an audience, and marchers were grouped in order of their society's founding, by district branch and age group. In this way, reformers and the rank and file presented themselves as members of communities, witnesses to a moral cause. In case the uninitiated missed the point, banners declared that temperance was the only way to a happy life.[106]

In July 1838, the temperance procession wound an elaborate route through the center of town and the suburbs, arriving at Pratt's Garden on Lemon Hill for a cold-water picnic and combined temperance with religious and patriotic service, including the singing of a temperance version of the "Star-Spangled Banner."[107] In following years, the procession and the popularity of the cold-water feast grew. In 1839 the *Public Ledger* observed that temperance clubs made a "very numerous and respectable body of men, each with a badge to designate association . . . each [club] with a banner and a band of music."[108] In 1840, the procession brought together more than seven hundred men and a few young women and took several hours to circulate through downtown Philadelphia. The emphasis shifted to total abstinence and the marchers invented a new enactment, "a water cooler capable of supplying fourteen gallons per hour, drawn by two grey horses" accompanied by girls dressed in white who passed cold ladles of water to the marchers.[109] This literal demonstration of temperance principles fit the reformers' belief that women, the naturally pure, ought to take responsibility for men, who were more easily tempted. The temperance processions showed an unusual tolerance of female participation, although women were still rare in street parades, probably because women were critical to the life of the associations. In 1841 the Protestant Temperance Association extended tolerance and parade space to the Irish Catholic Total Abstinence Association.[110]

In form and rationale, temperance processions attempted to create respectability and to promote a particular standard of worthiness.[111] This was done in part through the solemn demeanor of the processions, the accompaniment by elegant bands playing hymns and patriotic airs. Temperance processions displayed no frivolity along the line, no Turkish turbans or Indian war paint. Women in the procession, though few, were protected by white dresses and the sacred nature of their role in the cause. Banners explaining the somber joy of liberation from demon rum outlined the pledge's terms and results. Painted flags showed the drunkard's last trip—over the hill to the poorhouse in a blinding blizzard.[112] Marchers appeared as orderly, faithful battalions, organized by neighborhoods. White flags, brass bands, and mounted divisions raised neighborhood organizations above the painstaking routines of work, prayer, and visiting, turning them into warriors in a colorful battle. Through the use of military devices such as marshals, division flags, bands, and badges, neighborhood organizations became an army that took over the streets with a rich and righteous presence. The individual struggle for self-restraint and discipline against the trials of poverty was transformed into a moral and patriotic cause. That the processions took place on July Fourth—well known for its intemperance and rowdiness—increased its power, bringing to bear the day's connotations of release from work (leisure) and from tyranny (independence). This fusion eschewed older plebeian forms of sociability and connected that rejection with the definition of Americanism itself.

The themes of Americanism and the rejection of the irrational way of life of the poor resurfaced in the Grand Native American Procession of July 4, 1844. The nativist movement had close connections to temperance and evangelical Protestantism, and its leaders were the same type of class-boundary straddlers who led fire companies and temperance associations. Belief in Protestant superiority and the racial inferiority of the city's poor Irish inhabitants fused in nativism. The procession staged by the American Republican Party was a public announcement of the nativists' proposals to limit citizenship rights to men of American birth and to purify public education of popery.[113]

The processional form suited nativists well. Like temperance associations, they presented themselves as networks of neighborhoods. Thousands of marchers appeared in somber citizen's dress, arranged by ward and division. A stately variety of allegories and enactments unfolded in the line: a cenotaph for the "martyrs" of the "Battle of Kensington," barouches for the widows and "ancient revolutioners," and military bands. The rolling ships *Union* and *Washington* appeared again, recalling great civic days and announcing the sponsorship of master shipwrights. Scores of pennants, flags, and streamers bristled in the ranks of the ward organizations, and a rich display of painted silk banners depicted nativist sentiments and demands for the limitation of Catholic civil rights in heavy-handed allegory.[114]

The banners made explicit the procession's meaning for the marchers. Flag bearers literally stood under the outstretched arms of Washington, the symbol of national virtue, who shielded school buildings, sustained the open Bible, and warned with gesture and motto against the serpent "Foreign Influence." George Shiffler, the "martyr" of the spring's anti-Irish mobbings, clutched his breast and saved the tattered flag. Liberty and the eagle, favored national symbols, joined the ballot, Bible, and flag in repetitive reworkings of ideas about purity and threat, insult and danger. Feminine symbols were prevalent: Liberty and angels played prominent roles. Washington's mourning mother leaned over his tomb in a Protestant Pietà. These banners, like firemen's and temperance banners, were designed, sewed, and presented by affiliated ladies' clubs. Banners testified to the support of numerous women's circles and added to the sense of neighborhood solidarity. The nativist procession portrayed the masses gathered to defend the home, church, and schoolhouse—center points of the domestic, respectable life promoted by reformers.

As in earlier street displays, highly constructed objects in the native American procession bespoke a high level of collective resources brought to bear for the cause. For example, the rolling ships were reported to have cost the master shipwrights thousands of dollars. Expense underlined respectable support for nativism and impressed the eye with the gorgeous organization of detail. Organized strength was the central message of the Native American Procession. As the American Republicans wound their way through south and central Philadelphia, they seemed to sweep all before them, catching spectators and smaller parades in their wake.[115]

The nativists finished the day camped like an army at Snyder's woods, surrounded by their flags. A temperance picnic, oration, readings of Washington's Farewell Address and the Declaration of Independence were topped off with lavish fireworks. Although the nativists portrayed themselves as engaged in a defensive battle for church and country, their rhetoric and procession were offensive actions. Like the May riots, which were sparked by brazen nativist provocation, the procession incited violence by claiming that Irish-Americans threatened the country's purity and safety. If nativists challenged the Irish to fight on this Fourth, it was the nativists who did finally attack. When rioting broke out the next day, it was started by Protestants and focused on a rumored arms cache in a Catholic church in largely Protestant Southwark.[116]

RESPECTABILITY IN WORKERS' PARADES

The pressure to find respectable and worthy ways of acting in the street defined parades by Philadelphia's workers, whether on strike or celebrating firehouse life. While temperance processions provide the clearest example, the issue of respectability surfaced in trade union parades, demonstrations, and strikes as well as in fraternal self-promotions. For all processions, the decorous, orderly splendor of the volunteer militias seems to have served as model and referent. To appear patriotic, neat, regular, colorful, and expensive was to make a good parade, and these standards applied even when workingmen challenged the city's powerful. Not until the labor movement gathered mass strength after the Civil War would strikers and unionists be able to begin to define more fully how they would represent class conflict in public. More often, workingmen used parades to claim respectability for their organizations and for themselves.

This acceptance of canons of respectable street performance testifies to the pressure on what Bruce Laurie has called "traditional" working-class culture. The majority of Philadelphia's workers indulged independent, relaxed, and rowdily defiant styles of living—partly in compensation for the horrors of poverty and insecurity—and this pattern of culture would persist among some groups for most of the nineteenth century. Yet some workers responded to reformers' calls for close adherence to standards of self-restraint, piety, and thrift.[117] This change was being accomplished in part by the pressure from the new industrial order, which broke down older patterns of life and forced men and women to rearrange ways of living and acting. Working-class temperance advocates were among the first to register and respond to this transformation. The restructuring of values, however, was also a directed and intentional process. As people were forced to learn new ways of working appropriate to the factory, their social superiors aimed more specific moral reform efforts at them. Public schools, Sunday Schools, Sabbatarianism, religion, the poorhouse, popular literature, and the press were all tools in the promotion of piety, hard work, and self-control.[118]

To the dismay of reformers, however, culture could not be neatly reorganized by exhortation and attempts at control. Economic and social changes at once created "problems" and gave urban workers opportunities to build unprecedented, disturbingly autonomous ways of life, which could prove resistant to assaults from above.[119] The continuing controversy over the culture and condition of workers shows, on one hand, how disturbing poverty and difference were to propertied city dwellers, and on the other, how unevenly reformers succeeded in penetrating and changing workers' lives. Philadelphia's persistent burlesque street traditions show that in many ways the working class simply ignored the efforts and demands of the respectable. But the pressure for respectability in street parades reveals that Philadelphia's workers sometimes acknowledged the criticisms of social superiors and grasped and manipulated the standards of respectability. As the affluent adopted new manners and decorum for public interaction, so the upper levels of the working class would use, especially in street displays, the new standard.[120] The pressures of ordinances, policing, and proselytizing were felt, but they connected with some workers' will to distance and distinguish themselves from the ragged, immigrant poor. Striving for respectability, some workers found it—as they helped create it—in parades.

CHAPTER SIX

Patterns of Communication

Transformation of Repertoire

Between 1788 and 1860, Philadelphians developed a distinctive calendar of festivity and a repertoire of public ceremonial events. Parades and street ceremonies made the core of popular public events; parades were flexible, visible, and multifarious enough to ritualize a wide range of social questions and relations. Class, race, ethnicity, power and its legitimacy, patriotism, and the memory of history could be defined and debated in street dramas made by paraders.

Analysis of major contexts, varieties, styles, and uses of parades leads to the following questions. First, what kinds of communication were parades, and how did they communicate? Second, how did the antebellum parade repertoire affect what came later in the nineteenth and twentieth centuries?

Like all kinds of communication, from speech to artifacts to electronic media, parades became meaningful through patterns conceived by their makers and perceived by their audiences. Looking at pattern clarifies how parades could be so unusually varied and, at the same time, ultimately limited and constrained in what they could communicate. Meaningful patterns should be considered in terms of parades' uses in public performances, by performers, and within Philadelphia's range of styles and ways of being "on parade."

Philadelphia's Parade Makers

The city's parade makers can be divided roughly into two groups, although it is possible that some individuals participated in more than one sort of parade. Following the city's class lines, these groups consisted of men who owned property and men who did not. Philadelphia's well-reported parades were "economical spectacles" and military extravaganzas, made by men with material resources. Parades such as the Grand Federal Procession of 1788, Washington's Centennial of 1832, and the Native American Procession of 1844 presented, in addition to specific political messages, the elaborate organization of Philadelphia's social and material resources. Similarly, the enactments of work processes and the industrial displays of larger patriotic spectacles were sponsored and sometimes performed by factory owners, employers, and master craftsmen. On a more regular basis, militia parades displayed the symbolic dominance of the professionals and the propertied, just as the volunteer militias themselves represented the business class in street wars and public disturbances. The voluntary organization leaders who produced temperance and nativist processions also came from business and mercantile circles, although many association members were artisans and poorer workers.

In contrast, maskers, mummers, and burlesque parade makers seem to have come exclusively from the working class, and they set their performances in the context of working-class festivity. Strikers, while sometimes led by skilled workers, were often from the most miserably poor neighborhoods in the city. In fact, Philadelphia's workers usually struck because of industrial instability and because employers continually attacked their wages and standards of living. The militant strike parade, with its origins in the charivari and tarring and feathering, belonged to the milieu of Christmas revelry and militia burlesques.

Parade making, a select and privileged activity in the decades before the Civil War, was dominated by white men who often acted on and enforced their understanding that street theatricality was their exclusive domain. Because parades communicated group presence, conviction, and solidarity, whites found black street parades threatening; hence, when blacks tried to claim the right to street parades, they were ridiculed and threatened by mob violence. The parade's dramatic allusion to a unified community suggested that blacks might be in a position to collectively reduce white prerogatives. Similarly, Irish immigrants were discouraged from displaying ethnic unity and moral strength in the streets. Women's participation in street parades and other public manifestations elicited scorn, scandal, and near riot.

Parade-Making Occasions

Philadelphians' uses for parades were patterned, varying according to paraders' identities and intentions. Reasons for parading, though varied, were repetitive; although used for a dignitary's arrival or a workers' uprising, parades did not accompany every public or private event. The official uses of parades were limited—no processions marked the investiture of governors or judges, as in the eighteenth century, and criminals were no longer punished by being marched through the streets with shaved heads.[1] At the same time, some parades, such as July Fourth militia processions, recurred with such regularity that they stood as the definition of parading itself.

Popular militarism, linked to patriotism, was the most common street enactment. Using street displays to strengthen their legitimacy and social power, the volunteers created their own popularity. This prominence facilitated economic and political advancement and the exclusive sociability of the militia fraternity. The volunteers' legitimacy, however, undermined the public companies, excluding workers and the poor from playing a role in the domestic defense system as well as from a popular tradition of street displays.

The Uses of Performance

Employers and master artisans used displays of industrial prowess for their own purposes. Whether celebrating a governmental ideal, promoting a railroad or canal, or advertising Philadelphia as a site for industrial expansion, employers and manufacturers found the imagery of labor a fine advertising technique. Older craft meanings persisted within these promotions; artisans proudly displaying their skills and the quality of their products simultaneously portrayed the producer's moral and political role in the republic. Only the skilled workers enacted industry's virtues, however, and this meant that many other workers were excluded from participation in the symbolic republic. Parades enacting the world of work obscured the economic and political role played by the unskilled and cast the worth of labor in terms of craft knowledge. Artisan republicanism was dramatized within events sponsored, produced, and costumed, by employers and masters.

Strike and trade-union processions, on the other hand, signaled the breach of obligation and identification between men and masters. In strike parades, men declared themselves their own masters. Strike parades promoted the strikers' cause as morally just, circulated it through neighborhoods, and called others to turn out. In continuation of eighteenth-century traditions of direct action and folk drama, strikers also used parades to defend their communities, threatening retribution to those who betrayed the occupational group by taking boycotted work. Strikers' fife and drum parades not only intimidated blacklegs, but also broadcast the accusation of betrayal, labeling the offender a traitor to the community. Strike parades thus presented striking workers as morally upright, and helped create and unify opposition to the masters.

Working-class burlesque parades were explicitly political, again preserving eighteenth-century practice: Mock militias used ridicule in an attempt to destroy the oppressive militia system. More generally, however, the burlesquers expressed a widespread working-class perception that petty tyrants, wielding unjustly gained power, had infiltrated the republic's institutions and threatened to corrupt the nation. This perception was based on the realities of local class inequalities, and laughter directed at officers and the display of affluence often carried more than an undertone of class hostility. The festive revels of Christmas maskers extended criticism of the militia to other unpopular figures of authority. Insofar as fantastical traditions created and perpetuated neighborhood solidarities, this laughing unity was also expressed in the identification and impersonation of "others" and outsiders. In times of crisis, hostility, and racism, impersonating an outsider was not a far step from attacking him physically. Thus, both the burlesque militias and Christmas fantasticals drew on older traditions of folk drama, which had earlier links to folk justice, social protest, and violence—but they found different targets. The militia burlesques aimed up the social scale, while they remained firmly within the world of laughter; Christmas impersonations entered on the terrain of racial and ethnic violence.

These, then, were the uses of parades: self-promotion and the legitimation of private interests through patriotic, military, and historic ritual; legitimation of the power of the propertied, and challenges to that legitimacy; and mockery of institutions and politics, and delineation of the traits of outcasts and inferiors. At its heart, the repertoire of parades and ceremonies framed questions about power and legitimacy. These moving performances defined social issues. What was the nature of social power? Was it based on inheritance and birth, appearance and demeanor, or in natural rights? What did the Revolution mean, and who might claim to be its heirs? Were Irish immigrants (or Afro-Americans) more or less like human beings? Should they have equal rights, or be driven out of the city? Were employers legitimate, fatherly superiors, or did they betray the ideals of the republic when they profited off employees?

Parade Styles

Parades communicated through the recurrent uses of conventions and ways of being on parade. Conventions and styles fell into recognizable patterns that were closely linked to, but not coextensive with, parade makers' social identities and purposes. Orderly and disorderly, or respectable and antirespectable, describe the two predominant ways of being on parade. Order and respectability were accomplished through the division of the line of march into leaders and followers, into branches and units, according to the military practice popularized by the volunteers. This technique was used not only by the citizen soldiers but also by temperance advocates, nativists, firemen, and some trade unions. The unity of motion acquired through drilling and practice implied unanimity, collective control, and self-control. Uniforms reduced variety and effaced individualism, heightening the image of order created by concerted movement. At the same time, costumes caught the eye with a gorgeous and colorful organization of detail. Tokens of identity, such as badges, sashes, ribbons, and banners, unified marchers and separated them from their audience. Such details also advertised affluence: Bright colors, gilt weapons and buttons, and rich textures focused attention on the elaborate display of collective resources. In the same way, bands of musicians hired by voluntary organizations and the militias added aural complexity to the visual spectacle, announced the parade from afar, and testified to the expense of the production.

Decoration and the display of affluence became the prevalent standards for street parades and the means by which audiences recognized respectability. The frequency of orderly and elaborate parades, especially those of the volunteer militias, and the audiences' approval show that military interpretations of patriotism, especially with fancy, foreign costumes, were popular. One could imagine, however, that observers had differing interpretations. Poor working-class people probably envied and resented the firemen's glittering spectacles and the volunteers' flashy displays. What was it like for people who barely earned subsistence wages to watch the superfluous displays of their upwardly mobile neighbors or employers? Envy of the resources and leisure associated with stylish parades may have been tempered by the delight at the disruption of everyday routine, but anger at the spectacles of wealth may also have been dampened by the growing legitimacy of the spectacular. In the 1820s, for example, workingmen had found an alternative style of respectability, "plain republican" or "citizen's dress," but it was overshadowed by the successes of the militias and the fire companies.

The opposite of respectable parades were the tattered drills of the public militias, the angry fife and drum marches of the strikers, and the organized antistructure of the maskers and burlesque militias. Contrasted with the parades of the propertied, some working-class parades were orderly, but they were rarely splendid. Elaborate floats and elegant matching uniforms exceeded the means of most working Philadelphians. Strikers could rarely hire bands and usually relied on a drummer or fifer to announce their parade. The public militias, forced to march, were ridiculed for lacking uniforms, equipment, and adequate training.

Burlesque militiamen and mummers used irregularity and disorder to develop their own parade conventions. With rough instruments, such as pots, pans, horns, and bells, they flouted harmony and melody. In dress and makeup, burlesquers exaggerated the audience's diversity, making racial and sexual recombinations the centerpieces of their performances. The costumes of the burlesque militias pulled apart and satirized the use of dress to create order and signal affluence. Uneven legs, mismatched shoes, patches and tatters, and hats and swords that dwarfed the wearer mocked and destroyed uniformity.

Self-restraint and self-control were also the subject of burlesque antics. Mummeries grew out of and structured the noisy, mixed-up, drunken atmosphere of Battalion Day, July Fourth, and Christmas. Both street performances and crowd revels challenged the works of self-disciplined volunteers and voluntarists, defying the stress laid on propriety and temperance by the proponents of urban moral order.

Burlesque parade conventions aimed at the self-differentiation of moral reformers and private militias. In this sense, Mikhail Bakhtin's formulation of the uses of laughter applies to the difference between respectable and disorderly parade conventions. Laughter, according to Bakhtin, reduces distance.[2] Private militias and volunteer reformers attempted to distance themselves from the poor of the working class by creating distinct behavioral styles in public performances and public life. Mock militias tried to reduce social distance by aiming parodies at commanders from the upper reaches of local society. Humorous costume, makeup, and cacophony were used to confuse and cross boundaries, thus temporarily breaking down social barriers.

Respectable parades worked to define members, separate them from nonmembers, and explicate membership standards, such as those of military demeanor or abstinence. The different intentions of respectable and rowdy parades were apparent in relationships between performers and audiences. Disorderly maskings and burlesques were spontaneous performances that encouraged audience participation. Burlesques did not create distance between audience and performers—they reduced it. Fantasticals circulated in the streets, toured their own neighborhoods, and surprised the crowds. In contrast, respectable parades were announced ahead of time to gather audiences, and they followed defined, published routes. Planning and devices such as uniforms and marching skills not only heightened the sense of performance, but also discouraged bystanders from joining in, clearly separating performers and audience.

Strike parades exemplified the tension between respectable and disorderly styles. Strikers who needed to present themselves as respectable citizens engaged in a moral struggle using techniques such as bands, orderly marching, and uniformlike sashes, badges, and hats. These strikers often employed labor's corporate imagery on their banners and in their self-presentations as producers. Other strikers, however, were militant and overtly hostile, calling for community support against employers and heralding violence against traitors. These two different ways of making strike parades—asserting order versus suggesting violence—reflect the division between the skilled and the unskilled poor of the working class. The poor and unskilled hinted at violence, not because they were ignorant or lacked self-control, but because the militant display of solidarity best suited their desperate situation.

The uses of parades and parade styles were part of a discourse unfolding in the streets about class relations and ways of life in the city. In this discourse no one would have the final word, although propertied citizens had more resources and opportunities to communicate their viewpoint through enactment. The opposed valuations of competing ways of life were part of the problem of urban class relations, and street theatre addressed this opposition. New economic relations increased the number of poor employees, a condition that angered working people. At the same time, the newly affluent of the business class wished to justify power and money as theirs by tradition and right, not by acquisition. To create this image, the propertied distinguished themselves in dress, manners, residence, social life, religion, and language from older urban ways of life and the visible, voluble workers. But property owners, worried about how urban life and working-class degeneracy would affect society, believed that wide-ranging measures were needed to make the working class reform itself.[3]

For the propertied and those aiming for respectability, making a parade was an act accomplishing or advocating respectability. In the street, the respectable didactically displayed the standards they wished everyone would strive for.

Respectable parade making accepted the stratification of society into the propertied and the propertyless, urging inferiors to accept the blame for their poverty and to change their situation by adopting new behavior patterns. But since orderly parades were being performed largely by those who had already internalized standards of respectability, we must allow the possibility that many of the working class refused to accept stratification and the imposition of behavioral control. The best evidence on nineteenth-century working-class culture indicates that most workers laughed at—and turned away from—these proselytizing dramas.[4]

Set against the performances of the propertied, the parades of the working poor challenged and denied respectability and the social order based on property and power. Inasmuch as working-class culture looked inward or celebrated itself in maskings and burlesques, it rejected the validity of the way of life stressing piety and self-control. Disorderly street dramas set during festivals, the temporary rupture of labor discipline, countered the hegemony of the ideology of self-control and self-denial. As long as festive crowds enjoyed and understood the fun poked at militia volunteers and patriot rhetoricians, they remained open to other possibilities for political and cultural criticisms.

Strike parades addressed most directly the problem of urban class relations. Strikers, especially those who destroyed looms and persuaded others not to work, made manifest a growing knowledge that their labor was the main source of their power. Withholding labor was the one lever workingmen could use effectively against employers. Parades asserted the (legally unrecognized) right to strike and presented strikers' understandings of power relations clearly and publicly. Conversely, the respectable style of skilled workers' processions toned down the strike's direct reference to class relations and the power of the propertied over those who owned only their labor. Making themselves look like militiamen or voluntarists, some strikers denied the threat of direct action implied by their mustering of group power. Workers who did this may have bordered the working and propertied classes and may well have drawn on their experiences with other kinds of cross-class fraternities.

Strike parades shared more than the threat of disorder with the parades of maskers and burlesquers. These kinds of parades all sprang directly from the culture of working-class neighborhoods. Masked parodists mocked the pretensions of social superiors and delineated the traits of inferiors. Mock militias cast the artisan-republican critique of privilege and corruption into laughter, and strikers announced workers' unique power. The alternative parade traditions, therefore, held the potential to make alternate images of the social order. This power was recognized in the scorn of the propertied and in attempts to suppress oppositional parades, popular street culture, and festivity.

In all its variety and flexibility, the parade was well suited to the shape and structure of the early-nineteenth-century city, with its close and busy but open streets and its compact arrangement of differentiating neighborhoods. The questions parades could powerfully address—about the nature of power, the sources of legitimacy, and the criteria for belonging—were those of early-nineteenth-century urban politics. These questions were also addressed in party politics, symbolic crusades such as temperance and nativism, and urban rioting. For many Philadelphians experiencing a new urban life, parades—as images of social relations—were ways of interpreting and knowing a changing city. Yet, paradoxically, as ways of communicating, parades were limited and narrow. Access to the full power of public performance could not be shared equally—the right to street parades was restricted to members of the polity and constrained by conventions of respectability. Therefore, the meanings that parades could communicate were limited; parades could not be used to challenge the legitimacy of the social order nor to make claims on society, except through laughter and derision. Claiming citizens' rights, blacks would be mobbed, women derided, and strikers cordoned off or arrested. Festive license apparently sheltered some burlesquers and maskers from outrage, but they too could suffer for their performances.

Attempts at controlling public behavior and suppressing undesirable forms of popular culture had been continuous since the eighteenth century, with incremental and uneven success. With the emergence of the consolidated city and professional law enforcement in the 1850s, civil authorities' attempts to contain street life and performance became more concerted and more effective.⁵ The emergence of respectable conventions for street parades shows that cultural change and control were being effected in the symbolic, as well as behavioral, domain. The dominance of order and respectability in public performance implies that unlike recurrent attempts at suppression, the performance and popularization of new standards could attain more evenly successful results, at least in the sphere of public performance. Parades were, after all, only performances: There is no evidence that temperance processions themselves recruited many permanent members to the "white life." On the contrary, despite temperance marches, Christmas maskings continued to grow wildly intemperate. But the conventions of respectability did successfully define social legitimacy, and elegant spectacles became the standard for legitimacy in public performance. If parade makers had to eschew older traditions of militancy, and thus their identity as working-class citizens, to avoid arrest and attract favorable notice in the press, then the possibilities for communicating a genuine working-class stance through a parade were limited. One can conclude, then, that as a mode of communication, parades held surprising possibilities; they could reach large numbers of people and dramatize a variety of ideas. Yet respectability—a distillation of the social values of the propertied—permeated the generally accepted definition of a good parade. Parades were limited by their uses and by the social power of the predominant performers; thus they enabled respectable citizens to reproduce their own influence.

The limited uses for and the narrowed range of parades force an assessment of the publicness of street performance. Was the public sphere—of which the streets were only a part—infiltrated by all kinds of participants and open to all possible audiences? Or, to put it more broadly, what was the shape of the public sphere in the antebellum city? The answer gleaned from the cases examined here is that, while the streets may have been very open, they were not equally open to everybody; while the public sphere may have had room for a range of expression, it was shaped and limited by interests of the propertied and powerful. If those with little power forced new, oppositional meanings into street theatre, perhaps by means of a strike parade, this opening did not result from the public nature of street performance, but was effected by workers' determination and their recognition of their own class interests and collective power. When minorities, workers, and the poor used street theatre to present their ideas about social relations, they claimed a right that their betters wanted to deny them.

For all their multiplicity, parades were only public events if *public* means simply that which takes place in the open air. In fact, parade-making access was limited by wealth, opinion, custom, and everyday practice, and served interests that can be described as particular and private. As communication, the parade was a technique of the powerful, although as a resource it was not inaccessible to less-powerful citizens.

This conclusion has relevance for folklorists and historians working with notions of "public" versus "private" activities and cultural patterns. In general, *public* is contrasted with *domestic* and designates all that occurs outside the family circle. Public acts and activities are thought of as free, in limbo, rife with possibilities, accessible to all people, and open to kaleidoscopic meanings. In the case of the nineteenth-century city and its streets, such notions are incorrect. The public sphere is more accurately conceived of as a special, historically changing arena for action, one influenced by the conflicts that shape other domains, such as politics, industry, and education.

Toward the Twentieth Century

After the 1850s the uses of parades and street theatre and the shape of the public sphere shifted dramatically, until the traditions invented in the antebellum era would be barely recognizable. Because much of this history remains to be told, I can only offer some propositions and point interested readers in promising directions. On the one hand, spectacles of many kinds grew in scale, frequency, and popularity. On the other, the uses of the street and the possibilities of street performance were reshaped by several important, interacting forces: continuing assaults on working-class culture and the freedoms of the street; the growing partnership of commerce and government in the production of festivity and spectacle; the swelling strength of commercial mass media (and eventually electronic mediation); and the physical remaking of the city.

The cycle of festivals and ceremonial practices invented or refurbished during the antebellum years laid the foundation for late-nineteenth-century festivity; some traces, such as Washington's and Lincoln's birthday and the remembrance of July Fourth, exist today. What has vanished from memory is the wild disorder of festivals and holidays and the sense that festivity expresses parts of an oppositional working-class culture. After the Civil War these uproars persisted, and with them the notion that the working class could inject its own imagery and presence into the city's collective free time. Holidays could still contain oppositional meanings: Trade unions used July Fourth as a powerfully symbolic time—to call strikes and hold demonstrations—for most of the century.[6]

The antirespectable uses of the street continued to generate the antagonism of the propertied, especially while workers and the poor lived within the circle of their awareness, but late-nineteenth-century Philadelphians found new ways to crack the old problem. The introduction of a centralized police force was a breakthrough in the reform of street culture, one which shaped parade forms and uses. At their discretion, policemen could define and arrest disturbers of the peace, whether they were maskers, beggars, or street-corner orators.[7]

Labor's growing strength was the key reason for the invention of new techniques to preserve order. As more employees labored in the same workplaces, under the same employers, the collective power of the work force became disturbing and obvious. The Great Strike of 1877, the rise of a mass labor movement, the socialist movement, recurring economic depressions, and huge unemployment demonstrations all strengthened long-standing doubts about the people's right to assemble. From the late 1850s on, labor demonstrations became spectacular. Leaders could mass more people in the street than ever before, and recurring crises gave the poor more pressing reasons to protest. A series of huge processions in Philadelphia and other eastern cities culminated in New York in 1882 in a "Monster Demonstration" for the eight-hour day, the first Labor Day parade. Labor spectacles carried both the militant and respectable traditions. Inasmuch as the movement was made up of the skilled crafts and trades, respectability — dark suits, ceremonial banners, and marching bands — predominated, but mass processions could also be militant. In the 1870s, 1880s, and 1890s, parades could propagandize ideas ranging from the eight-hour day to workers' control of production and profits.[8]

After the Great Strike of 1877, the business class and government reached a decisive innovation in the maintenance of urban order: Legislation confirmed the privileged position of the volunteer militias. The volunteers became the state's National Guard, and after this elevation they served almost entirely as "policemen of industry," protecting strikebreakers and industrial property from workers, and helping contain strike parades and demonstrations.[9] Philadelphia also found use for the militias in festive times, especially Christmas, to keep revelry within spatial limits and to protect downtown property. It was partly through the use of the guard or "reserves" that the city was able to reform its wild holidays.[10]

Fear of strikes, gatherings, and mass meetings prompted some cities to legislate limits on public meetings and assemblies. Although we have no real history of this process, it is clearly crucial to the history of public communication. Mayors were given the prerogative of banning assemblies during civil emergencies, and Philadelphia began requiring parade and demonstration permits after the late 1870s.[11] In the twentieth century, as the right to organize and strike became more clearly recognized in law, legal refinements were developed to limit the possibilities of strike-related demonstrations, picketing, and secondary strikes. If parades and strikes went hand in hand in the early nineteenth century, today strike parades and mass picketing are rarely seen, and the relationship between the First Amendment and the traditions of picketing and demonstrating is cloudy.[12]

While business leaders worried about strikes and demonstrations, cultural reformers determined to apply example, intervention, and suppression to clean up working-class festivity and public behavior. One program for reform involved rationalizing the irrational side of city festivals.

The festive disorder of July Fourth and Christmas was becoming intolerable to elite Philadelphians. They in turn invented movements for a "safe and sane" Fourth and pressured city authorities to ban masking, revels, and noise-making.[13] Another strategy was a movement to reform and rewrite civic ceremony. By the late 1850s the most educated and elite of urbanites disavowed their heritage, claiming that the United States had no rituals comparable to those of Europe or worthy of the name "tradition."[14] But this allegation, evidence of the distance the most affluent placed between themselves and vernacular culture, forces us to recognize that most urban street theatre was beneath the notice of the wealthy by the last half of the century. To members of the elite, the old Fourth of July or Washington's Birthday, with orations and parades, were weak and disorganized ceremonies, outmoded and insufficient for the task of educating immigrants and the poor about American history and citizenship. As David Glassberg has detailed, the American Pageantry Movement, which blossomed in the 1890s, tried to replace the familiar antebellum patterns of ceremony with allegorical performances modeled on Elizabethan pageants. Such displays required knowledgeable pageant-masters trained in literature and art, scripts and casts, and financial resources. Blending allegory with local and national history, the pageants drew on local elites for support and actors; pageant-masters explicitly excluded the participation of local working-class clubs with their own performative traditions. For example, a Philadelphia civic pageant written by local historian Ellis P. Oberholtzer and performed in 1908 rejected the participation of Philadelphia Mummers clubs. The pageantry movement aimed not only to instruct, but also to put a city on the map; thus only accepted, respectable versions of local culture would be included, and the Mummers were still far too outrageous.[15] In the end, the pageantry movement was a failure, despite the important social and material resources its leaders marshaled. Its stiff neo-Elizabethan style and its educated allegories had little to do with local culture and neighborhood institutions.

If wholesome examples failed to reform urban public culture, commercial efforts had more success. After the Civil War, the production of spectacles was part of the display of the assured power of Philadelphia's manufacturing and commercial elite. The old techniques of parades as "economical spectacles" or industrial advertisements expanded into huge celebrations. The Centennial Exposition of 1876 was probably the turning point for Philadelphia, providing myriad opportunities for linking history with industrial prowess. The Centennial was the event that officially joined city government, industry, and commerce in the production of spectacles, not only because the city was the site of a national display of technology and manufactures, but also because downtown was the theatre for an entire year of historicizing and recommemoration, planned with the active participation of business leaders. This success was repeated in 1882, with the Bicentennial of the city's founding and a Grand Industrial Parade, and again in 1887, in the Centennial of the Constitution. For this occasion, business and military leaders reproduced a version of the Grand Federal Procession of 1788, complete with rolling ships and Greek edifices. All three spectacles aimed to bring visitors to the city, and all were reported in the press as national events.[16]

A new development of commercial culture, the department store, also linked festivity, commerce, and spectacle in ways that could redefine public culture. These huge emporia in the city's center led the way in producing parades and festivals, albeit along foreign and exotic lines, to advertise their wares and introduce female customers to commodity consumption.[17] In both the industrial historical spectacle and the department-store parade, late-nineteenth-century street theatre continued the businessman's practice of using the parade as a kind of advertising. But there was one important difference: In the displays produced by department stores, spectacle, goods, and consumption were becoming bound together in ways that are now entirely familiar—in, for example, the Thanksgiving Day parade, which kicks off the year's biggest purchasing season, the month before Christmas. And department-store spectacles and industrial displays showed city authorities that festivity itself—if properly organized and contained—might add to a city's importance, reputation, and wealth. Could not Christmas maskings and Saint Patrick's Day processions be turned into a respectable part of the city's self-image, enhancing the commercial downtown with a flash of local color?[18]

Indeed, they could and they would. In 1900 Christmas revelry finally became respectable in the form of the first New Year's Mummers Parade, with an official parade route, licenses for performers (as well as an official license for transvestism and acting crazy), and prizes offered by merchants. This pattern continues today; Philadelphia's Department of Commerce helps arrange sponsorship for the popular spectacles of patriotism, militarism, and ethnicity.[19]

Commercial mass media also helped change the uses and meanings of the street. Although Colonel Pluck's 1825 burlesque was publicized by the press up and down the east coast, it had still been appropriate for the colonel to take his message on tour. In the late nineteenth century, spectacular tours, such as that of President Grant, were popular, but accounts in the mass circulation dailies could reach much more dispersed audiences and ever-wider numbers of readers.[20] Parades and ceremonies were now experienced by much larger audiences than would ever witness them — audiences in the same city or across the country. At the same time, the experience of the spectacle for this vast audience was limited through the choices made by editors and reporters about which events — or parts of events — to report and how to report them. For most of the nineteenth century, parades probably played first and best to their live audiences; yet, as in the case of the early-nineteenth-century strike parades, marchers were concerned about the good opinion of the press as *part* of that audience. Strikers, as proponents of a controversial cause, strained to use devices of respectability and made sure they marched past newspaper offices. In the late nineteenth century, part of the rationale for labor and socialist spectacle may have been to garner impressive media reports. In the late twentieth century, the electronic media have pushed this tendency to its furthest limits. It is now necessary when planning a parade or a demonstration to consider the media first, to secure maximal coverage. Conversely, if a parade or demonstration receives no media coverage, it may as well not have happened; demonstration reports devoid of information about why demonstrators came together predominate.[21]

The spectacular and the commercial, linked by the last half of the nineteenth century, are now a major preoccupation of the mass media: The commercial parade, or the spectacles of the powerful, will be reported, dissected, and interpreted for a vast, remote audience. The political musterings of those with divergent, unfamiliar, or unpopular views must be spectacular to receive media notice. The first Solidarity Day labor parade, in 1981, in Washington, D.C., was overshadowed in the media by a free Simon and Garfunkel reunion concert in Central Park. On June 12, 1982, the largest demonstration in American history, the Rally for a Nuclear Freeze, received less national coverage than an annual Rose Bowl Parade.[22]

Finally, the restructuring of the early-nineteenth-century city and street helped destroy the older uses of parades and ceremonies. Philadelphia's central street layout has remained constant over two centuries, but its social geography and uses of the streets are radically different. The separation, first of home from workplace, and then the tripartite division of home, workplace, and business district accomplished by suburbanization meant that the once-close webs of family and neighborhood, labor and consumption were torn. In the twentieth century, the rise of private automotive transport added another rupture, making the streets conduits for traffic and pushing sociability and economic life to the city's edges. The movement of neighborhoods away from workplaces, and the ceding of streets to cars, changed the shape of mass parades and altered the meanings of smaller neighborhood street performances. Large, straight areas—Broad Street and Market Street, the parkways and boulevards—can be efficiently cut off, blockaded, and guarded for parades. Such spaces were not the context for earlier parades, which wound around blocks of coworkers, neighbors, and friends or circled Independence Hall. Parades are no longer performed where people live and work, but, for reasons of traffic flow, in special, denuded spaces designated by the city. In contrast, small neighborhood performances—lacking the media coverage and the prestige of official ceremonial performance space—seem invisible. Performances for neighbors have become, in a sense, private.

Nineteenth-century constraints and limitations on public uses of the street have thus been strengthened and dramatically extended. The collective uses of the streets and open spaces are now determined almost entirely by the interests of private enterprise. Private enterprise is now in the business of building privately owned spaces—such as shopping malls—which are publicly accessible and open but fit carefully selected criteria to maximize only one aspect of social existence—consumption. Because of the combined forces of commerce and the demand for order, open spaces have become much less lively milieux. Parades, as we know them today, give only a carefully prefabricated appearance of ties to a genuine community life.

A Note on Sources

Although there has been little historical writing on the public, ceremonial culture of American cities in the early nineteenth century, newspapers provide a rich, detailed, and varied data source. In the years between 1788 and 1860, scores of newspapers were published in Philadelphia, and many issues of these papers still survive. Accounts of quite a few early parades and public ceremonies exist in print, as terse as these accounts may be, but the researcher has to locate them amid the myriad other stories.

However, the variety and richness of these print sources offers the researcher an invaluable dividend. In the early nineteenth century, there was a wide spectrum of reporting and opinion in the press. Political parties, the labor movement, ethnic societies, fraternities, and religious groups all at times had their own newspapers. In addition, the emerging commercial press tried to develop news-reporting strategies to appeal to readers with different interests and affiliations. In this book I have tried, where possible, to compare the points of view of different papers in order to clarify their utility as sources.

I have relied on the following papers, published in Philadelphia except where noted. The years given after each citation refer to the issues of the paper I examined; these dates do not necessarily represent the full run of the paper's publication.

Aurora and General Advertiser, 1794—1835
Daily Chronicle, 1828—1834
Democratic Press, 1807—1829
Franklin Gazette, 1818—1824
Gazette of the United States, 1801—1804

Hazard's Register of Pennsylvania, 1828—1835
Inquirer, 1860—1900
Man (New York), 1834
Mechanics' Free Press, 1828—1832
National Gazette and Literary Register, 1820—1842
Niles' Weekly Register (Baltimore), 1811—1849
North American, 1839—1860
Pennsylvania Inquirer and National Gazette,
    1842—1850
Pennsylvanian, 1832—1861
Philadelphia Inquirer, 1829—1842
Poulson's American Daily Advertiser, 1800—1840
Public Ledger, 1836—1859
Saturday Evening Post, 1821—1850
True American, 1798—1823
United States Gazette, 1790—1847
Working Man's Advocate (New York), 1829—1833

Like other nineteenth-century serials, the vast majority
of these newspapers have never been microfilmed, and of
those that have been preserved on film, not all are available
to the public in libraries and archives. (The only copies
of many film sets are owned by private microfilming companies.) In Philadelphia, however, the Historical Society
of Pennsylvania has preserved many original issues and
series.

Notes

CHAPTER ONE

1. *United States Gazette* (Philadelphia), February 24, 1832.

2. Ibid.

3. Ibid.

4. Ibid.

5. Ibid.

6. This description of the Washington Centennial Procession is drawn from the *United States Gazette*, February 21, 22, and 24, and March 1, 1832; and *Poulson's American Daily Advertiser* (Philadelphia), February 17, 21, and 24, 1832.

7. For celebrations of Washington's Birthday by blacks, see *United States Gazette*, February 21, 1832; for women's complaints, see *Poulson's American Daily Advertiser*, February 17, 1832; for the role of the Cincinnati, see *United States Gazette*, February 24, 1832; for Philadelphia's workingmen, see Bruce Laurie, *Working People of Philadelphia, 1800–1850* (Philadelphia: Temple University Press, 1980), especially pp. 3–30, 85–104.

8. Kenneth Burke, *A Rhetoric of Motives* (New York: Prentice-Hall, 1950); following Burke, Roger D. Abrahams explores folklore as rhetorical communication in "Introductory Remarks to a Rhetorical Theory of Folklore," *Journal of American Folklore* 81 (1968): 143–58.

9. See, for example, Daniel Joseph Singal, "Beyond Consensus: Richard Hofstadter and American Historiography," *American Historical Review* 89, no. 4 (October 1984): 976–1004.

10. For the relationship between ritualization and social history, see Rhys Isaac, *The Transformation of Virginia, 1740–1790* (Chapel Hill: University of North Carolina Press, 1982).

11. E. P. Thompson, *The Making of the English Working Class*, rev. ed. (New York: Penguin Books, 1977); Thompson's important articles, especially "Patrician Society, Plebeian Culture," *Journal of Social History* 7 (1974): 382–405, have inspired much innovative work on the interrelations of popular culture, politics, and social history. Henry Glassie synthesizes trends in social history and existential approaches to anthropology in *Passing the Time in Ballymenone: Culture and History of an Ulster Community* (Philadelphia: University of Pennsylvania Press, 1982). Dell Hymes, in *Foundations in Sociolinguistics: An Ethnographic Approach* (Philadelphia: University of Pennsylvania Press, 1974), lays

out powerful premises for the study of social structures and uses of language, which suggest approaches for the study of nonlinguistic behavior in the past and the present. Although not cited extensively in this book, Hymes has shaped my concepts and strategies for the study of parades as communication. Raymond Williams has forced folklorists to think critically and historically about their discipline and has enriched the study of traditions and communities. See his *Marxism and Literature* (Oxford: Oxford University Press, 1977), and *The Country and the City* (New York: Oxford University Press, 1973).

12. Raymond Williams, *Marxism and Literature*; and Williams, "The Press and Popular Culture: An Historical Perspective," in George Boyce, James Curran, and Pauline Wingate, eds., *Newspaper History: From the 17th Century to the Present Day* (London and Beverly Hills: Constable, 1978), pp. 41–50.

13. See Kay Turner, "Introduction," *Texas Folklore Papers*, 9 (1980), pp. v–ix.

14. Raymond Williams, *Drama in a Dramatized Society* (Cambridge: Cambridge University Press, 1975).

15. Edward Muir, *Civic Ritual in Renaissance Venice* (Princeton: Princeton University Press, 1981); David M. Bergeron, *English Civic Pageantry, 1558–1642* (London: Edward Arnold, 1971); L. J. Morrissey, "English Street Theatre, 1655–1708," *Costerus* 4 (1972): 105–37; Morrissey, "English Pageant Wagons," *Eighteenth-Century Studies* 9 (1976): 353–74; Glynne Wyckham, *Early English Stages, 1300–1660*, 2 vols. (London: Routledge, Kegan Paul, 1959–1963); and Robert Darnton, "A Bourgeois Puts His World in Order: The City As Text," in Darnton, *The Great Cat Massacre and Other Episodes in French Cultural History* (New York: Basic Books, 1984), pp. 106–43.

16. Peter Burke, *Popular Culture in Early Modern Europe* (London: Temple Smith, 1978). Robert Muchembled, in *Culture populaire et culture des élites dans la France moderne (XVe–XVIIIe siècles)* (Paris: Flammarion, 1978), discusses plebeian and elite uses of processions and parades. See also, Peter Linebaugh, of Tufts University, "Silk Is the Difference," unpublished paper, 1984; and Donald Richter, "The Struggle for Hyde Park in the 1860s," *Research Studies* 42, no. 4 (December 1974): 246–55. For problems in the history of popular culture and its relation to social, economic, and religious upheavals, see Bob Scribner, "Religion, Society and Culture: Reorientating the Reformation," *History Workshop* 14 (Autumn 1982): 2–22; Natalie Z. Davis, *Society and Culture in Early Modern France* (Stanford: Stanford University Press, 1975). For nineteenth-century developments, see Robert Storch, ed., *Popular Culture and Custom in Nineteenth-Century England* (London: Croom Helm, 1982); Peter Bailey, *Leisure and Class in Victorian England: Rational Recreation and the Quest for Control, 1830–1885* (London: Routledge, Kegan Paul, 1978); Eileen Yeo and Stephen Yeo, eds., *Popular Culture and Class Conflict, 1590–1914: Explorations in the History of Labor and Leisure* (Sussex: Harvester Press, 1981); and Roy Rosenzweig, *Eight Hours for What We Will: Workers and Leisure in an Industrial City, 1870–1920* (Cambridge: Cambridge University Press, 1983).

17. Eric Hobsbawm, "The Invention of Tradition," and "Mass Producing Traditions, 1870–1914," in Eric Hobsbawm and Terence Ranger, eds., *The Invention of Tradition* (Cambridge: Cambridge University Press, 1982), pp. 1–14, 263–307; and George L. Mosse, *The Nationalization of the Masses* (New York: New American Library, 1977).

18. James Leith, *Media and Revolution: Molding a New Citizenry in France During the Terror* (Toronto: Hunter Rose, 1968); Mona Ozouf, *La fête révolutionnaire, 1789–1799* (Paris: Editions Gallimard, 1976); Ozouf, "Le Cortège et la ville: Les Itinéraires Parisiens des fêtes révolutionnaires," *Annales: Économies, sociétés, cultures* 26 (1972): 896–916; Ozouf, "Space and Time in the Festivals of the French Revolution," *Comparative Studies in Society and History* 17 (1973): 371–84; John Rearick, "Festivals in Modern France: The Experience of the Third Republic," *Journal of Contemporary History* 12 (1977): 435–60; Eugen Weber, *Peasants into Frenchmen* (Stanford: Stanford University Press, 1976); and Hobsbawm, "Mass Producing Traditions," and "Invention of Tradition."

19. Charles D. Deshler, "How the Declaration Was Received in the Old Thirteen," *Harper's New Monthly Magazine* 85 (June 1892): 165–87. For a Frazerian myth-ritualist and antihistorical interpretation of the uses of public ritual in Revolutionary War mobilization, see Peter Shaw, *American Patriots and the Rituals of Revolution* (Cambridge: Harvard University Press, 1981), pp. 204–31.

20. George W. Douglas, *The American Book of Days*, 3rd ed., Jane M. Hatch, comp. and ed. (1948; repr., New York: H. W. Wilson, 1978), pp. 197–204; Stewart Culin, "Note," *Pennsylvania Magazine of History and Biography* 24 (1900): 127–28.

21. For English popular royalism, see Thomas W. Lacquer, "The Queen Caroline Affair: Politics as Art in the Reign of George IV," *Journal of Modern History* 54 (1982): 417–66. For Washington's ceremonial activities, see W. S. Baker, "Washington After the Revolution, 1784–1799," *Pennsylvania Magazine of History and Biography* 20 (1896): 178, 334, 351, 473–74, 498–99; and 21 (1897): 34–35, 187–88.

22. William Duane, Irish-born Philadelphia editor, railed against the pretentious military displays of the city's antidemocratic elite. Planning to beat them at their own game, he outshone them in the street with his own well-trained, well-dressed Militia Legion; see Kim Phillips, "William Duane, Revolutionary Editor," doctoral dissertation, University of California, Berkeley, 1968, pp. 71–83, 97.

23. Michael Kammen, *A Season of Youth: The American Revolution and the Historical Imagination* (New York: Knopf, 1978); Alexis de Tocqueville, ed. J. P. Mayer, trans. George Lawrence, *Democracy in America* (Garden City, N.Y.: Doubleday Anchor Books, 1969), pp. 235–37, 465–70; "Holidays," *North American Review* 84 (April 1857): 331–63.

24. For Evacuation Day, see Sean Wilentz, "Artisan Republican Festivals and the Rise of Class Conflict in New York City, 1788–1837," in Michael H. Frisch and Daniel J. Walkowitz, eds., *Working-Class America: Essays on Labor, Community and American Society* (Urbana: University of Illinois Press, 1983), pp. 37–77.

25. Douglas, *Book of Days*, pp. 235–37, 359–62; "Historic Processions in Boston," *Bostonian Society Publications* 5 (1908): 65–119; and "Funeral Processions in Boston," *Bostonian Society Publications* 4 (1907): 125–49.

26. Baker, "Washington After the Revolution"; and Samuel Hazard, ed., *Register of Pennsylvania* (Philadelphia) 12 (October 1833): 251–52. This magazine appeared under slightly different names during this period. We shall refer to it as the *Register of Pennsylvania*, or *Register*, throughout.

27. Harold Donaldson Eberlein and Courtlandt Van Dyke Hubbard, *The Diary of Independence Hall* (Philadelphia: J. B. Lippincott, 1948), pp. 79–81, 325.

28. For the resurrection of "guild" pageantry and rituals, see Wilentz, "Artisan Republican Festivals."

29. The larger history of North American folk drama remains to be written.

30. Historical work on the techniques and uses of plebeian protest has increased in recent years with the rediscovery of "the crowd"; see George F. Rudé, *The Crowd in History: A Study of Popular Disturbances in France and England, 1730–1848* (New York: Wiley, 1964). For early American traditions of crowd action, see Alfred F. Young, "English Plebeian Culture and Eighteenth Century American Radicalism," in Margaret Jacob and James Jacob, eds., *The Origins of Anglo-American Radicalism* (London and New York: Allen Unwin, 1983), pp. 185–212. To understand what the so-called inarticulate aimed to communicate through direct action, whether violent or nonviolent, see Marcus Rediker, " 'Good Hands, Stout Heart and Fast Feet': The History and Culture of Working People in Early America," *Labour/Le Travailleur* 10 (1982): 123–44. See also Pauline Maier, *From Resistance to Revolution: Colonial Radicals and the Development of American Opposition to Britain, 1765–1776* (New York: Vintage, 1974); and Alfred F. Young, ed., *The American Revolution: Explorations in the History of American Radicalism* (DeKalb: Northern Illinois University Press, 1976).

31. Folklorists, concerned in recent years with the concept of performance, have tried to use it to better understand communication. Central to this goal is the development of tools for the careful analysis of context, the social factors and settings that infuse performance with meaning. The problem posed by the notion of context, however, is not how best to record and document contextual features of folkloric performance, but how to define it all. Which features are relevant to a description of the milieu (or medium) determining communication? See all the essays in Dan Ben-Amos and Kenneth Goldstein, eds., *Folklore: Performance and Communication* (Mouton: The Hague, 1975), and especially Dell Hymes, "Breakthrough into Performance," pp. 11–74. See also Ben-Amos, "Toward a Definition of Folklore in Context," *Journal of American Folklore* 84 (1971): 3–15.

32. Jurgen Habermas, "The Public Sphere: An Encyclopedia Article," *New German Critique* 1 (1974): 49–55; Eberhard Knodler-Bunte, "The Proletarian Public Sphere and Political Organization: An Analysis of

Osker Negt and Alexander Kluge's *The Public Sphere and Political Experience*," *New German Critique* 2 (1975): 51–75.

33. In recent cultural anthropology, conflict is studied as "symbolic"; after social conflict is ritually expressed in the public sphere, society returns to "normal." See Victor Turner, *The Ritual Process: Structure and Anti-Structure* (Chicago: Aldine, 1969); Turner, *Dramas, Fields and Metaphors: Symbolic Action in Human Society* (Ithaca: Cornell University Press, 1974); for criticism, see Jack Goody, "Against Ritual," in Sally F. Moore and Barbara Myerhoff, *Secular Ritual* (Amsterdam: Van Gorcum, 1977), pp. 25–35.

34. Émile Durkheim, quoted by Hilda Kuper, "The Language of Sites and the Politics of Space," *American Anthropologist* 74 (1972): 411–25.

35. For example, Peter Buckley, "To the Opera House: Culture and Society in New York City, 1820–1860," doctoral dissertation, State University of New York at Stony Brook, 1984, pp. 271–342.

36. Sandra K. D. Stahl, "The Oral Personal Narrative in Its Generic Context," *Fabula* 18 (1977): 18–39.

37. "Popular culture" is used here in its older sense; that is, of or relating to the people, especially that unofficial, noncommercial, and customary culture commonly shared among (but not necessarily limited to) the demographically dominant poor and working people (the majority in any culture). Here popular culture does not mean the industrially produced, standardized cultural forms produced for cheap sale to "mass" audiences (e.g., the comic book); nevertheless, popular culture in the sense of cheap, commercially produced materials (comic almanacs, forerunners of comic books) filled with imagery and ideas aimed at a working-class audience was being invented in the urban United States between 1800 and 1860. See Dan Schiller, *Objectivity and the News: The Penny Press and the Rise of Commercial Journalism* (Philadelphia: University of Pennsylvania Press, 1981); Stewart Ewen and Elizabeth Ewen, *Channels of Desire: Mass Images and the Shaping of American Consciousness* (New York: McGraw-Hill, 1982), pp. 13–38. There is no history of the relationship between popular culture of the first, oral, and customary variety and the cheap, commercially produced variety, yet their chronologies overlap. Commercial culture undoubtedly drew heavily on oral traditions, and the oral tradition and mass media continue to share genres, forms, and content. See, for examples, Jerry Palmer, *Thrillers: Genesis and Structure of a Popular Genre* (London: Edward Arnold, 1978); Victor Neuberg, *Popular Literature: A History and Guide* (New York: Penguin, 1977); and Martha Vicinus, *The Industrial Muse: A Study of Nineteenth-Century British Working-Class Literature* (London: Croom Helm, 1974).

The proprietors of popular culture were often called "the populace," the "lower sort," or (sarcastically) "the public" in the late eighteenth and early nineteenth centuries. Today these people are sometimes discounted by historians' labels, such as "the inarticulate," or "ordinary people." For "inarticulate" people, the bearers of popular culture have left a record in print, material culture, and oral tradition of an astonishing and extraordinary range of expression. See Peter Burke, *Popular Culture in Early Modern Europe* (London: Temple Smith, 1978); and Henry Glassie, *Pattern in the Material Culture of the South Eastern United States* (Philadelphia: University of Pennsylvania Press, 1969). In the early nineteenth century, the people to whom popular culture belonged were no undifferentiated mass, various as they were in the United States by their regional and ethnic origins, languages, and occupations.

38. Dell Hymes, "Folklore's Nature and the Sun's Myth," *Journal of American Folklore* 88 (1975): 35–69.

39. Williams, *Marxism and Literature*, pp. 108–27.

40. Luigi Lombardi-Satriani, "Folklore as Culture of Contestation," *Journal of the Folklore Institute* 11 (1975): 99–121. Cf. M. A. K. Halliday, "Anti-Languages," *American Anthropologist* 78 (1976): 570–84; for vernacular culture as oppositional culture, see Marcus Rediker, "Under the Banner of King Death: The Social World of Anglo-American Pirates, 1716–1726," *William and Mary Quarterly*, 3rd ser., 38 (April 1981): 203–27.

41. Peter Burke, *Popular Culture in Early Modern Europe*; E. P. Thompson, "Patrician Society, Plebeian Culture," pp. 382–405.

42. For an important assessment of commercial culture's role in transforming vernacular culture, see Rosenzweig, *Eight Hours for What We Will*; see also, Francis Couvares, "The Triumph of Commerce: Mass Culture and Class Culture in Pittsburgh," in Frisch and Walkowitz, eds., *Working-Class America*, pp. 123–52.

43. Couvares, "The Triumph of Commerce."

44. A full and critical history of American culture would examine the blending of public, commercial, and state influences in such perennials as Christmas, Thanksgiving, and Memorial Day, and their implications for Raymond Williams's notion of the selective tradition (*Marxism and Literature*, pp. 108–27).

45. The notion of tradition bearers is familiar to folklorists from Carl Von Sydow's *Selected Papers in Folklore* (Copenhagen: Rosenkilde and Bagger, 1948). Von Sydow's crucial insight that people rather than abstract "forces" shape traditions is applicable beyond the psychological study of the individual in culture. Von Sydow recommends studying the processes of making or producing cultural forms, as does Raymond Williams in *Marxism and Literature*.

46. E. P. Thompson, "The Moral Economy of the English Crowd in the Eighteenth Century," *Past and Present* 50 (1971): 76–136; Henry Glassie, *Folk Housing in Middle Virginia* (Knoxville: University of Tennessee Press, 1976); and Isaac, *Transformation of Virginia*.

47. "Peter Single" (pseud.), "Existing Things," *Mechanics' Free Press* (Philadelphia), April 19 and October 18, 1828, January 9, 1830.

CHAPTER TWO

1. Diane Lindstrom, *Economic Development in the Philadelphia Region, 1810–1850* (New York: Columbia University Press, 1978), pp. 1–54; Bruce Laurie, *Working People of Philadelphia, 1800–1850* (Philadelphia: Temple University Press, 1980), pp. 3–30.

2. Lindstrom, *Philadelphia Region*, pp. 24–25; Laurie, *Working People*, pp. 8–10; James T. Lemon, *The Best Poor Man's Country: A Geographical Study of Early Southeastern Pennsylvania* (Baltimore: Johns Hopkins University Press, 1976), pp. 73–92; Sam Bass Warner, *The Private City: Philadelphia in Three Periods of Its Growth* (Philadelphia: University of Pennsylvania Press, 1968), pp. 56–57.

3. Cynthia Jane Shelton, "The Mills of Manayunk: Early Industrialization and Social Conflict in the Philadelphia Region, 1787–1837," doctoral dissertation, University of California, Los Angeles, 1982, pp. 110–69.

4. Lindstrom, *Philadelphia Region*, pp. 1–24; and Jeffrey Williamson and Peter Lindert, "Long Term Trends in American Wealth Inequality," in James D. Smith, ed., *Modelling the Distribution and Intergenerational Transmission of Wealth* (Chicago: University of Chicago Press, 1980), pp. 9–93.

5. Edward Pessen, *Riches, Class, and Power Before the Civil War* (Lexington, Mass.: D. C. Heath, 1973), pp. 73–163.

6. For information on the eighteenth century, see Gary B. Nash, "Up from the Bottom in Franklin's Philadelphia," *Past and Present* 77 (1977): 58–83; for the rise of economic inequality, see Laurie, *Working People*, pp. 3–104. Historians disagree about how to name early-nineteenth-century American class structure; nevertheless, the rise of systematic, structural inequalities of wealth and power has been amply demonstrated. The distinction between two classes, the working class and the propertied or business class, follows Michael B. Katz, Mark J. Stern, and Michael Doucet, *The Social Organization of Early Industrial Capitalism* (Cambridge: Harvard University Press, 1982). The term *middle class* has been avoided because of its theoretical vagueness. Despite evidence of some social mobility and the fact that some workers and artisans straddled the boundaries between the working class and the business class, it is not clear that a "middle class" existed in early-nineteenth-century America as a discrete entity, separate in interests and sources of power from both labor and capital; see ibid., and Anthony Giddens, *The Class Structure of Advanced Societies* (New York: Harper & Row, 1975). As Chapter Five will show, new values that mediated between the working class and the propertied were emerging—and very important—in the antebellum era.

7. Pessen, *Riches, Class, and Power*, pp. 281–301.

8. Louis H. Arky, "The Mechanic's Union of Trade Associations and the Formation of the Workingmen's Movement," *Pennsylvania Magazine of History and Biography* 76 (1952): 142–76; William A. Sullivan, "A Decade of Labor Strife," *Pennsylvania History* 17 (1950): 23–38; William A. Sullivan, *The Industrial Worker in Pennsylvania, 1800–1840* (Harrisburg: Pennsylvania Historic and Museum Commission, 1955); Laurie,

Working People, pp. 67–83, 161–87; and Sean Wilentz, *Chants Demo-cratic: New York City and the Rise of the American Working Class, 1788–1850* (New York: Oxford University Press, 1984).

9. Lindstrom, *Philadelphia Region,* pp. 24–54; Walter S. Glazer, "Participation and Power: Voluntary Associations and the Functional Organization of Cincinnati in 1840," *Historical Methods Newsletter* 5 (1972): 151–68; Mary P. Ryan traces the formation of male and female networks of interest and sociability in *Cradle of the Middle Class: The Family in Oneida County, New York, 1790–1865* (Cambridge: Cambridge University Press, 1981), pp. 105–44; Katz, Stern, and Doucet, *Early In-dustrial Capitalism,* pp. 50–53, 64–107, 356–62; and Pessen, *Riches, Class, and Power,* pp. 251–80.

10. Michael Feldberg, "The Crowd in Philadelphia History," *Labor History* 15 (1974): 323–36; Elizabeth Geffen, "Violence in Philadelphia in the 1840s and 1850s," *Pennsylvania History* 36 (1969): 381–410; and W. M. Thackeray, quoted in Joseph Jackson, *Literary Landmarks of Philadelphia* (Philadelphia: David McKay, 1939), frontis.

11. For the history of European cities as stages for culture, see An-thony Vidler, "The Scenes of the Street: Transformations in Idea and Reality, 1750–1871," in Stanford Anderson, ed., *On Streets* (Cambridge: M.I.T. Press, 1978), pp. 29–111. For medieval cities, see Lewis Mumford, *The City in History: Its Origins, Its Transformations, and Its Prospects* (New York: Harcourt, Brace and World, 1961), pp. 163, 167, 277–80. For the North American commercial city forms, see Ian Davey and Michael Doucet, "Appendix One: The Social Geography of a Commercial City, ca. 1853," in Michael B. Katz, *The People of Hamilton, Canada West: Family and Class in a Mid-Nineteenth-Century City* (Cambridge: Har-vard University Press, 1975), pp. 319–42.

12. Sylvia Doughty Fries, *The Urban Idea in Colonial America* (Phil-adelphia: Temple University Press, 1977), pp. 97–101.

13. Harold Donaldson Eberlein and Courtlandt Van Dyke Hubbard, *The Diary of Independence Hall* (Philadelphia: J. B. Lippincott, 1948), pp. 13–14, 23, 59, 92.

14. J. Thomas Scharf and Thompson Westcott, *The History of Phila-delphia, 1609–1884,* 3 vols. (Philadelphia: L. H. Everts, 1884) 1:649 and 2:857; and John F. Watson, *The Annals of Philadelphia and Pennsyl-vania,* (Philadelphia: Carey & Hart, 1830), and rev. ed. in 3 vols., ed. Willis P. Hazard (Philadelphia: Edwin S. Stuart, 1900) 1:350–51.

15. Watson, *Annals* 1:276–81, 436–41, 477–83, 485–98.

16. In the eighteenth century, the city was tightly clustered along the north-south streets close to the Delaware; after 1800 it spread west, north, and south. For the social geography of late-eighteenth-century Philadel-phia, see Mary Schweitzer's unpublished paper, "Occupation, Residence and Real Estate Values in Philadelphia, 1790" (Philadelphia Center for Early American Studies Seminar, October 26, 1984). See also, Fries, *Urban Idea in Colonial America,* pp. 89–96; Gwendolyn Wright, *Build-ing the Dream: A Social History of Housing in America* (Cambridge: M.I.T. Press, 1981), pp. 24–40; and Pessen, *Riches, Class, and Power,* pp. 183–89.

17. Class and occupational neighborhoods were recognized by Phila-delphians at least as early as 1790; see Schweitzer, "Occupation, Resi-

dence and Real Estate Values." For speculation in housing and real estate, see Sam Bass Warner, *The Private City*, pp. 49–62, 126–40; for territoriality, see Bruce Laurie, "Fire Companies and Gangs in Southwark," in Allen F. Davis and Mark Haller, eds., *The Peoples of Philadelphia: A History of Ethnic Groups and Lower Class Life, 1790–1940* (Philadelphia: Temple University Press, 1973), pp. 71–87; for Philadelphia's wealthy neighborhoods, see Pessen, *Riches, Class, and Power*, pp. 183–89.

18. Fries, *Urban Idea in Colonial America*, pp. 89–96. Frances Trollope, *Domestic Manners of the Americans* (London, 1832), p. 210; for Rebecca Davis, see Tillie Olsen, "Rebecca Harding Davis," in *Silences* (New York: Dell, Laurel Ed., 1978), p. 116.

19. Thomas Czarnowski, "The Street As Communications Artifact," in Anderson, ed., *On Streets*, pp. 207–12; and François Bedarida and Anthony Sutcliffe, "The Street and The Structure of Life in the City," *Journal of Urban History* 6 (1980): 379–96.

20. For prohibition of theatre and entertainments in the city, see William S. Dye, "Pennsylvania Against the Theatre," *Pennsylvania Magazine of History and Biography* 55 (1931): 333–71. For the history of theatricals in the early nineteenth century, see Arthur H. Wilson, *A History of the Philadelphia Theatre, 1835–1855* (Philadelphia: University of Pennsylvania Press, 1935); and Lawrence W. Levine, "William Shakespeare and the American People: A Study in Cultural Transformation," *American Historical Review* 89 (February 1984): 34–66.

21. For class relations in the theatre, see Alexander Saxton, "Blackface Minstrelsy and Jacksonian Ideology," *American Quarterly* 27 (1975): 3–28; and Peter Buckley, " 'A Privileged Place': New York Theatre Riots, 1817–1849" (paper presented at the annual meeting of the Organization of American Historians, Philadelphia, April 1, 1982). For criticism of the moral effects of theatres and plays, see A Friend to the Theatre, *An Enquiry into the Conditions and Influence of the Brothels in Connection with the Theatres at Philadelphia* (Philadelphia, pamphlet, 1834). Peter Buckley and Michael Meranze generously shared their research on reformers' opposition to the theatre.

22. Christine Stansell, "Women, Children and the Uses of the Street: Class and Gender Conflict in New York City, 1850–1860," *Feminist Studies* 8 (1982): 308–35.

23. Sean Wilentz, "Crime, Poverty and the Streets of New York: The Diary of William H. Bell, 1850–51," *History Workshop* 7 (1979): 126–55; and "Disgusting Exhibitions," *Public Ledger* (Philadelphia), June 26, 1844. Philadelphia instituted a Department of Beggar Detectives during the Panic of 1857; City of Philadelphia, Department of the Beggar Detectives, *Report*, 1857–58, Philadelphia City Archives.

24. See, for example, a letter from "Veron," *Mechanics' Free Press* (Philadelphia), April 26, 1828. Objections to the suppression of charcoal vendors and scavengers claimed vendors' customary right to use a cry or bell and commented on the unquestioned use of rattles by the night watch; ibid, October 23, 1830.

25. For resistance to fines collectors, see *Niles' Weekly Register* (Baltimore), April 4, 1835, p. 76; July 20, 1833, p. 344; and September 14, 1833, p. 47. For resistance to the destruction of markets to make way for rail-

roads, see *United States Gazette* (Philadelphia) June 5, 1835. For opposition to the corporate use of streets to build rail lines, phrased in terms of the streets' public nature, see *Public Ledger*, June 22, 1842. For resistance to strikebreakers, see *Public Ledger*, August 19, 1842.

26. Stansell, "Class and Gender Conflict"; and Nancy F. Cott, *The Bonds of Womanhood: 'Woman's Sphere' in New England, 1780–1835* (New Haven: Yale University Press, 1977).

27. Warner, *Private City*, pp. 49–62, 126–40; Stuart Blumin, "Residential Mobility in Nineteenth-Century Philadelphia," in Davis and Haller, eds., *Peoples of Philadelphia*, pp. 37–51. The Schuylkill side of the city, for example, had a neighborhood named "Rotten Row," and the Schuylkill docks were thought of as an underworld; see Howard O. Sprogel, *The Philadelphia Police, Past and Present* (Philadelphia, privately published, 1887), pp. 622–30. For a description of Southwark as a demonic region, see *Public Ledger*, January 3, 1854.

28. Fries, *Urban Idea in Colonial America*, pp. 97–101; Scharf and Westcott, *History of Philadelphia* 3:1845; Watson, *Annals* 2:397; and Samuel Hazard, ed., *Register of Pennsylvania* (Philadelphia) 12 (July 1833): 8.

29. Watson, *Annals* 2:265; and Eberlein and Hubbard, *Independence Hall*, pp. 175–80.

30. Ibid., pp. 219, 286, 312, 358. For the importance of public reading aloud, proclamation, and ritual in the Revolution, cf. Rhys Issac, "Dramatizing the Ideology of Revolution: Popular Mobilization in Virginia, 1774–1776," *William and Mary Quarterly*, 3rd ser., 37 (1980): 29–52.

31. Watson, *Annals* 1:397.

32. *United States Gazette*, July 1, 1823; Scharf and Westcott, *History of Philadelphia* 1:649 and 2:857. For the history of the movement to abolish spectacular public punishment in Pennsylvania, see Michael Meranze, "The Penitential Ideal in Late Eighteenth-Century Philadelphia," *Pennsylvania Magazine of History and Biography* CVIII, no. 4 (October 1984): 419–40.

33. *Mechanics' Free Press*, October 3, 1829.

34. *Pennsylvanian* (Philadelphia), June 3–7, 9, 10, 12, 1835. The *North American* (Philadelphia), November 12, 1857, provides an example of the need to obtain a permit to use the Square.

35. See, for example, Donald M. Scott, "The Popular Lecture and the Creation of the Public in Mid-Nineteenth Century America," *Journal of American History* 66 (1980): 791–809.

36. Gary E. Nash, " 'To Arise Out of the Dust': Absalom Jones and the African Church of Philadelphia, 1785–1795" (paper presented to the Philadelphia Center for Early American Studies Seminar, September 24, 1982).

37. Geffen, "Violence in Philadelphia"; *History of Pennsylvania Hall, Which Was Destroyed by a Mob on the 17th of May, 1838* (Philadelphia, 1838; repr. ed., New York: Negro Universities Press, 1969).

38. Christopher Hill, "The Uses of Sabbatarianism," in *Society and Puritanism in Pre-Revolutionary England*, 2nd ed., (New York: Schocken, 1967), pp. 145–218; Peter Burke, *Popular Culture in Early Modern Europe* (London: Temple Smith, 1978); and R. W. Malcolmson,

Popular Recreations in English Society, 1700–1850 (Cambridge: Cambridge University Press, 1973).

39. Dye, "Pennsylvania Against the Theatre."

40. Eric Foner, *Tom Paine and Revolutionary America* (New York: Oxford University Press, 1976), pp. 50–51.

41. Hazard, *Register* 1 (April 1828): 154 (a complaint from 1732), 255 (from 1738), 271 (from 1741).

42. The most dramatic eruption of popular radicalism in the city was the Fort Wilson riot, which is analyzed by Steven J. Rosswurm in "Arms, Culture and Class: The Philadelphia Militias and the 'Lower Orders' in the American Revolution," doctoral dissertation, Northern Illinois University, DeKalb, 1977, pp. 430–61.

43. *Democratic Press* (Philadelphia), May 12, 1825. Crowds also got out of control at pleasure gardens; see *Niles' Weekly Register*, October 31, 1819, pp. 143–44; and Geffen, "Violence in Philadelphia."

44. Geffen, "Violence in Philadelphia"; David Grimstead, "Rioting in Its Jacksonian Setting," *American Historical Review* 77 (1972): 361–97.

45. Laurie, *Working People*, pp. 3–30; and Shelton, "Mills of Manayunk," pp. 192–94.

46. Laurie, *Working People*, pp. 33–52; Douglas Reid, "The Decline of Saint Monday, 1766–1876," *Past and Present* 71 (1976): 76–101; E. P. Thompson, "Time, Work, Discipline and Industrial Capitalism," *Past and Present* 38 (1967): 56–97; and Sidney Pollard, "Factory Discipline in the Industrial Revolution," *Economic History Review*, 2nd ser., 16 (1963): 254–71.

47. Laurie, *Working People*, pp. 53–104.

48. The history of how festivity, industrial work, and poverty are related remains to be written. For some contributions, see J. H. Plumb, "The Commercialization of Leisure in Eighteenth-Century England," in J. H. Plumb, Neil McKendrick, and John Brewer, eds., *The Birth of a Consumer Society: The Commercialization of Eighteenth-Century England* (Bloomington: Indiana University Press, 1982); Roy Rosenzweig, *Eight Hours for What We Will: Workers and Leisure in an Industrial City, 1870–1920* (Cambridge: Cambridge University Press, 1983); James Walvin, *Leisure and Society, 1830–1950* (New York and London; Longmans, 1978); Peter Bailey, *Leisure and Class in Victorian England: Rational Recreation and the Quest for Control, 1830–1885* (London: Routledge, Kegan Paul, 1978); Reid, "Decline of Saint Monday"; and Herbert H. Gutman, *Work, Culture and Society in Industrializing America* (New York: Vintage, 1977), pp. 3–78.

49. Susan G. Davis, "'Making Night Hideous': Christmas Revelry and Public Order in Nineteenth-Century Philadelphia," *American Quarterly* 34 (1982): 185–99; and Alfred Shoemaker, *Christmas in Pennsylvania: A Folk-Cultural Study* (Kutztown: Pennsylvania Folklife Society, 1959).

50. Davis, "'Making Night Hideous.'"

51. *Daily Chronicle* (Philadelphia), December 26, 1833.

52. J. Ritchie Garrison, "Battalion Day: Militia Muster and Frolic in Pennsylvania Before the Civil War," *Pennsylvania Folklife* 26 (1976–77): 2–12.

53. See, for example, *Democratic Press*, April 30, 1808.

54. *Public Ledger*, May 10, 1836.

55. *Saturday Evening Post* (Philadelphia), June 4, 1828.

56. *Public Ledger*, July 12, 1837.

57. Dinners organized by political clubs are described in papers sponsored by parties and factions. The party press was the predominant newspaper form in the United States until the rise of the labor press and the cheap or "penny" press in the 1830s. Some examples of these accounts appear in *Poulson's American Daily Advertiser* (Philadelphia), July 3, 1801; *True American* (Philadelphia), July 4, 1805; and *Democratic Press*, July 6, 1810. The dinner as a forum for oratory is discussed in Howard H. Martin, "Orations on the Anniversary of American Independence, 1776–1876," doctoral dissertation, Evanston, Northwestern University, 1955, pp. 11–94. Fletcher M. Green details the context of southern toasting traditions in "Listen to the Eagle Scream: One Hundred Years of the Fourth of July in North Carolina, (1776–1876)," *North Carolina Historical Review* 31 (1954): 295–320, 529–49.

58. See, for example, "Extracts from the Diary of Thomas Franklin Pleasants, 1814," *Pennsylvania Magazine of History and Biography* 39 (1915): 322-31.

59. For size of the party presses' readership, see Frank Luther Mott, *American Journalism—A History, 1690–1960*, 3rd ed., (New York: Macmillan, 1962), pp. 202–3, 303; and Dan Schiller, *Objectivity and the News: The Public and the Rise of Commercial Journalism* (Philadelphia: University of Pennsylvania Press, 1981), pp. 12–13.

60. For numerous examples, see W. A. Newman Dorland, "The Second Troop Philadelphia City Cavalry," *Pennsylvania Magazine of History and Biography* 47 (1923): 264, 269, 362–63; see also *United States Gazette*, July 5, 1821, and July 5, 1834.

61. Martin, "Orations," pp. 11–94.

62. *Record of Burials, 1730–1831*, Old Swedes' Church (Gloria Dei), Philadelphia, contains notes on informal July Fourth frolics, or dances, in the Southwark district; for an example from 1801, see p. 176. This source was brought to my attention by Susan Klepp.

63. Some Philadelphia crafts and trades celebrated traditional occupational holidays, such as the shoemakers' holiday, St. Crispin's Day. Early in the nineteenth century Philadelphia printers celebrated Benjamin Franklin's birthday. These practices seem to have been more vigorous and popular in New York City than in Philadelphia. See Sean Wilentz, "Artisan Republican Festivals and the Rise of Class Conflict in New York City, 1788–1837," in Michael H. Frisch and Daniel J. Walkowitz, eds., *Working-Class America: Essays on Labor, Community and American Society* (Urbana: University of Illinois Press, 1983), pp. 37–77.

64. Shelton, "Mills of Manayunk," pp. 199–200; and William Sisson, "From Farm to Factory: Work Values and Discipline in Two Early Textile Mills," *Working Papers from the Regional Economic History Research Center* 4 (1981): 15.

65. *Poulson's Daily Advertiser*, July 6, 1822.

66. *United States Gazette*, July 1, 1823.

67. *Public Ledger*, July 4, 1839.

68. Ibid., July 4, 1844.

69. *Pennsylvanian*, July 6, 1850.

70. *Mechanics' Free Press*, June 6, 1829.

71. Ibid., June 20, 1829.

72. Nativists' uses of the Fourth of July have never been studied in their own right, but see David Montgomery, "The Shuttle and the Cross: Weavers and Artisans in the Kensington Riots of 1844," *Journal of Social History* 5 (1972): 411–46.

73. Sidney Fisher, for example, loathed the day; see Nicholas B. Wainwright, ed., *A Philadelphia Perspective: The Diary of Sidney George Fisher* (Philadelphia: Historical Society of Philadelphia, 1967), pp. 224, 258, 476, 518; and *North American*, September 4, 1839.

74. This story is still untold, but see Davis, "'Making Night Hideous'"; and Rosenzweig, *Eight Hours for What We Will*, pp. 153–68.

75. Frederick Douglass, "What to the Slave is the Fourth of July?" *Black Scholar* 7 (1976): 32–37; Philip S. Foner, "Black Participation in the Centennial of 1876," *Phylon* 39 (1974): 283–86; Leonard I. Sweet, "The Fourth of July and Black Americans in the Nineteenth Century: Northern Leadership Opinion Within the Context of Black Experience," *Journal of Negro History* 61 (1976): 256–75; and Benjamin Quarles, "Antebellum Free Blacks and the 'Spirit of '76,'" *Journal of Negro History* 61 (1976): 229–42.

Philadelphia had a long-standing free black community clustered at the southeastern edge of the old city center and along Cedar (South) Street. From the early nineteenth century on, blacks competed with white neighbors for jobs and resources, achieving relative strength in unskilled trades, in a few guilds, and in the exclusivity of black-defined occupations before the Civil War. Social and political conditions worsened for Philadelphia blacks after the 1830s, when Pennsylvania rescinded their right to vote and interracial attempts at labor organization collapsed. See Emma J. Lapsansky, "A Haven for Those Low in the World: South Street Philadelphia, 1762–1854," doctoral dissertation, University of Pennsylvania, 1975; and W. E. B. DuBois, *The Philadelphia Negro* (repr. ed.; New York: Schocken, 1970).

76. Sweet, "Fourth of July and Black Americans."

77. *Public Ledger*, August 2 and 3, 1842. In contrast, late-eighteenth-century black and white Philadelphians working together in the antislavery cause appeared together in ceremonial, public roles. See Nash, "'To Arise Out of the Dust.'"

78. *Public Ledger*, December 28, 1840.

79. Watson, *Annals* 2:261.

80. Doris Yoakum, "Women's Introduction to the American Platform," in William N. Brigance, ed., *A History and Criticism of American Public Address*, vol. 1 (New York and London: McGraw-Hill, 1943), pp. 153–89; Gerda Lerner, *Black Women in White America: A Documentary History* (New York: Pantheon, 1972), p. 83; Gerda Lerner, *The Grimké Sisters of North Carolina: Pioneers for Women's Rights and Abolition* (New York: Schocken, 1971), pp. 187–89; Eleanor Flexner, *Century of Struggle: The Women's Rights Movement in the United States* (New York: Athenaeum, 1973), pp. 21–28, 51; and Angela Y. Davis, *Women, Race and Class* (New York: Random House, 1981), pp. 30–69. Delores Hayden has expanded

our understanding of women's relation to public spaces in *Redesigning the American Dream: The Future of Housing, Work and Family Life* (New York: Norton, 1984), pp. 24–28, 209–24.

Historians who argue that nineteenth-century American women had no public role overstate the case and underestimate women's social and political activism: Antebellum women in the eastern part of the country had invented a variety of influential public roles and stances. Public roles and public *ceremonial* presence, however, are not the same thing. The limitations on female self-representation in the streets and on hustings, despite women's political energies, underscore the special, highly charged nature of public terrains; see Nancy A. Hewitt, *Women's Activism and Social Change: Rochester, New York, 1822–1872* (Ithaca: Cornell University Press, 1984).

81. *Poulson's American Daily Advertiser*, February 17, 1832. Women dressed as figures of purity appeared in temperance processions; see *Public Ledger*, July 2–4, 6, 1840.

82. Dennis Clark, *The Irish Relations: Trials of an Immigrant Tradition* (Rutherford, N.J.: Fairleigh Dickinson University Press, 1982), pp. 193–203; and *Niles' Weekly Register*, April 3, 1819, pp. 71–72, and April 5, 1823, pp. 105–7.

Philadelphia was home to many Protestant (Ulster) Irish and Catholic Irish. Thus, July 12 (the anniversary of defeat of the Catholic Republican forces by William of Orange at the Battle of the Boyne) and Saint Patrick's Day became traditional days for parades and factional brawling between Orangemen and the Sons of Erin (Hibernians).

CHAPTER THREE

1. Samuel Hazard, ed., *Register of Pennsylvania* (Philadelphia), 6 (October, 1830): 245–46; for details and rhetoric of the ceremony, the following account is quoted from the *Register*:

The day was ushered in with a national salute of artillery; and at all points, from the theatres, large buildings and public houses, the tri-colored flag and the American Standard waved together.

At an early hour, the members of various volunteer companies were seen hastening to their several places of *rendezvous*, and the citizens were on the alert to enjoy the sight which each separate parade offered.

A battalion of volunteers was formed in Library Street, in front of the Military Hall, under the command of Captain James Page. We noticed among these, Capt. Page's handsome company of State Fencibles, and Capt. Niles' company of Greys, whose soldierly appearance and deportment always reflect so much honor on the officers and individuals of the corps. Capt. Charles Schreiner's well appointed and handsome company was on the ground . . . Captain Niles' company of Greys bore a splendid *tri coloured banner*, handsomely decorated, with a likeness of Lafayette in the center (white) stripe. About 10 o'clock A.M. this battalion marched into north Eighth Street, and formed a line fronting east on the dwelling of John M. Chapron, Esq., where Captain Page's company was to receive a *Standard*.

PRESENTATION

The two bands of music were drawn up, on the right and left of the door, and a guard placed to preserve order—and we ought to do credit to the persuasion of Capt. Page, which fairly conquered the turbulency of the crowd.—The TRI COLORED FLAG was then brought from the house and greeted with shouts from the people, the band playing the Marseillaise Hymn. Miss EMILIE CHAPRON then came forward, supported by Mr. Tetterill and Mr. Brazier, and presented to Capt. Page the standard, with the following

ADDRESS

"Captain Page:—It is with feelings of the most joyful emotion, that I perform the pleasing duty of presenting to the citizen soldiers under your command the Tri-Colored Banner, which has so lately been the signal, round which the brave citizens of France, in the successful defense of their right to be represented in the councils of their nation, to the free exercise of their religion after that form of worship which shall seem most proper to each, to the uncontrolled expression and communication of their opinion on all subjects and to perfect equality in the eyes of the law, between every individual in the nation.

"America had marked from afar, with mingled feelings of indignation and sympathy, of disappointment and hope, the long protracted sufferings of France, successively from popular frenzy and misguided zeal, from the brilliant and dazzling but oppressive rule of the mighty conqueror, and from the gradual encroachments of an imbecile and obstinate dynasty. But now when she beholds the children of France rising in all the majesty of virtuous indignation, proclaiming and vindicating with unparalleled bravery those heaven born principles which she herself first promulgated and maintained and sealing their devotion to them with their blood; now then she hails her loudly and rapturously as worthy of her sisterly love and with tears of Joy, throws out her arms to clasp her to her heart.

"To you then, brave children of America, the hope and pride of your country, this noble standard is committed, to wave in harmonious folds with our own glorious 'Star Spangled Banner,' an emblem of that friendship which should always unite two nations, who boast of having for their fathers, WASHINGTON and LAFAYETTE."

When the standard had been given to the Sergeant and one of the bands had played a national air, Capt. Page made the following

REPLY:

"Recent events in France have elicited in behalf of her people the undivided and intense interest of a large portion of the civilized globe. Wherever the intelligence of her mighty struggles has been carried, admiration of the courage of her citizens, sympathy in their afflictions and joy for their success have commingled and her regeneration has been greeted as an epoch teeming with the happiest consequences for all mankind.

"In our own tranquil republic, such a change from the extreme despotism to the full enjoyment of civil and religious liberty, effected by the spontaneous and wonderful exertions of an intelligent population, with a rapidity and heroism unknown in the annals of history, is indeed loudly hailed by millions of freemen. The intrepidity and prudence of the citizens of Paris and the devotion and forebearance of the National Guard form a theme for every tongue and deserve to be cherished in the hearts of all who are not dead to that homage which high and honorable feeling never refuses to extend the choicest virtues of human character. Long will the citizens of America remember the glorious conduct of their brethren of France. They fought to vindicate and restore laws insulted and trampled upon—and they succeeded in establishing their reign, were the first to acknowledge their influence and submit to their power. Thus it is always with the soldiers of freedom; they can never be other than friends to their country.

"I accept, then, fair lady, this beautiful standard, to be cherished by the men I have the honor to command, as an object with which every inspiring sentiment is associated—reminding them as it will, not only of *patriotism* but of the *innocence* and *beauty* which it is their happiness to admire—their duty to protect. On this auspicious day, set apart by our citizen soldiers to celebrate the triumph of a nation, which gratitude will not permit us to forget; its folds shall harmoniously unite with those of the 'Stars and Stripes' and while they gently mingle in the breeze, sacred emblems of *'liberty and order,'* the names of WASHINGTON and LAFAYETTE immortal champions of both, shall be wafted to heaven with the purest aspiration["].

The standard was beautifully decorated, and was, in point of elegance, worthy of the occasion.

The battalion then took up the line of march and proceeded to form with the division.

The division was formed in Arch Street, and a little before 1 o'clock, the procession under the command of Major General Cadwalader took up the line of march. An advanced mounted guard led the way. At a considerable distance from these were the past military officers—officers who had joined the Lafayette procession, United States officers &c all mounted; following which was Major General Cadwalader, as commander in chief, with his staff: on the left of General Cadwalader rode Colonel JOHN G. WATMOUGH in uniform. Following these were Brigadier General PATTERSON, with his aids. Gen. P. [*sic*] was at the head of the first brigade of Pennsylvania Volunteers, in which were included troops from Chester and Montgomery Counties. The artillery commanded by Colonel PREVOST took the lead of the brigade. Several fine troops of horse, with the first city troop at the head were in this brigade as well as one or two companies of *Riflemen.*

At the head of the second Brigade, was General GOODWIN followed immediately by Captain CHILDS' company of Artillery. We noticed immediately succeeding this company, the Montgomery Guards from Norristown.

The company of cadets from a neighboring school, attracted much attention.

In the brigade were several handsome companies from the country; and the numerous and well mounted troop of horse from Jersey, which attracted so much notice in the Lafayette procession. In the rear of the troops were several hundred citizens mounted and formed into a file, with a tri-colored flag.

The houses along the streets through which the procession moved were many of them decorated with flags, and two were suspended over the street at the Coffee House. The windows were crowded with ladies, and the side walks filled with spectators of the enlivening scene, which had new attractions from the excellent music employed by the military.

In the procession we noticed a barouche, containing four gentlemen of the '76 stamp, viz: ex-sheriff STREMBECK, Sheriff REESE, Doctor WHITE and one gentleman whose face we could not see. The division moved through several of the principal streets and having closed its march, was dismissed by the major general.

In the evening, several handsome transparencies were exhibited. The Walnut Street Theatre was illuminated, and was honored with the company of many military gentlemen, as was the Arch and

Chestnut Street Theatres [sic]. We learn that another standard was presented to a volunteer company—we did not learn the name of the donor, nor of the receivers.

2. My argument that women had little access to public ceremonial activities in antebellum Philadelphia necessitates a comment on Miss Chapron's appearance. Public speeches by women (except for self-identified radicals like Frances Wright) were rare in this period. Flag and standard presentations, however, were well known; they allowed women supporters of causes like temperance and nativism to inject a female presence into the public sphere without eliciting ridicule. Standards and flags, and ceremonies built around them, were significant because women had made the banners being presented. Newspapers reported not only the gift of a banner, but also the identities of those who designed and executed it, and the details of its imagery. Volunteer militia troops may have had informal ladies' auxiliaries, or "sweethearts clubs," as did fire companies in this period.

3. Hazard, *Register* 6 (October 1830): 245–46.

4. Ibid.

5. For a summary of the militia controversy and its connection to social and military debates in this period, see John K. Mahon, *History of the Militia and the National Guard* (New York: Macmillan, 1983), pp. 46–96. The militia system is usually treated as an example of the failure of United States military policy in the early national and Jacksonian eras. I have found no detailed study of them as ceremonialists.

6. For the formation of the Associators, see Steven J. Rosswurm, "Arms, Culture and Class: The Philadelphia Militias and the 'Lower Orders' in the American Revolution," doctoral dissertation, Northern Illinois University, DeKalb, 1977. Sources for the history of Philadelphia's volunteers include the Annual Reports of the Pennsylvania Adjutant General; Joseph Jackson, *Encyclopedia of Philadelphia*, 5 vols. (Harrisburg: National Historical Association, 1931–33) 1:133–39; J. L. Wilson, John C. Groome, J. F. McFadden, and J. Willis Martin, eds., *Book of the First Troop Philadelphia City Cavalry, 1774–1915* (Philadelphia, 1915); Captain Thomas S. Lanard, *One Hundred Years with the State Fencibles* (Philadelphia: Neilds, 1913); General James W. Latta, *History of the First Regiment Infantry, National Guard of Pennsylvania (Grey Reserves), 1861–1911* (Philadelphia: J. B. Lippincott, 1917); J. Thomas Scharf and Thompson Westcott, *History of Philadelphia: 1609–1884*, 3 vols. (Philadelphia: L. H. Everts, 1884) 1:1016–20; W. A. Newman Dorland, "The Second Troop Philadelphia City Cavalry," *Pennsylvania Magazine of History and Biography* 45 (1921): 257–91, 356–87; 46 (1922): 57–77, 154–72, 262–71, 346–65; 47 (1923): 67–79, 147–77, 262–76, 357–75; 48 (1924): 270–84, 372–82; and William P. Clarke, *Official History of the Militia and National Guard of the State of Pennsylvania, from the Earliest Period of Record to the Present Time*, 2 vols. (Philadelphia: C. J. Hendler, 1909–1912).

7. Rosswurm, "Arms, Culture and Class," pp. 112-73, 461–62.

8. Ibid., pp. 270–380; and Eric Foner, *Tom Paine and Revolutionary America* (New York: Oxford University Press, 1976), pp. 63–67.

9. Rosswurm, "Arms, Culture and Class," pp. 270–380.

10. Eric Foner, *Tom Paine*, pp. 63–67; and Laurence D. Cress, "The Standing Army, the Militia and the New Republic: Changing Attitudes Toward the Military in American Society, 1786–1820," doctoral dissertation, University of Virginia, Charlottesville, 1976, p. 235.

11. Mahon, *Militia and National Guard*, pp. 46–62; see also Cress, "Militia and the New Republic," pp. 1–20, for early evidence of divisions in militia duties. For local and regional differences in the militia as a social institution, see Marcus Cunliffe, *Soldier and Civilian: The Martial Spirit in America, 1775–1865* (Boston: Little, Brown, 1968). For the best summary of Pennsylvania's militia laws and their history, see Joseph L. Holmes, "The Decline of the Pennsylvania Militia, 1815–1870," *Western Pennsylvania Historical Magazine* 57 (1974): 199–217.

12. For the suppression of Fries's Rebellion, see Kim T. Phillips, "William Duane, Revolutionary Editor," doctoral dissertation, University of California, Berkeley, 1968, pp. 67–72. Philadelphia cavalries helped put down the Whiskey Rebellion; see Dorland, "Second Troop City Cavalry," 47 (1923): 6. For use of militia against postwar upheaval generally, see Mahon, *Militia and National Guard*, pp. 54–55.

13. Holmes, "Decline of Pennsylvania Militia"; and J. Ritchie Garrison, "Battalion Day: Military Exercise and Frolic in Pennsylvania Before the Civil War," *Pennsylvania Folklife* 26 (1976–77): 2–12.

14. There is good evidence—including the overlap of volunteer company officership, political party activity, and elected officeholding—that the volunteers functioned as proto-parties: Small local organizations, they may have been the building blocks of larger party organizations. Information on the structure and political party function of the volunteers is based on militia drill and meeting announcements, published rosters of musters and militia elections, as well as secondary sources. While there is no detailed social history of Philadelphia politics in this era (and it is misleading to apply conclusions about state politics to the city), and until there is a social history of the urban militias, statements about the volunteers' political role must remain speculative. The author who studies militias will have to locate and examine the manuscript local muster rolls and reports from local adjutants to the state's Adjutant General.

Volunteer companies served as adjuncts to political factions during the conflicts of the 1790s; see Phillips, "William Duane," pp. 64–97, 278–393; Dorland, "Second Troop City Cavalry," 49 (1925): 93–94; Harold Donaldson Eberlein and Cortlandt Van Dyke Hubbard, *Diary of Independence Hall* (Philadelphia: J. B. Lippincott, 1948), pp. 323–26. Mahon, *Militia and National Guard*, pp. 46–62, outlines the positions of Federalists, Jeffersonians, and others on the role of the militia in the republic. For the Jacksonian uses of volunteer troops and officerships by politicians, see Philip S. Klein, *Pennsylvania Politics: A Game Without Rules* (Philadelphia: Historical Society of Pennsylvania, 1940), pp. 13–14, 32–34.

Militia drill announcements indicate that commanders, especially of the oldest and "best" troops, were men of "old Philadelphia" families, sometimes descendants of Revolutionary War officers. Elite militia commanders bore surnames like Chew, Ingersoll, Morris, Biddle, Childs, Cadwalader, Prevost, Patterson, Wetherill, Fotteral, and Powel.

Precise knowledge of volunteer troops' occupational makeup depends on the still-unwritten social history of militias. I compared samples of names from published lists of militia officers (majors, captains, colonels, brigadier majors, and brigadier generals) against city directories for 1828, 1835, and 1850. These admittedly unscientific samples indicate that men who were active over a number of years—those who turned up again and again in election and muster announcements—tended to be "gentlemen," attorneys, merchants, and master craftsmen in luxury trades. High division offices such as brigadier general were held by attorneys and prominent merchants, and militia office sometimes overlapped with governmental appointment, such as alderman, tax collector, justice of the peace, notary, or customs-house official.

For example, James Page led the State Fencibles from the 1830s through the 1850s: Page was an attorney at law and a postmaster. C. C. Biddle, a well-known volunteer leader, was colonel of the First Regiment Volunteer Light Artillery, a lawyer, and a bank president in the 1830s. He was the son of Colonel Clement Biddle, a Revolutionary War veteran who helped put down the Whiskey Rebellion. Between the 1820s and 1840s, Major General Robert Patterson was in charge of the First Division, commander of a regiment of cavalry, a wholesale grocer, and a director of the Philadelphia Bank. T. W. L. Freeman was a captain in the "Corps City Phalanx," an auctioneer, and the founder of a long-time house of auctioneers. Peter Fritz was a master marble-mason whose men built the Merchants' Exchange; president of the Philadelphia Savings Institution in the 1830s, Fritz was a captain in the National Greys from the early 1830s into the 1850s, was active in Democratic Party politics, and ran for brigadier general in 1842. George Cadwalader, one of Philadelphia's very wealthy gentlemen, was a militia enthusiast, leading the Washington Greys in the 1830s and participating in the Washington Hose (fire) Company.

15. For the antidemocratic nature of Philadelphia's volunteer establishment, see John F. Watson, *Annals of Philadelphia and Pennsylvania* (Philadelphia: Carey & Hart, 1830), and rev. ed. in 3 vols., ed. Willis P. Hazard (Philadelphia: Edwin S. Stuart, 1900) 1:330. For rich detail about the Washington Greys, see "Extracts from the Diary of Thomas Franklin Pleasants, 1814," *Pennsylvania Magazine of History and Biography* 39 (1915): 322–31, 410–24. See also Cunliffe, *Soldier and Civilian*, pp. 215–54; and Mahon, *Militia and National Guard*, pp. 57–62.

16. Jackson, *Encyclopedia* 1:133–39; Scharf and Westcott, *History of Philadelphia* 2:1016–20; and Klein, *Game Without Rules*, pp. 13–14, 32–34.

17. Ibid., pp. 13–14, 32–34, and "Diary of Thomas Franklin Pleasants."

18. *Mechanics' Free Press* (Philadelphia), April 10, 1830. For information on artisans' wages in this period, see Richard McLeod, "Philadelphia Artisans, 1828–1850," doctoral dissertation, University of Missouri, Columbia, 1971, pp. 102, 149–56. See also Bruce Laurie, *Working People of Philadelphia, 1800–1850* (Philadelphia: Temple University Press, 1980), pp. 10–12; and Mahon, *Militia and National Guard*, p. 82.

19. *Mechanics' Free Press*, April 10, 1830.

20. The surviving Annual Reports of Pennsylvania's Adjutant General show wildly fluctuating estimates of enrollments in Philadelphia's public companies. For sources on why these reports are unreliable, see Paul Tincher Smith, "Militia of the United States from 1846–1860," *Indiana Magazine of History* 15 (1919): 21–47; and Holmes, "Decline of Pennsylvania Militia." It is reasonable to estimate, however, that the vast majority of eligible men in the city belonged to public companies. In 1830, if the population of the city area was about 200,000, the number of white men between 18 and 45 years of age must have run into the tens of thousands, compared to the 1,089 members of volunteer companies counted by a writer for the *Mechanics' Free Press*, April 10, 1830. For comparison, in 1847 when the city's population neared 400,000, enrollees totaled 50,063 for Philadelphia and the county; of these, 48,033 were public company members and 2,030 belonged to private troops. Private companies, for all their prominence in street parades, were a small part of the white male citizenry. In 1847 the volunteers were also ranked in a pyramid of status, with 237 members in cavalries, 247 in rifle companies, 571 as artillerymen, and 977 as infantrymen. See Pennsylvania Adjutant General, *Annual Report for the Year of 1847* (Harrisburg: 1847), pp. 10–13.

21. McLeod, "Philadelphia Artisans," pp. 149–56; Laurie, *Working People*, pp. 18–19, 103–4, 107–33; and Philip S. Foner, *History of the Labor Movement in the United States*, Vol. I: *From Colonial Times to the Founding of the American Federation of Labor* (New York: International Publishers, 1947; rev. ed., New World Paperbacks, 1975), pp. 48–64.

22. Philadelphia's unpopular fines collectors were also dealt with violently (*see Chapter Four*).

23. Holmes, "Decline of the Pennsylvania Militia"; Walter J. Hugins, *Jacksonian Democracy and the Working Class: A Study of the New York Workingmen's Party, 1829–1837* (Stanford: Stanford University Press, 1967), pp. 33, 138; and Philip S. Foner, *History of the Labor Movement*, Vol. I, pp. 123–24, 467–68, 473–74.

24. Holmes, "Decline of the Pennsylvania Militia," pp. 208–13.

25. Ibid.

26. Ibid. See also "A Plea for Militia Reform," *New England Magazine* 3 (July 1834): 51–65.

27. See, for example, Cunliffe, *Soldier and Civilian*, pp. 179–235; and Mahon, *Militia and National Guard*, pp. 78–96.

28. Membership in a militia company was frequently announced along with other qualifications in newspaper advertisements for political candidates. See, for example, "A Plea for Militia Reform."

29. *Mechanics' Free Press*, April 10, 1830.

30. "A Plea For Militia Reform"; and *North American* (Philadelphia), August 27, 1839.

31. Prominent militiamen who held public office included Robert Wharton (mayor), Samuel P. Wetherill (councilman and "gentleman"), Peter Fritz (councilman), Rudolph H. Bartle, (alderman), Alexander Henry (mayor), and Morton McMichael (alderman and mayor).

32. *Mechanics' Free Press*, November 28, 1829, January 9 and May 8,

15, 22, 1830; Hugins, *Jacksonian Democracy and the Working Class*, pp. 11–23, 148–71; and Sean Wilentz, "Artisan Republican Festivals and Rise of Class Conflict in New York City, 1788–1837," in Michael H. Frisch and Daniel J. Walkowitz, eds., *Working-Class America: Essays on Labor, Community and American Society* (Urbana: University of Illinois Press, 1983), pp. 37–77.

33. Local reform campaigns—in the springs of 1833, 1834, 1837, and 1842—often featured an "anti-aristocratical" "mechanic's ticket": *Pennsylvania Gazette* (Philadelphia), May 22, 1833; *United States Gazette* (Philadelphia), May 2, 1835; *Public Ledger* (Philadelphia), June 12, 1837; and *Public Ledger*, May 4, 1842. There is no account of the campaigns for militia reform in Philadelphia, and histories of the labor movement and workingmen's movements only briefly mention the issue. Yet militia reform was a plank in both the Workingmen's and, later, Democratic Party platforms. The volunteer militia troops were clearly parts of local political machines, but we need to learn much more about how they functioned.

34. For analysis of a comparable problem of legitimation and its solution through public display, see Abner Cohen, *The Politics of Elite Culture: Explorations in the Dramaturgy of Power in a Modern African Society* (Berkeley: University of California Press, 1981).

35. "A Plea for Militia Reform," p. 59.

36. Dorland, "Second Troop City Cavalry" 47 (1923): 262; W. S. Baker, "Washington After the Revolution—1784–1799," *Pennsylvania Magazine of History and Biography* 20 (1896): 178, 334, 351, 473–75, 498–99; 21 (1897): 34–35, 187–88; and Stewart Culin, "Note," ibid., 24 (1900): 127–28. Eberlein and Hubbard describe colonial celebrations of Georgian birthdays in *Independence Hall*, pp. 79–81; Washington's Birthdays, p. 335; and George III's birthday, as celebrated after the Revolution, p. 325.

Criticism of the aristocratic tone of the holiday surfaced early; see George W. Douglas, *The American Book of Days* (New York: H. W. Wilson, 1948), pp. 137–38. The image of Washington is analyzed in Peter Karsten, *Patriot Heroes in England and America: Political Symbolism and Changing Values over Three Centuries* (Madison: University of Wisconsin Press, 1978), pp. 57–110; and Robert P. Hay, "George Washington, American Moses," *American Quarterly* 21 (Summer 1969): 780–91.

37. Baker, "Washington After the Revolution," p. 178.

38. Ibid., p. 351.

39. *Democratic Press* (Philadelphia), February 23, 1810; *Pennsylvania Gazette*, March 1, 1815; and *Poulson's American Daily Advertiser* (Philadelphia), February 19, 1825.

40. *United States Gazette*, February 27, 1821.

41. *Niles' Weekly Register* (Baltimore), February 25, 1832, p. 467; Hazard, *Register* 9 (February 1832): 102–3, 109; and Scharf and Westcott, *History of Philadelphia* 1:633–35.

42. Garrison, "Battalion Day."

43. See, for example, "Diary of Thomas Franklin Pleasants."

44. Men like Richard Bache, William Duane, and John Binns published party papers and headed volunteer companies: Bache, the *Frank-*

lin Gazette and Franklin Flying Artillery; Duane, the *United States Gazette* (later, the *Aurora*) and the Militia Legion Regiment; and Binns, the *Democratic Press* and the Independent Volunteers.

45. *Saturday Evening Post* (Philadelphia), May 7, 1825.

46. *Democratic Press*, May 23, 1826.

47. *United States Gazette*, May 2, 1826.

48. Ibid., May 24, 1836.

49. *Public Ledger* May 3, 1837.

50. *Pennsylvanian* (Philadelphia), May 28, 1850; see also *Public Ledger*, May 3, 1842, April 30, 1844.

51. *United States Gazette*, July 5, 1821; *Public Ledger*, February 23, 1841, September 13, 1842, May 12, 1840; and *Pennsylvanian*, May 28, 1842.

52. *Niles' Weekly Register*, October 10, 1835.

53. Robert F. Ulle, "Popular Black Music in Nineteenth-Century Philadelphia," *Pennsylvania Folklife* 25 (1975–76): 20–28.

54. For fife-and-drum bands, see Dena J. Epstein, *Sinful Tunes and Spirituals: Black Folk Music to the Civil War,* (Urbana: University of Illinois Press, 1977), pp. 119–20, 155. Volunteer militia companies also employed bands and orchestras for their Washington's Birthday and May Night balls. See, for example, *Public Ledger*, May 1, 4, 1838; and *Poulson's American Daily Advertiser*, February 19, 1825.

55. *Mechanics' Free Press*, May 15, 1830; *Democratic Press*, May 12, 1825; *Public Ledger*, May 10, 1836; and *North American*, November 13, 1857.

56. Volunteers lobbied for an end to nonuniformed drills and musters at privately organized militia conventions, such as the one held in Harrisburg in 1842 and reported in the *Military Magazine and Record of the Volunteers of the City and County of Philadelphia* (Philadelphia) 3 (1842).

57. July Fourth parades by volunteers were reported in detail. See Dorland, "Second Troop City Cavalry" 47 (1923): 264, 363–64; *Democratic Press*, July 5, 1808, July 3, 1809, and July 5, 1810; *True American* (Philadelphia) July 5, 1810; *Aurora and General Advertiser* (Philadelphia), July 5, 1812; "Diary of Thomas Franklin Pleasants," p. 330; *Franklin Gazette* (Philadelphia), July 4, 1818; *United States Gazette*, July 10, 1821; and *Poulson's American Daily Advertiser*, July 6, 1826.

58. *Poulson's American Daily Advertiser*, July 4, 1821, July 6, 1822; and *United States Gazette*, July 10, 1823.

59. *Poulson's American Daily Advertiser*, June 24, 1835, reprinted a song composed for a militia dinner.

60. Visits and excursions were recorded in *Poulson's American Daily Advertiser*, July 6, 1826; *Mechanics' Free Press*, July 24, 1830; *United States Gazette*, July 2, 1832, July 1, 4, 6, 1834; and *Public Ledger*, July 6, 1838.

61. This Red Bank is located a little south of downtown Camden, an easy boat ride across the Delaware from Philadelphia's Navy Yard. (It is not the more northerly Red Bank, on the Atlantic shore.)

62. Hazard, *Register* 2 (November 29, 1829): 297.

63. For example, in 1828 the beginning of work on the Baltimore and

Ohio Railroad in Baltimore was celebrated with an enormous procession of the militias, trades, and Freemasons, planned and sponsored by the officers of the railroad company; see *Niles' Weekly Register*, July 6, 1828, p. 233. Philadelphia's first and most spectacular ceremony combining trades and militia imagery was the Grand Federal Procession of 1788, an allegorical parade foregrounding manufactures in the city.

64. Hazard, *Register* 10 (September 29, 1832): 206.

65. Ibid.

66. Fred Somkin, *Unquiet Eagle: Memory and Desire in the Idea of American Freedom, 1815–1860* (Ithaca: Cornell University Press, 1967), pp. 131–74.

67. Hazard, *Register* 12 (October 1833): 251–52.

68. *Poulson's American Daily Advertiser*, September 28, 30 and October 4, 1824.

69. See accounts of receptions for the following: Martin Van Buren, in *Niles' Weekly Register*, March 16, 1833, p. 39; Henry Clay, in *North American*, August 26, 1839; Andrew Jackson, in *Niles' Weekly Register*, March 16, 1819, pp. 28–29; and the Hungarian patriot Louis Kossuth, in *Public Ledger*, December 24, 1851.

70. Hazard, *Register* 11 (June 15, 1833): 376–78. Competing "anti-aristocratical" receptions were held for Jackson.

71. *American Museum* (Philadelphia) 4 (July 1788): 57–75.

72. *Niles' Weekly Register*, October 30, 1813, pp. 145–47.

73. Elaborate public obsequies were popular in France during the First Republic; Americans may have borrowed this ceremonial tradition from the French. Cf. Mona Ozouf, *La Fête révolutionnaire, 1789–1799* (Paris: Editions Gallimard, 1976), pp. 7–43.

74. George Morgan, *The City of Firsts, Being a Complete History of the City of Philadelphia from its Founding, in 1682, to the Present Time* (Philadelphia: The Historical Publishing Society, 1926), pp. 334–35. Washington's sham funeral is described in Dorland, "Second Troop City Cavalry" 48 (1924): 378–81. Ceremonies for Thomas Jefferson and John Adams are found in *Saturday Evening Post*, July 29, 1826; and Lyman Butterfield, "The Jubilee of Independence," *Virginia Magazine of History and Biography* 61 (April 1953): 119–40. The history of spectacular funerals is a worthy topic for a folklorist. These early-nineteenth-century obsequies were part of a tradition that reached its apotheosis in Lincoln's funeral train, and is now a mass-media staple.

75. *United States Gazette*, July 18, 21–22, 1834.

76. *Pennsylvania Inquirer and National Gazette* (Philadelphia), March 9, 1846.

77. To a certain extent, the links between the nineteenth-century volunteers and the Revolution were not fictitious, but expressed family history and connections: Some volunteer leaders were the descendants of Revolutionary officers. Many more leaders, however, had their titles and links to the past from commissions held during the War of 1812. Locally, the militia's performance between 1812 and 1814 was hardly a glorious memory; see Holmes, "Decline of Pennsylvania Militia."

78. For contested versions of the July Revolution's meaning for New York artisans, mechanics, and political leaders, see Wilentz, "Artisan

Republican Festivals," pp. 53–56. In Philadelphia, workingmen viewed the events of July 1830 differently from militia leaders. For artisans, that revolution was a successful if timid first step; in their speeches and toasts they urged the Paris workingmen to finish the revolution they had begun. See Hazard, *Register* 6 (October 1830): 221–22 ("Workingmen's Meeting"); and *Mechanics' Free Press*, January 15, 1831 (toasts to the Paris workingmen).

79. Alfred F. Young, "George Robert Twelves Hewes (1742–1840): A Boston Shoemaker and the Memory of the American Revolution," *William and Mary Quarterly*, 3rd ser., 38 (1981): 561–623.

80. "Old Revolutioners" appeared in the July Fourth procession of 1844, "gentlemen of the '76 stamp" in the July Days procession (see note 1).

81. "Timbertoes" made use of the popular "hick's letter home" genre, thus his New England "dialect." This description of a New York parade was reprinted from the July 7 issue of the *New York Constellation* in the *Mechanics' Free Press*, July 24, 1830.

82. The culmination of the Philadelphia Associators' antiprofiteering campaign occurred on October 4, 1779, at the "Battle of Fort Wilson," when radical militiamen attacked the house of a prominent Loyalist. During this riot, the "silk-stocking cavalry" fought back the crowd and defended the collaborators; see Rosswurm, "Arms, Culture and Class," pp. 430–61. This pattern of the use of upper-class cavalries to maintain law and order persisted in nineteenth-century Philadelphia, in strikes and riots; see Robert Reinders, "The Militia and Public Order in Nineteenth-Century America," *Journal of American Studies* 11 (1977): 81–101. For the Revolt of the Pennsylvania Line in January 1781, see Hazard, *Register* 2 (September 1828): 137–38.

83. Michael Kammen, in *A Season of Youth: The American Revolution and the Historical Imagination* (New York: Knopf, 1978), pp. 3–110, argues that the American Revolution underwent changes in popular memory. Especially after 1830, he claims, the Revolution, while never repudiated, was thought of and remembered more ambiguously; it gradually became a noncontroversial phenomenon, while it, and events after 1783, had been very controversial before 1830. Was the Revolution just? Was it a mistake, divinely ordained, the culmination of human civilization to date? Did it go far enough? Did it go too far? Had it been preserved or subverted since 1783? All these questions were open and contested in the Early National period. Kammen never explores the possibility of competing traditions of historical interpretation *outside* elite and literary spheres, except to note that George Bancroft was aware of abundant oral traditions surrounding Revolutionary events and deemed them "rubbish." Kammen writes mildly that "Revolutionary origins managed or perpetuated by an elite . . . offer certain problems" in a democracy (p. 34). For ways to think about ill-recorded traditions of popular historicizing, see Young, "Hewes"; see also Alfred F. Young, "English Plebeian Culture and Eighteenth-Century American Radicalism," in Margaret Jacob and James Jacob, eds., *The Origins of Anglo-American Radicalism*, (London: George Allen & Unwin, 1983), pp. 185–222. Detailed analysis of shifts in oratorical interpretation of the

meaning of the Revolution is found in Howard H. Martins, "Orations on the Anniversary of American Independence, 1776–1876," doctoral dissertation, Northwestern University, Evanston, Ill., 1955, pp. 138–95.

84. Wilentz, "Artisan Republican Festivals"; and *Mechanics' Free Press*, July 25 and September 21, 1829.

85. These ideas on the relationship between reenactments and popular historicizing were improved in a panel discussion on folklore and history at the annual meetings of the American Folklore Society, Nashville, Tennessee, October 27, 1983. Thanks are due to co-panelists Henry Glassie, John Dorst, Sandy Ives, and Sam Schrager.

86. Karsten, *Patriot Heroes*, pp. 79–110; Somkin, *Unquiet Eagle*, pp. 131–74; and Marcus Cunliffe, *George Washington: Man and Monument* (Boston: Little, Brown, 1958).

87. *Mechanics' Free Press*, April 10, 1830.

88. "A Plea for Militia Reform"; and Cunliffe, *Soldier and Civilian*, pp. 215–35.

89. *Workingman's Advocate* (New York), January 21, 1832.

90. For examples of exchanges and presentations, see *Democratic Press*, May 15, 1807, June 28, 1825; Hazard, *Register* 6 (October 1830): 245–46; *United States Gazette*, July 4, 22, 23, 1834; and *Public Ledger*, April 4, 1836.

91. *Democratic Press*, May 19, 1826; *Mechanics' Free Press*, May 17, 1828, May 15, 1830; *Saturday Evening Post*, June 4, 1828; and *Public Ledger*, May 10, 19, 1836, June 12, 1837.

92. Christopher Hill, *Society and Puritanism in Pre-Revolutionary England*, 2nd ed. (New York: Schocken, 1967), pp. 145–218; and Paul Boyer, *Urban Masses and Moral Order in America, 1820–1860* (Cambridge: Harvard University Press, 1978), pp. 3–66.

93. Examples of civic-private ceremonial collaboration include Washington Square's redesign and dedication, Lafayette's reception in 1824, and ceremonies for consolidation of the city in 1854. See Eli K. Price, *The History of the Consolidation of the City of Philadelphia* (Philadelphia: J. B. Lippincott, 1873), pp. 90–109.

94. Holmes, "Decline of the Pennsylvania Militia," pp. 204–9.

95. Ibid., pp. 211–17. For the militia's prominence, see Philip S. Foner, *The Great Labor Uprising of 1877* (New York: Monad Press, 1977), pp. 55–77.

CHAPTER FOUR

1. Throughout this study, I have designated parades of all kinds as folkloric or vernacular communication. However, in this chapter, the term *folk drama* has a precise meaning taken from folkloristics. Here, folk drama refers to a collection of genres and dramatic practices that folklorists have studied, mainly among rural Western Europeans. The vast literature on folk drama has rarely had a base in social history. Broadly, these dramatic traditions are calendrical and festive; some forms include traditional texts or plays that are thought to have been disseminated mainly by oral tradition and example, although evidence shows some dissemination via chapbooks. Until recently, folklorists working on folk drama have mainly tried to find "texts" of these "plays." Basic sources for texts include R. J. E. Tiddy, *The Mummers Play* (Oxford: Oxford University Press, 1923); E. K. Chambers, *The English Folk Play* (New York: Russell and Russell, 1964); and E. Cawte, A. Helm, and N. Peacock, *English Ritual Drama: A Geographical Index* (London: Publications of the Folklore Society, 1967). Considered performatively, folk dramatic customs also include processing, begging, dancing, and miming. Folk dramas have been defined by community locus and focus, and by noncommercial production, usually by age cohorts. Folklorists have discerned two major themes of European festive folk dramas: folk plays on life, death, and regeneration and processional performances to outline, constitute, and construct communal bonds at critical and festive times. See Herbert Halpert, "A Typology of Mumming," in Herbert Halpert and G. M. Story, eds., *Christmas Mumming in Newfoundland: Essays in Anthropology, Folklore and History* (Toronto: University of Toronto Press, 1969), pp. 35–61. For the best ethnographic study of folk drama in a community setting, see Henry Glassie, *All Silver and No Brass: An Irish Christmas Mumming* (Bloomington: Indiana University Press, 1969).

A portion of the first half of this chapter was published in Susan G. Davis, "The Career of Colonel Pluck: Folk Drama and Popular Protest in Early Nineteenth-Century Philadelphia," *Pennsylvania Magazine of History and Biography* 109, No. 2 (April 1985): 179–202. Copyright 1985, The Historical Society of Pennsylvania. Material in the second half of this chapter appeared, in different form, in my article "'Making Night Hideous': Christmas Revelry and Public Order in Nineteenth-Century Philadelphia," *American Quarterly* 34 (Summer 1982): 185–99, published by the University of Pennsylvania. Copyright 1982, Trustees of the University of Pennsylvania.

2. Alfred F. Young, "Pope's Day, Tarring and Feathering and Cornet Joyce, Jun.: From Ritual to Rebellion in Boston, 1745–1775" (paper presented to the Anglo-American Conference on Comparative Labor History, Rutgers University, April 26–28, 1973); Alfred F. Young, "English Plebeian Culture and Eighteenth-Century American Radicalism," in Margaret Jacob and James Jacob, eds., *The Origins of Anglo-American Radicalism* (London: George Allen & Unwin, 1983), pp. 185–212; Dirk Hoerder, "Boston Leaders and Boston Crowds, 1765–1776," in Alfred F. Young, ed., *The American Revolution: Explorations in the*

History of American Radicalism (DeKalb: Northern Illinois University Press, 1976), pp. 233–71; Edward Countryman, "'Out of the Bounds of the Law': Northern Land Rioters in the Eighteenth Century," in Young, *American Revolution*, pp. 37–69. In Philadelphia, sailors defended customary smuggling prerogatives with the tar brush; see Howard O. Sprogle, *The Philadelphia Police, Past and Present* (Philadelphia, 1887), pp. 51–52.

3. Steven J. Rosswurm, "Arms, Culture and Class: The Philadelphia Militia and the 'Lower Orders' in the American Revolution," doctoral dissertation, Northern Illinois University, DeKalb, 1977, pp. 84–106.

4. *Pennsylvania Packet* (Philadelphia), September 30, 1780.

5. Ibid. Another use of ritual shaming by the crowd occurred on the Fourth of July after General Howe's evacuation of the city: A procession bore a prostitute dressed in a high British headdress through the streets, cheering and banging drums. Ridicule turned on the "filth" (social and physical) of the woman. See Henry D. Biddle, ed., *Extracts from the Journal of Elizabeth Drinker, from 1759–1807, A.D.* (Philadelphia: J. B. Lippincott, 1889), p. 107.

6. Young, *American Revolution*, pp. 449–61, especially p. 458; and Kim T. Phillips, "William Duane, Revolutionary Editor," doctoral dissertation, University of California, Berkeley, 1968, p. 67.

7. Michael Meranze, "The Penitential Ideal in Late-Eighteenth-Century Philadelphia," *Pennsylvania Magazine of History and Biography* 108, no. 4 (October 1984): 419–50.

8. Young, "Pope's Day"; and Joseph Reidy, "Negro Election Day and Black Community Life in New England, 1750–1860," *Marxist Perspectives* 13 (Fall 1978): 102–17.

9. Peter Burke, *Popular Culture in Early Modern Europe* (London: Temple Smith, 1978); and Peter Buckley, "'A Privileged Place': New York Theatre Riots, 1817–1849" (paper presented at annual meetings of the Organization of American Historians, April 1, 1980, Philadelphia).

10. H. E. Scudder, ed., *The Recollections of Samuel Breck* (Philadelphia: Porter and Coates, 1877), quoted in William Wells Newell, "Christmas Maskings in Boston," *Journal of American Folklore* 9 (1896): 178.

11. Raymond Williams, "The Press and Popular Culture in the Nineteenth-Century," in George Boyce, James Curran, and Pauline Wingate, eds., *Newspaper History: From the 17th Century to the Present Day* (London: Constable, 1978); Dan Schiller, *Objectivity and the News: The Penny Press and the Rise of Commercial Journalism* (Philadelphia: University of Pennsylvania Press, 1980); Victor Neuberg, *Popular Literature: A History and Guide* (New York: Penguin Books, 1977); Peter Buckley, "An Essay on New York Publics" (paper presented to the Social Science Research Council, New York City Working Group, November 18, 1983); and Susan G. Davis and Dan Schiller, "The Delineation of Deviance in Street Literature, 1820–1860," in Mario Sismondi, Roberto Grandi, and Massimo Pavarini, eds., *I Segni di Cainó* (The Sign of Cain) (Florence: Festival dei Popoli, 1985).

12. Elizabeth C. Keiffer, "John Durang, the First Native American Dancer," *Pennsylvania Dutchman* 6 (1954): 26–38; and Alfred Shoemaker, "Stoffle Rilbp's Epistle," *Pennsylvania Dutchman* 6 (1954): 39.

13. Richard M. Dorson, "Mose the Far Famed and World Reknowned," *American Literature* 15 (1943): 288–300; and Francis Hodge, *Yankee Theatre: The Image of America on Stage* (Austin: University of Texas Press, 1964).

14. The terms *masking* and *disguising* are used here to describe a practice often called "mumming" in the British Isles, but a distinction should be maintained. Although Philadelphia's early masking traditions were the antecedents of its present-day Mummers Parade and Mummers and Shooters Clubs, the phenomena are conceptually distinct. Nineteenth-century Philadelphians were not performing the mummers' plays of British Isles tradition, and Philadelphia's twentieth-century Mummers and Shooters barely resemble mummers elsewhere. What Philadelphians called "maskers" revealed origins and intentions; the term "mummers" was assigned to Christmas revelers only at the end of the nineteenth century.

15. Rosswurm, "Arms, Culture and Class," pp. 25–32, 44; *Niles' Weekly Register* (Baltimore), April 4, 1835, p. 76, July 20, 1833, p. 344, and September 14, 1833, p. 47.

16. *Niles' Weekly Register*, May 14, 1825, p. 176.

17. *Saturday Evening Post* (Philadelphia), May 7, 1825.

18. Ibid.

19. Ibid.

20. *Democratic Press* (Philadelphia), May 9, 1825.

21. Ibid.; and *Saturday Evening Post*, May 15, 1825.

22. Natalie Z. Davis, *Society and Culture in Early Modern France* (Stanford: Stanford University Press, 1975), pp. 97–123; Burke, *Popular Culture in Early Modern Europe*; Roger D. Abrahams and Richard Bauman, "Ranges of Festival Behavior," in Barbara A. Babcock, ed., *The Reversible World: Symbolic Inversion in Art and Society* (Ithaca: Cornell University Press, 1978), pp. 193–208.

23. John Brewer, "Theatre and Counter-Theatre in Georgian Politics: The Mock Elections at Garrat," *Radical History Review* 22 (Winter 1979–80): 7–40; cf. Thomas W. Lacquer, "The Queen Caroline Affair: Politics as Art in the Reign of George IV," *Journal of Modern History* 54 (1982): 417–66. The Wilkesite agitations occurred from the late 1760s into the 1790s. They were a long series of election protests in support of John Wilkes and, more generally, in support of the right to protest, the right to meet publicly, of the Bill of Rights, and of the right of electors to return members of Parliament of their choice.

24. Francis Grose, *A Classical Dictionary of the Vulgar Tongue*, 3rd ed. corrected and enlarged (London: Hooper and Wigstead, 1796), p. 161.

25. *Saturday Evening Post*, May 15, 1825.

26. Ibid., May 21, 1825.

27. Ibid.

28. *United States Gazette* (Philadelphia), May 20, 1825.

29. For citation of a "corn toppers" parade (the date is unclear), see John F. Watson, *The Annals of Philadelphia and Pennsylvania* (Philadelphia: Carey and Hart, 1830), and rev. ed. in 3 vols., ed. Willis P. Hazard (Philadelphia: Edwin S. Stuart, 1900) 3:363–64.

30. *Democratic Press*, May 26, 1825.

31. *United States Gazette*, June 1, 1825; and *Democratic Press*, May 19, 24, 1825, May 18, 1826.

32. *Niles' Weekly Register*, August 12, 1826, p. 413; *United States Gazette*, May 11, 13, 1826; *Democratic Press*, May 13, 17, 1826.

33. *Niles' Weekly Register*, August 12, 1826, p. 413, September 16, 1826, p. 48; *Saturday Evening Post*, September 9, 23, 1826.

34. *Niles' Weekly Register*, September 16, 1826, p. 48, October 28, 1826. Pluck died a pauper in Blockley Almshouse in 1839 and was buried in the almshouse grounds. *United States Gazette*, September 26, 1839.

35. *United States Gazette*, June 1, 1825.

36. *Democratic Press*, May 19, 1825.

37. *Saturday Evening Post*, May 7, 1825.

38. *United States Gazette*, June 1, 1825.

39. Ibid.

40. Ibid.

41. *Niles' Weekly Register*, June 27, 1829, p. 284.

42. *Workingman's Advocate* (New York), May 4, 1831, October 5, 7, 14, 21, 26, 29, 1831. For New England, see Anthony J. Marro, "Vermont's Local Militia Units, 1815–1860," *Vermont History* 40 (1972): 28–42; Telfer Mook, "Training Day in New England," *New England Quarterly* 11 (1938): 675–97; Charles W. Burpee, *The Military History of Waterbury, New Hampshire* (Connecticut: Price, Lee and Adkins, 1891), p. 31; Marcus Cunliffe, *Soldier and Civilian: The Martial Spirit in America, 1775–1865* (Boston: Little, Brown, 1968), p. 190. One artist registered the parades' protest against illegitimate authority and illustrated the connections between transatlantic cultural experiences by using the pseudonym "Hassan Straightshanks." This was a direct reference to the social and political criticism in the popular cartoons of the English artist George Cruikshank (*see "The Grand Fantastical Procession of the City of New York" in the illustrations section*).

43. Walter J. Hugins, *Jacksonian Democracy and the Working Class: A Study of the New York Workingmen's Movement, 1829–1837* (Stanford: Stanford University Press, 1960), pp. 33, 138; and Philip S. Foner, *History of the American Labor Movement*, Vol. I: *From Colonial Times to the Founding of the American Federation of Labor*, rev. ed. (New York: International Publishers, New World Paperbacks, 1975), pp. 123–24, 467–68, 473–74.

44. *Pennsylvania Gazette* (Philadelphia), May 21, 1833.

45. Ibid.

46. Ibid.

47. *Pennsylvanian* (Philadelphia), September 17, 1833.

48. *Pennsylvania Gazette*, May 22, 28, 1833.

49. *Pennsylvanian*, October 29, 1833.

50. Ibid.

51. Ibid.

52. *New Haven Standard*, quoted in *Pennsylvania Gazette*, June 6, 1833; *Easton Sentinel*, January 10, 1834; Ethan Allen Weaver, *Local Historical and Biographical Sketches* (Germantown, Pa., 1906), pp. 90–91; the *Chambersburg Repository* is quoted in *Niles' Weekly Register*, June 6, 1835, p. 234.

53. Augustus B. Longstreet, *Georgia Scenes* (New York: 1840), p. 145; Cunliffe, *Soldier and Civilian*, pp. 190–92; Theodore Gromert, "The First National Pastime in the Middle West," *Indiana Magazine of History* 29 (1933): 171–75; and Richard Walser, "Don Quixote Invincibles," *North Carolina Folklore* 24 (1976): 95–100.

54. *Military Magazine and Record of the Volunteers of the City and County of Philadelphia* (Philadelphia) 3 (1842): 11.

55. Ibid.

56. Similar dramatic techniques of folk justice share many different names: in England, skimmington riding, skimmity ride, riding the stang, and rough music; in France, *charivari*; in Germany, *katzenmusick*; in North America, shivaree; and many others. Violet Alford, "Rough Music," *Folklore* 70 (1959): 505–18; E. P. Thompson, "'Rough Music': Le Charivari Anglais," *Annales: Economies, sociétés, civilisations* 27 (1972): 285–315; and Bryan D. Palmer, "Discordant Music: Charivaris and White Capping in Nineteenth-Century North America," *Labour/Le Travailleur* (Halifax) 3 (September 1973): 5–62.

57. Thompson, "'Rough Music'"; and Palmer, "Discordant Music," p. 24.

58. E. P. Thompson, "The Moral Economy of the English Crowd in the Eighteenth Century," *Past and Present* 50 (1971): 76–136; and Countryman, "'Out of the Bounds of the Law,'" in Young, ed., *American Revolution*.

59. Palmer, "Discordant Music," pp. 26–33; cf. G. M. Story, "Mummers in Newfoundland History: A Survey of the Printed Record," in Halpert and Story, eds., *Christmas Mumming in Newfoundland*, pp. 165–85.

60. Henry Christman, *Tin Horns and Calico: A Decisive Episode in the Emergence of Democracy* (New York: Holt, 1945); and David Maldwyn Ellis, *Landlords and Farmers in the Hudson-Mohawk Region, 1790–1850* (Ithaca: Cornell University Press, 1946), pp. 225–67. Disguised rent rioters were known in the Helderberg region at least as early as the 1790s, according to Ellis (p. 242).

61. Hans Kurath, *A Word Geography of the Eastern United States* (Ann Arbor: University of Michigan Press, 1949), p. 78; and Joseph Wright, *The English Dialect Dictionary*, 6 vols. (London: Henry Frowde, 1898–1905) 2:543.

62. Norman Simms, "Ned Ludd's Mummers Play," *Folklore* 89 (1978): 166–78; and David Jones, *Before Rebecca* (London: Allen Lane, 1973).

63. *Mechanics' Free Press* (Philadelphia), September 20, 1828.

64. *Philadelphia Comic Almanac for 1835* (Philadelphia: G. Strong, 1835), n.p.; this almanac also contains a woodcut of Colonel Pluck.

65. Grose, *Classical Dictionary of the Vulgar Tongue*, p. 140.

66. Thelma Niklaus, *Harlequin; or, the Rise of the Bergamask Rogue* (New York: George Braziller, 1956), pp. 22–34; and Simon Lichman, "The Gardener's Story and What Came Next: A Contextual Analysis of the Marshfield Paper Boys' Mumming Play," doctoral dissertation, University of Pennsylvania, 1981, pp. 254–63.

67. Bruce Laurie, *Working People of Philadelphia, 1800–1850* (Philadelphia: Temple University Press, 1980), pp. 5–6, 77–78; and Richard A.

McLeod, "Philadelphia Artisans, 1828–1850," doctoral dissertation, University of Missouri, Columbia, 1971, pp. 59–74.

68. *Mechanics' Free Press*, September 6, 1828.

69. Ibid., April 19, October 18, 1828.

70. Ibid., January 9, 1830.

71. Mikhail Bakhtin, *Rabelais and His World*, trans. Helene Iswolsky (Cambridge: M.I.T. Press, 1968).

72. *Public Ledger* (Philadelphia), June 16, 1837, July 1, 6, 1839.

73. Ibid., June 6, 1838.

74. "Fourth of July: The Day We Celebrate, 1836–1860," *Atlantic* 94 (1904): 108–13; George W. Douglas, *The American Book of Days* (New York: H. W. Wilson, 1948), p. 376; Alfred L. Shoemaker, "Fantasticals," *Pennsylvania Folklife* 9 (1957–58): 28–31; the *San Francisco Evening Bulletin*, July 5, 1872, cites a burlesque July Fourth parade; fantasticals and callithumpians took part in Philadelphia's Centennial celebration. The Fourth also prompted burlesque speeches; see Howard H. Martin, "Orations on the Anniversary of American Independence, 1776–1876," doctoral dissertation, Northwestern University, Evanston, Ill., 1955, pp. 93, 317–43.

75. Fragments of the history of Philadelphia's masking traditions and its later Mummers have been brought together; see Charles E. Welch, "The Philadelphia Mummers Parade," doctoral dissertation, University of Pennsylvania, 1968. For a more detailed historical study, see Susan G. Davis, "'Making Night Hideous': Christmas Revelry and Public Order in Nineteenth-Century Philadelphia," *American Quarterly* 34 (1982): 185–99. For a close historical examination of masking in one North American region, see Story, "Mummers in Newfoundland History." For a discussion of mummers and fantasticals, see Alfred L. Shoemaker, *Christmas in Pennsylvania: A Folk-Cultural Study* (Kutztown, Pa.: The Pennsylvania Folklife Society, 1959), pp. 21–23, 102–3. For Afro-American connections and analogues, see Ira D. Reid, "The John Canoe Festival," *Phylon* 3 (1942): 348–70; and Richard Walser, "His Lordship, John Kuner," *North Carolina Folklore* 19 (1971): 160–72.

76. An argument for the cultural universality of Christmas folk dramas and for deeper historic continuity of mumming in Philadelphia than I can find evidence for is presented by Welch, "Philadelphia Mummers Parade," pp. 28–33.

77. Shoemaker, *Christmas in Pennsylvania*, pp. 73–85.

78. Halpert, "A Typology of Mumming"; and Richard Bauman, "Belsnickling in Nova Scotia," *Western Folklore* 31 (1972): 229–43.

79. Shoemaker, "Fantasticals"; Don Yoder, "The Folk-Cultural Background," in Shoemaker, *Christmas in Pennsylvania*, pp. 5–17; *United States Gazette*, January 12, 1825; and *Daily Chronicle* (Philadelphia), December 26, 1833.

80. *Public Ledger*, December 25, 1844.

81. Ibid., January 2, 1844.

82. *North American* (Philadelphia), December 25, 1854.

83. Ibid., December 25, 1855. The name "Shanghai Guards" may have born anti-authority connotations as well; the once-obscene nose-thumbing "shanghai" gesture had a long history of such use. See Archer

Taylor, "The Shanghai Gesture," *Folklore Fellows Communication No. 116* (Helsinki: Suomalainen Tiedekatemia, 1956).

84. *North American*, January 1, 1856. Both the Santa Anna Cavalry and the Ampudia Guards celebrated the defeats in late 1856 of the Mexican generals. Pedro de Ampudia had just surrendered to Zachary Taylor. Pennsylvania cities and towns appear to have had a tradition of burlesquing the defeated, although this has never been investigated. My cousin, Dr. Irene Laub, a lifelong resident of Easton, Pennsylvania, recalls that, in the early twentieth century, it was customary to celebrate elections with "Salt River Parades" "honoring" the loser. The expression "up Salt River" preceded the contemporary "up Shit Creek without a paddle," meaning totally lost or in trouble without a means of escape.

85. *Public Ledger*, January 2, 1846.

86. Ibid.

87. Ibid., December 27, 1845.

88. Alexander Saxton, "Blackface Minstrelsy and Jacksonian Ideology," *American Quarterly* 27 (1975): 3–28; *United States Gazette*, December 27, 1829; *Sunday Dispatch* (Philadelphia), December 27, 1857 (a recollection of Christmases in the 1830s); and *Public Ledger*, January 2, 1847.

89. In 1877 the Philadelphia *Inquirer* (January 1 and 2) described the serenaders' custom of demanding free drinks as more effective than a city ordinance for keeping bars closed on Christmas Day. For ransacked taverns, see *Public Ledger*, January 4, 1849; *North American*, January 3, 1854, and January 25, 1855.

90. Ibid., January 3, 1854.

91. *Public Ledger*, January 2, 1850; Bruce Laurie, "Fire Companies and Gangs in Southwark: The 1840s," in Allen F. Davis and Mark H. Haller, eds., *The Peoples of Philadelphia: A History of Ethnic Groups and Lower-Class Life, 1790–1940* (Philadelphia: Temple University Press, 1973), pp. 71–87.

92. *North American*, January 2, 3, 1857.

93. *Public Ledger*, December 27, 1837, December 28, 1840, December 28, 1846. For full-blown race riots, see *Public Ledger*, December 27, 1848. For attacks on black churches, see *North American*, January 3, 1853. For attacks on the watch, see *Public Ledger*, January 1, 1839, December 27, 1845, and December 28, 1846.

94. Davis, " 'Making Night Hideous.' "

95. *North American*, December 25, 1855.

96. Davis, " 'Making Night Hideous,' " pp. 196–98.

97. David Grimsted, "Rioting in Its Jacksonian Setting," *American Historical Review* 77 (1972): 361–97; Michael Feldberg, "The Crowd in Philadelphia History," *Labor History* 15 (1974): 323–36; David Montgomery, "The Shuttle and the Cross: Weavers and Artisans in the Kensington Riots of 1844," *Journal of Social History* 5 (1972): 411–46; and Elizabeth Geffen, "Violence in Philadelphia in the 1840s and 1850s," *Pennsylvania History* 36 (1969): 381–410.

98. Davis, " 'Making Night Hideous,' " pp. 197–98; and *Inquirer*, January 2, 1884, and January 2, 3, 1887.

CHAPTER FIVE

1. On the diversity of Philadelphia's workers' cultures, see Bruce Laurie, *Working People of Philadelphia, 1800–1850* (Philadelphia: Temple University Press, 1980), pp. 33–107.

2. Alfred F. Young, "English Plebeian Culture and Eighteenth-Century American Radicalism," in Margaret Jacob and James Jacob, eds., *The Origins of Anglo-American Radicalism* (London: George Allen & Unwin, 1983), pp. 185–212; and Herbert G. Gutman, *Work, Culture and Society in Industrializing America* (New York: Vintage, 1977), pp. 3–78. The Carpenters' Company is the best-known survivor of that crossing, but it was an association of wealthy and powerful master builders and was by no means representative of the city's craftsmen.

3. Laurie, *Working People*, pp. 3–33.

4. For example, see *Public Ledger* (Philadelphia) August 29, 1842.

5. David Bergeron, *English Civic Pageantry, 1558–1642* (London: Edward Arnold, 1971); and his, "Civic Pageants and Historical Drama," *Journal of Medieval and Renaissance Studies* 5 (1975): 89–105; Glynne Wickham, *Early English Stages, 1300–1660*, 2 vols. (London: Routledge, Kegan Paul, 1959; and New York: Columbia University Press, 1963); and J. L. Morrissey, "English Street Theatre: 1665–1708," *Costerus* 4 (1972): 105–37.

6. David Montgomery, "The Working Class in the Pre-Industrial City," *Labor History* 9 (1968): 3–22; Richard B. Morris, *Government and Labor in Early America* (New York: Columbia University Press, 1946), pp. 1–54; and Marcus B. Rediker, "'Good Hands, Stout Hearts, Fast Feet': The History and Culture of Working People in Early America," *Labour/ Le Travailleur* 10 (Autumn 1982): 123–44.

7. Montgomery, "The Working Class in the Pre-Industrial City."

8. "Account of the Federal Procession of July 4, 1788," *American Museum* 4 (July 1788), repr. in Samuel Hazard, ed., *Register of Pennsylvania* (Philadelphia) 2 (July 1828): 417–25. Similar happenings in New York have been analyzed by Sean Wilentz in "Artisan Republican Festivals and the Rise of Class Conflict in New York City, 1788–1837," in Michael H. Frisch and Daniel J. Walkowitz, eds., *Working-Class America: Essays on Labor, Community and American Society* (Urbana: University of Illinois Press, 1983), pp. 37–77. See also, Sarah H. J. Simpson, "The Federal Procession of the City of New York," *New-York Historical Society Quarterly Bulletin* 9 (1925): 39–58.

9. "Federal Procession," p. 418.

10. Ibid.

11. Cynthia Jane Shelton, "The Mills of Manayunk: Early Industrialization and Social Conflict in the Philadelphia Region, 1787–1837," doctoral dissertation, University of California, Los Angeles, 1982, pp. 110–69.

12. "Federal Procession," p. 419.

13. Ibid.

14. Ibid.

15. Ibid.

16. Ibid.

17. Ibid.
18. Ibid., p. 420.
19. Ibid., p. 425.
20. Ibid., p. 420.
21. Ibid., p. 422.
22. Laurie, *Working People*, p. 40. For artisans' political attitudes and support for the Constitution, see Eric Foner, *Tom Paine and Revolutionary America* (New York: Oxford University Press, 1976), pp. 19–69.
23. "Federal Procession," p. 422.
24. Ibid., p. 423.
25. Alan Kulikoff comes to a similar conclusion about the representation of the wealthy in a Boston procession for George Washington in "The Progress of Inequality in Revolutionary Boston," *William and Mary Quarterly*, 3rd ser. 28 (1971): 375–412.
26. Gary B. Nash, "Up From the Bottom in Franklin's Philadelphia," *Past and Present* 17 (1977): 58–83.
27. Laurie, *Working People*, pp. 3–33, 40; Eric Foner, *Tom Paine*, pp. 19–69; and Nash, "Franklin's Philadelphia," pp. 55–83.
28. *Poulson's American Daily Advertiser* (Philadelphia), August 31, September 1, 11, 1824.
29. Ibid., September 8, 1824.
30. Ibid., September 21, 24, 1824.
31. Ibid., September 3, 1824. See also Laurie, *Working People*, pp. 3–33; and Wilentz, "Artisan Republican Festivals."
32. "Holidays," *North American Review* 84 (April 1857): 331–63. For employers' ceremonies promoting enterprise and the opening of the Baltimore and Ohio Railroad, see *Niles' Weekly Register* (Baltimore), July 6, 1828, p. 233. For opening of the Philadelphia Merchants' Exchange, see Hazard, *Register* 12 (September 1833): 293; for opening of the Germantown Railroad, ibid. 14 (November 1834): 276–77; for the Philadelphia and Norristown Railroad, see ibid. (October 1834): 264; for canal-opening ceremonies, ibid. 4 (October 1829): 254. In the 1830s master butchers sponsored elaborate processions of cattle, using medieval craft symbolism, to announce the arrival of their wares at the slaughterhouses and markets; see Ellis Paxson Oberholtzer, *Philadelphia: A History of the City and Its People, a Record of 225 Years*, 4 vols. (Philadelphia: S. J. Clarke, 1911) 2:85.
33. *United States Gazette* (Philadelphia), February 17, 21–23, March 1, 3, 1832; and *Poulson's American Daily Advertiser*, February 17, 21, 24, 1832.
34. *United States Gazette*, March 1, 1832.
35. Ibid., February 24, 1832.
36. Ibid.
37. Ibid.
38. Ibid., July 12, 17, 22, 1834.
39. Hazard, *Register* 11 (June 1833): 376–78.
40. Thomas Cochran, *Pennsylvania: A Bicentennial History* (New York: W. W. Norton, 1978), pp. 66–85; and Charles M. Snyder, *The Jacksonian Heritage: Pennsylvania Politics, 1833–1848* (Harrisburg: Pennsylvania Historic and Museums Commission, 1958), pp. 35–49.

41. *Niles' Weekly Register*, April 5, 1834, pp. 92–94.

42. Snyder, *Jacksonian Heritage*, pp. 35–49; in April 1834 the Whigs staged several mass "jubilees" to consolidate gains in anti-Jackson opinion, and trade symbols such as miniature ships were prominently displayed at these gatherings. See also Hazard, *Register* 13 (May 1834): 282–83.

43. Ibid. (March 1834): 204–5.

44. *Pennsylvanian* (Philadelphia), March 21, 22, 1834.

45. For example, the machinery and technology prominently displayed in the Centennial Exhibition of 1876.

46. *Mechanics' Free Press* (Philadelphia), June 20, 1829; and Wilentz, "Artisan Republican Festivals." Wilentz shows that a wide variety of republican and patriotic ceremonies were observed by New York's artisans. The record for Philadelphia makes it difficult to determine whether Philadelphia workingmen structured their ceremonial culture differently from New Yorkers, or whether gaps in local records make autonomous artisan ceremonies seem rarer. Certainly, the complete absence of trades association records for Philadelphia's antebellum years shapes what can be known; a comparative study of ceremonialism in the two cities would be useful.

47. David Montgomery, "Strikes in Nineteenth-Century America," *Social Science History* 4 (1980): 81–104.

48. E. P. Thompson, *The Making of the English Working Class*, rev. ed. (New York: Penguin, 1977), pp. 181–84; Peter Linebaugh, "Silk Is the Difference," unpublished paper, 1984, and Keith Thomas, "Work and Leisure in Pre-Industrial Societies," *Past and Present* 29 (1964): 55.

49. *Oxford English Dictionary*, s.v. "strike." Marcus Rediker provided this etymological clue.

50. Reprinted from *Albany Argus* in *Democratic Press* (Philadelphia), May 16, 1826.

51. Ibid.

52. Reprinted from an unidentified New Orleans newspaper in *Democratic Press*, June 17, 1825.

53. For an antistrike evangelical July Fourth sermon, see Laurie, *Working People*, pp. 89–90.

54. Philip S. Foner, *History of the Labor Movement in the United States*, Vol. I: *From Colonial Times to the Founding of the American Federation of Labor* (New York: International Publishers, 1947; rev. ed., New World Paperbacks, 1975), pp. 118–20.

55. Laurie, *Working People*, pp. 90–91.

56. *United States Gazette*, June 4, 1835.

57. Ibid., June 12, 1835.

58. Ibid.

59. Ibid.

60. *Pennsylvanian*, June 15, 1835.

61. Ibid.

62. Ibid., June 18, 1835.

63. Laurie, *Working People*, p. 91.

64. *Pennsylvanian*, June 4, 1835.

65. Ibid., June 3–7, 9–10, 12, 1835.

66. *United States Gazette*, July 11, 1835.

67. *Mechanics' Free Press*, April 19, June 28, 1828.

68. *Pennsylvanian*, June 20, 1835.

69. Laurie, *Working People*, pp. 85–106.

70. Ibid., pp. 107–36. See also David Montgomery, "The Shuttle and the Cross: Weavers and Artisans in the Kensington Riots of 1844," *Journal of Social History* 5 (1972): 411–46.

71. Richard A. MacLeod, "Philadelphia Artisans, 1828–1850," doctoral dissertation, University of Missouri, Columbia, 1971, pp. 102–69.

72. *Public Ledger*, August 30, 1839.

73. Ibid., August 19, 1842.

74. Ibid.

75. Ibid., August 26, 1842.

76. Ibid., August 29, 1842.

77. Ibid., September 3, 7–9, 1842.

78. Ibid., September 26, 1842.

79. Ibid., October 27, 1842.

80. Ibid., February 24, 1846. See also MacLeod, "Philadelphia Artisans," pp. 149–69.

81. *Public Ledger*, February 24, 27, 28, and March 2, 5, 1846.

82. Ibid., March 9, 1846.

83. *Pennsylvania Inquirer and National Gazette* (Philadelphia), March 9, 1846.

84. Young, "Eighteenth-Century American Radicalism"; and Alfred F. Young, "Pope's Day, Tarring and Feathering and Cornet Joyce, Jun.: From Ritual to Rebellion in Boston, 1745–1775" (paper presented to the Anglo-American Conference on Comparative Labor History, Rutgers University, April 26–28, 1973).

85. *Public Ledger*, March 9, 1846.

86. Henri Moulierac, "The Strike: War or Festival?" *Diogenes* 98 (Summer 1977): 55–70.

87. Norman Simms, "Ned Ludd's Mummer's Play," *Folklore* 89 (1978): 166–78; and E. P. Thompson, "The Moral Economy of the English Crowd in the Eighteenth Century," *Past and Present* 50 (1971): 76–136.

88. The classic statement of this is Florence Reece's song about the Harlan County, Kentucky, coal miners' strikes, "Which Side Are You On?," originally recorded for the Library of Congress in 1937. Edited and transcribed by Pete Seeger, it was reprinted in Alan Lomax, comp., *Hard-Hitting Songs for Hard-Hit People* (New York: Oak Publications, 1967), pp. 176–77.

89. Shelton, "The Mills of Manayunk," p. 299.

90. *United States Gazette*, June 5, 1835.

91. *Public Ledger*, August 2, 1842.

92. *North American* (Philadelphia), November 10–13, 1857.

93. *Pennsylvanian*, October 1, 1850.

94. For example, on August 11, 1828; see J. Thomas Scharf and Thompson Westcott, *The History of Philadelphia, 1609–1884*, 3 vols. (Philadelphia: L. H. Everts, 1884) 1:623.

95. John F. Szwed, "Race and the Embodiment of Culture," *Ethnicity* 2 (1975): 19–33.

96. Andrew Neilly, "Violent Volunteers: A History of the Philadelphia Volunteer Fire Department, 1736–1871," doctoral dissertation, University of Pennsylvania, 1959; and Bruce Laurie, "Fire Companies and Gangs in Southwark: The 1840s," in Allen F. Davis and Mark Haller, eds., *The Peoples of Philadelphia: A History of Ethnic Groups and Lower-Class Life, 1790–1940* (Philadelphia: Temple University Press, 1973), pp. 71–87.

97. Scharf and Westcott, *History of Philadelphia* 1:636; Hazard, *Register* 16 (October 1835): 218–19; *Philadelphia Gazette and Daily Advertiser* (Philadelphia), March 28, 1833, March 27, 28, 1834; and *Public Ledger*, January 1, 1836 (a special centennial parade), March 10, 1846. Other important firemen's parades included escort parades for visiting firemen or returning local companies. Firemen were fond of cotillions and dances. See *Pennsylvanian*, December 25, 1850.

98. *Philadelphia Gazette and Daily Advertiser*, March 28, 1833.

99. *Pennsylvanian*, March 28, 1834.

100. Ibid. See also *Philadelphia Gazette and Daily Advertiser*, March 28, 1833.

101. *Pennsylvanian*, March 28, 1834; and *Philadelphia Gazette and Daily Advertiser*, March 28, 1833.

102. *Pennsylvanian*, March 28, 1834.

103. Grand marshals who held militia offices and city council offices included Peter Fritz, Alexander Henry, George K. Childs, and John Price Wetherill. *Pennsylvanian*, May 12, 1835, and October 4, December 25, 30, 1850; and *Public Ledger*, September 9, 1839, February 20, 1841.

104. Laurie, *Working People*, pp. 72–73, 115–33.

105. Ibid., pp. 115–24, 141–42; and Mary P. Ryan, *Cradle of the Middle Class: The Family in Oneida County, New York, 1790–1865* (Cambridge: Cambridge University Press, 1981), pp. 105–35.

106. *Public Ledger*, June 30, 1838, June 29, 1839, July 2, 6, 1840, June 29, July 7, 1841, and July 1, 1842.

107. Ibid., June 30, July 6, 1838.

108. Ibid., June 29, July 2, 6, 1839.

109. Ibid., July 2–4, 6, 1840.

110. Ibid., June 29, July 7, 1841; and Dolores Hayden, *Redesigning the American Dream: The Future of Housing, Work and Domestic Life* (New York: W. W. Norton, 1984), pp. 30–31.

111. Respectability is discussed by Bruce Laurie in "Nothing on Compulsion: Lifestyles of Philadelphia Artisans, 1820–1850," *Labor History* 15 (1974): 337–66; and R. Q. Gray, "Styles of Life, the 'Labor Aristocracy' and Class Relations in Later Nineteenth-Century Edinburgh," *International Journal of Social History* 18 (1973): 428–52.

112. For example, the banner designed by the "Misses Fackney"; see *Public Ledger*, July 7, 1841.

113. Montgomery, "Shuttle and the Cross."

114. *Public Ledger*, June 26, 28, 29, and July 1, 2, 4, 6, 1844.

115. Ibid., July 6, 1844.

116. Montgomery, "Shuttle and the Cross."

117. Laurie, *Working People*, pp. 33–52, and his "Nothing on Compulsion," pp. 337–66.

118. Paul Boyer, *Urban Masses and Moral Order in America, 1820–1860* (Cambridge: Harvard University Press, 1978), pp. 3–66; and Michael B. Katz, *The Irony of Early School Reform: Educational Reform in Mid-Nineteenth-Century Massachusetts* (Cambridge: Harvard University Press, 1968), pp. 40–50.

119. Roy Rosenzweig, *Eight Hours for What We Will: Workers and Leisure in an Industrial City, 1870–1920* (Cambridge: Cambridge University Press, 1983); Francis Couvares, "The Triumph of Commerce: Class Culture and Mass Culture in Pittsburgh," in Frisch and Walkowitz, eds., *Working-Class America*, pp. 123–52; and Gareth Stedman-Jones, "Class Expression versus Social Control? A Critique of Recent Trends in the Social History of Leisure," and "Working-Class Culture and Working-Class Politics in London, 1870–1900: Notes on the Remaking of a Working Class," in Jones, *Languages of Class: Studies in English Working-Class History, 1832–1982* (Cambridge: Cambridge University Press, 1983), pp. 76–89, 179–238, respectively.

120. Karen Haltunnen, *Confidence Men and Painted Women: A Study of Middle-Class Culture in America, 1830–1870* (New Haven: Yale University Press, 1982).

CHAPTER SIX

1. Alfred F. Young, "Pope's Day, Tarring and Feathering and Cornet Joyce, Jun.: From Ritual to Rebellion in Boston, 1745–1775" (paper presented to the Anglo-American Conference on Comparative Labor History, Rutgers University, April 26–28, 1973); and Michael Meranze, "The Penitential Ideal in Late Eighteenth-Century Philadelphia," *Pennsylvania Magazine of History and Biography* 108, no. 4 (October 1984): 419–40.

2. Mikhail Bakhtin, *Rabelais and His World*, trans. Helene Iswolsky (Cambridge: M.I.T. Press, 1968), pp. 59–144.

3. Paul Boyer, *Urban Masses and Moral Order in America, 1820–1860* (Cambridge: Harvard University Press, 1978), pp. 33–66; and R. Q. Gray, "Styles of Life, the 'Labor Aristocracy,' and Class Relations in Later Nineteenth-Century Edinburgh," *International Journal of Social History* 18 (1973): 428–52.

4. Gareth Stedman-Jones, "Working-Class Culture, Working-Class Politics in London, 1870–1900: Notes on the Remaking of a Working Class," in his *Languages of Class: Studies in English Working-Class History, 1832–1982* (Cambridge: Cambridge University Press, 1983), pp. 179–238; and Roy Rosenzweig, *Eight Hours for What We Will: Workers and Leisure in an Industrial City, 1870–1920* (Cambridge: Cambridge University Press, 1983).

5. Philadelphia established a professional police force with the city's consolidation in 1854; see Howard O. Sprogel, *The Philadelphia Police, Past and Present* (Philadelphia, 1887), pp. 89–113. Compare John C. Schneider, "Mob Violence and Public Order in the American City, 1830–1865," doctoral dissertation, University of Minnesota, Minneapolis, 1971.

6. Philip S. Foner, *History of the Labor Movement in the United States*, Vol. I: *From Colonial Times to the Founding of the American Federation of Labor* (New York: International Publishers, 1947; rev. ed., New World Paperbacks, 1975), p. 47 and passim.

7. Boyer, *Urban Masses*; and Roger Lane, *Policing the City: Boston, 1822–1885* (Cambridge: Harvard University Press, 1967).

8. Philip S. Foner, *The Great Labor Uprising of 1877* (New York: Monad Press, 1977); Herbert G. Gutman, "The Tompkins Square 'Riot' in New York City on January 13, 1874: A Reexamination of Its Causes and Aftermath," *Labor History* 6, no. 1 (Winter 1965): 44–70; and Theodore F. Watts, *The First Labor Day Parade, Tuesday, September 5, 1882: Media Mirrors to Labor's Icons* (Silver Spring, Md.: Phoenix Rising, 1983).

9. Robert Reinders, "The Militia and Public Order in Nineteenth-Century America," *Journal of American Studies* 11 (1977): 81–101.

10. Susan G. Davis, "'Making Night Hideous': Christmas Revelry and Public Order in Nineteenth-Century Philadelphia," *American Quarterly* 34 (1982): 185–99.

11. Ibid. See also "Right of Street Parades," *Every Saturday* 11 (1871): 146.

12. Tom Dove, ed., *The Law and Political Protest: A Handbook to Your Political Rights Under the Law* (Berkeley: Boalt Hall Action Com-

mittee, 1974), pp. 24–27. Dove and his collaborators make it clear that while picketing and demonstrations seem unequivocally protected by the First Amendment, both the rights of free speech and peaceable assembly are hedged in by hazy qualifications of what is an "appropriate" and "public" space. Definitions of "appropriate" and "public" are contingent, and the right to define them rests with civil authorities. Cf. Staughton Lynd, *Labor Law for the Rank and Filer* (San Pedro, Calif.: Singlejack, 1978); and Julius Getman, "Labor Law and Free Speech: The Curious Policy of Limited Expression," *Maryland Law Review* 43, no. 1 (1984).

13. Rosenzweig, *Eight Hours for What We Will*, pp. 153–70; and Davis, "'Making Night Hideous.'"

14. "Holidays," *North American Review* 84 (April 1857): 331–63.

15. David Harold Glassberg, "American Civic Pageantry and the Image of Community, 1900–1930," doctoral dissertation, Johns Hopkins University, Baltimore, 1982, pp. 7–32.

16. Jane Campbell Scrapbook #62, Boies Penrose Pictorial Collection, Historical Society of Pennsylvania, Philadelphia.

17. William R. Leach, "Transformations in a Culture of Consumption: Women and Department Stores, 1890–1925," *Journal of American History* 71, no. 2 (September 1984): 319–42.

18. Davis, "'Making Night Hideous'"; for a suggestion that Saint Patrick's Day could be turned to promotional purposes, see *Philadelphia Inquirer*, March 19, 1861.

19. City of Philadelphia, Department of Commerce, Office of the City Representative, Public Information Division, files 1962–1966, Philadelphia City Archives, Records Group #64.3; and Department of Commerce, Office of the City Representative, Ceremonial Division files, 1966–, Philadelphia City Archives, Records Group #64.4.

20. Mark Farber, "The Structure of Spectacles in Late Nineteenth-Century New York" (paper presented to the Annual Meetings of the Organization of American Historians, Philadelphia, April 1, 1982).

21. Compare James D. Halloran, Philip Elliot, and Graham Murdock, *Demonstrations and Communication: A Case Study* (Harmondsworth, England: Penguin, 1970).

22. The June 12, 1982 demonstration has been impressively documented by Political Art Documentation/Distribution (PADD) in a slide tape, "We Want to Live."

Index

Independence, as social ideal, 25; linked to manufacturing and industry, 125

Independence Day. *See* Fourth of July

Independence Day burlesques. *See* Fourth of July

Independence Hall. *See* State House

Independence Square. *See* State House Square

"Indians," in parades, 128, 145

Industrial capitalism, 17–18, 20; and culture change, 20, 24–25, 152–53, 162–65; and festivals, 36–37, 187 n. 48; growth and crisis of, 12; parades and, 12, 128–29; political change and, 25; and popular culture, 152–53; social change and, 162; and social conflict, 26; spatial exploitation and, 28–29; time and, 36–38, 134; work patterns and, 114

Industrial exhibitions, 132, 155–56, 170

Industrial production: small-scale, 37–38; Philadelphia's system of, 12, 24–25

Industrialization. *See* Industrial capitalism

Inequality, economic, 24–25; criticized in folk drama, 110–11. *See also* Class, social; Class relations

Inequality, social, 24–26; and folk dramas, 73, 110–11; working-class critique of, 24–26. *See also* Class, social; Class relations

Infantry, volunteer membership in, in 1830, 55. *See also* Volunteer militia companies

Interpretation of parades, 14; *See also* Audiences, for parades

Invention of tradition. *See* Tradition, invention of

"Ires" (pseud.), 137

Irish, 190 n. 82; immigrants, 28, 47, 110–11, 150, 157, 159; viewed as subspecies, 143, 150

Jackson, Andrew, 66, 70; and Bank War, 130–32; demonstrations against, 131–32; national tour of, 66, 82; receptions for, 66, 130–31; "sham funeral" for, 66; and volunteer militia companies, 66

Jackson Day (January 8), 132; burlesque of, 95

Jeffersonians, celebrants of Fourth of July, 41

"Jim Crows," 106

Johnson, Frank (Francis), 61–62

Jokes, antimilitia, 99

Journeymen, in parades, 127, 129

July Revolution (1830), ceremonies celebrating, 49–51, 68, 191–94 n. 1

Kammen, Michael, 201 n. 83

Kensington (district of Philadelphia Co.), 24, 145; weavers' riots in (1844), 143, 150–51; weavers' strike in, 138–39

Krimmel, John Lewis, "Independence Day in Centre Square," 42

Labor: in colonial America, 116–17; corporate imagery of, 116–32, 162; iconography of, 21; and leisure, 36–37; mass processions by, 167–68; in parades, 21, 118–23, 164; and public order, 167; seasonality of, 37; unfree, 34–35

Labor, as social good, 2, 117, 122–23, 157; artisan republican ideology of, 122–23

Labor Day, 167–68

Labor movement, 167; in Philadelphia, 5, 26, 115–16; in politics, 25–26; and the press, 116; and street theatre, 116

Labor press, 134

Labor processes: as enacted in parades, 2, 21, 117, 120–21; and ideology, 37–38; and social life, 37–38

"Lafayette" (pseud.), 61

Lafayette, Marquis de, 50–51; as patriot hero, 70; receptions for, 15, 65, 126–27; "sham funeral" of, 66, 129; tour of, 65; and volunteer militia companies, 51, 65

Landscape, of Philadelphia, 27–28

Laughter, 78, 80, 100–101, 103, 158, 161

Laurie, Bruce, 37, 136, 144, 151

Legislators, as members of volunteer militia companies, 53–54

Legislature, Pennsylvania, and militia laws, 56

Von Sydow, Carl, 182 n. 45

Wage labor: fear of crowds and, 35; growth of, 24–25, 124–25; seasonal rhythms and, 39
Wages, 137–38; at issue in strikes, 137–40
War of 1812: celebration of victories of, 66; volunteers of, 2
"Washington" (pseud.), 84
Washington (rolling ship), 150
Washington, George, 10, 51, 65; Farewell Address of, 2, 128, 151; as "father" of volunteer militia companies, 69–70; grand national tour of, 11, 65; as icon, 3, 70; as nativist symbol, 150; as patriot hero, 10, 30, 50–51, 65
Washington Blues (volunteer militia company), 59
Washington Greys (volunteer militia company), 50–51, 61, 67
Washington Guards (volunteer militia company), 54, 59, 61
Washington Monument, Philadelphia, 31
Washington Square, 27, 60; redesigned, 31
Washington's Birthday, 1–5, 9–10, 58–60; parades on, 59–60; volunteer militia companies and, 58–60, 67
Washington's Birthday Centennial, 1832, 1–5, 12, 31, 60, 127–29, 156
Watchmen, 30, 44, 110–11, 145; attacks on, 107
Water power, 36–37
Watson, John F., 32, 47
Wealth: distribution of, in Philadelphia, 24–25; displayed in parades, 146–47, 151, 159–60; social origins of, in Philadelphia, 24–25
Wealthy families, 51, 61
Weavers: in Grand Federal Procession, 119; Irish, 143; and strikes, 133, 137–40, 143; in Washington Centennial Procession, 126–27
Whig Party, 26; as celebrants of Fourth of July, 41; mass demonstrations and, 131
Wilentz, Sean, 212 n. 46
Williams, Raymond, 7, 16–17, 77
Winter, pace of labor in, 36–37

Women: exclusion of, from parades, 47; public and ceremonial roles of, 189–90 n. 80, 194 n. 2; in street parades, 4, 47, 119, 149, 157; of working class, 37, 47, 119
Women's clubs, 151
Women's dress, as maskers' costume, 105–6, 110. *See also* Transvestism
Work: adjacent to domestic life, 34; on Fourth of July, 42. *See also* Labor
Work discipline, Muster Day and, 40
Work processes: changes in, 100, 134; enacted in parades, 4, 21, 126–29, 156–57
Workers: as celebrants of Washington's Birthday, 10; in Christmas festivity, 108–9; and militia laws, 55–57; in parade traditions, 160–61; in political associations, 25; in public culture, 113, 157, 160–61; and receptions for Andrew Jackson, 65; in reform movements, 21; in "sham funerals," 66; and styles of parade performance, 114; views of economic progress of, 69; in voluntary associations, 115–16
Workforce: artisans in, in 1788, 125; composition of, in nineteenth century, 37–38
Working class, 30–39; and critique of corruption, 158; as "demons," 105; divisions within, 123–24, 127, 143, 162–63; parade traditions of, 161, 163–65; street theatre and, 73, 156; in twentieth-century civic pageantry, 169–70
Working-class culture: attempts to reform, 71–72, 115, 147–49, 152–53, 162–69; business-class concern over, 29–30, 113; and commercial theatre, 77; divisions in, 152–53; festival and, 162; in firemen's parades, 145–47; and folk drama, 74; press as source on, 116; resistance in, 163; respectability in, 152–53; temperance associations and, 115; time and autonomy in, 36; as "traditional," 152
Working-class radicalism, 35. *See also* Artisans, radical